THE
VANISHING
CONSCIENCE

JOHN F. MacARTHUR, JR.

THE VANISHING CONSCIENCE

NELSON BOOKS
A Division of Thomas Nelson Publishers
Since 1798

www.thomasnelson.com

The Vanishing Conscience

Nelson Books may be purchased in bulk for educational, business, fundraising, or sales promotional use. For information, please email SpecialMarkets@ThomasNelson.com.

All Scripture quotations in this book, except those noted otherwise, are from the New American Standard Bible, © 1960, 1962, 1963, 1968, 1971, 1972, 1973, 1975, and 1977 by The Lockman Foundation, and are used by permission.

Quotations marked KJV are from the King James Version.

Appendixes 2 and 3 are selected from an unpublished collection of Puritan and Reformed essays adapted for modern readers, © 1994 by Phil Johnson. Used by permission.

Library of Congress Cataloging-in-Publication Data

MacArthur, John, 1939–
    The vanishing conscience / John F. MacArthur, Jr.
      p. cm.
    Includes bibliographical references.
    ISBN 0–8499–0842–6 (hc)
        0–7852–7181–3 (sc)
    1. Sin. 2. Conscience—Religious aspects—Christianity. 3. Guilt—Religious aspects—Christianity. 4. Church and the world. I. Title.
BT715.M126 1994
241'.3—dc20
                                    93—47503
                                       CIP

Printed in the United States of America

05 06 07 08 09 RRD 5 4 3 2 1

To Al Sanders

*with gratitude for half a century
of loyal service to the Savior
and thanks for many years
as a wise and generous friend.*

Contents

Contents

Preface

We live in a culture that has elevated pride to the status of a virtue. Self-esteem, positive feelings, and personal dignity are what our society encourages people to seek. At the same time, moral responsibility is being replaced by victimism, which teaches people to blame someone else for their personal failures and iniquities. Frankly, the biblical teachings about human depravity, sin, guilt, repentance, and humility are not compatible with any of those ideas.

The church has been far too willing to embrace the fads of worldly opinion—particularly in the area of psychology and self-esteem. Christians often merely echo worldly thinking on the psychology of guilt and the importance of feeling good about oneself. The adverse effect on the life of the church can hardly be underestimated.

Nowhere has the damage registered more than in the way professing Christians deal with their own sin. In speaking to Christians around the country, I have seen a disheartening trend developing for at least two decades. The church as a whole is growing less concerned with sin, and more obsessed with self-exoneration and self-esteem. Christians are rapidly losing sight of sin as the root of all human woes. And many Christians are explicitly denying that their own sin can be the cause of their personal anguish. More and more are attempting to explain the human dilemma in wholly unbiblical terms: temperament, addiction, dysfunctional families, the child within, codependency, and a host of other irresponsible escape mechanisms promoted by secular psychology.

The potential impact of such a drift is frightening. Remove the reality of sin, and you take away the possibility of repentance. Abolish the doctrine of human depravity and you void the divine plan of salvation. Erase the notion of personal guilt and you eliminate the need for a Savior. Obliterate the human conscience, and you will raise an amoral and unredeemable generation. The church cannot join hands with the world in such a grossly satanic enterprise. To do so is to overthrow the very gospel we are called to proclaim.

This book is not merely a lament about society's deplorable moral state or the damage we see caused by sin all around us. Nor is it an attempt to stir Christians up to tackle the impossible task of reconstructing society. Awakening the *church* to the awful reality of sin is my only point of concern. That alone would have a positive effect on the world.

Is social reconstruction even an appropriate way for Christians to spend their energies? I recently mentioned to a friend that I was working on a book dealing with sin and our culture's declining moral climate. He immediately said, "Be sure you urge Christians to get actively involved in reclaiming society. The main problem is that Christians haven't acquired enough influence in politics, art, and the entertainment industry to turn things around for good." That, I acknowledge, is a common view held by many Christians. But I'm afraid I don't agree. The weakness of the church is not that we're too uninvolved in the politics or administration of our society, but that we too easily absorb the false values of an unbelieving world. The problem is not too little activism, but too much assimilation. As I noted in a recent book, the church is fast becoming like the world in several respects. Those most active in the social and political realms are often the *first* to absorb the world's values. Social and political activists cannot have any worthwhile impact on society if their own consciences are not clear and strong.

"Reclaiming" the culture is a pointless, futile exercise. I am convinced we are living in a post-Christian society—a civilization that exists under God's judgment. As we will note in an early chapter of this book, abundant evidence suggests that God has abandoned this culture to its own depravity. Certainly He is not interested in superficial moral reform for an unregenerate society. God's purpose in this world—and the church's only legitimate commission—is the proclamation of the message of sin and salvation to individuals, whom God sovereignly redeems and calls *out* of the world. God's purpose is to save those who will repent of their sins and believe the gospel—not to work for external corrections in a morally bankrupt culture.

If that sounds the least bit pessimistic or cynical to you, it isn't. Scripture predicted times exactly like these:

In the last days difficult times will come. For men will be lovers of self, lovers of money, boastful, arrogant, revilers, disobedient to parents, ungrateful, unholy, unloving, irreconcilable, malicious gossips, without self-control, brutal, haters of good, treacherous, reckless, conceited, lovers of pleasure rather than lovers of God; holding to a form of godliness, although they have denied its power. . . . [And] evil men and impostors will proceed from bad to worse, deceiving and being deceived (2 Tim. 3:1–5, 13).

God's purposes *are* being fulfilled, no matter how vainly people strive against Him. Titus 2:11 assures us that God's grace appears, bringing salvation in the midst of the lowest human depravity, teaching us to live "sensibly, righteously and godly in the present age" (v. 12).

There is great hope, even in the midst of a wicked and perverse generation, for those who love God. Remember, He will build His church and "the gates of hades will not prevail against it" (Matt. 16:18). He also is able to make all things work together for the good of His elect (Rom. 8:28). Christ Himself intercedes for His chosen ones, people who are not of this world, even as He is not of this world (Jn. 17:14). What is His prayer? "I do not ask Thee to take them out of the world, but to keep them from the evil one. . . . Sanctify them in the truth; Thy word is truth" (vv. 15, 17).

As believers, then, our duty with regard to sin is not to try to purge all society's ills, but to apply ourselves diligently to the work of our own sanctification. The sin we need to be most concerned with is the sin in our own lives. Only as the church becomes holy can it begin to have a true, powerful effect on the outside world—and it won't be an external effect, but a changing of hearts. That is the focus of this book. This is a message for believers—Christians who are aliens and strangers in a hostile world (1 Pet. 2:11). It is an appeal that we commit ourselves to *biblical* thinking, that we see ourselves as God sees us, and that we deal honestly with our own sin.

To understand how to deal honestly with our own sin, we must first fully understand the problem. Part I of this book describes the decadent state of contemporary society, how sin has been treated, and consequently how the conscience has been affected. Part II examines the nature of sin. Part III provides practical solutions to gaining victory over sin. Three appendixes provide additional treatments of topics that are central in this book. Appendix 1 looks at the apostle Paul's instructions for gaining victory over sin as outlined in Romans 6. Appendixes 2 and 3 provide modern renderings of sermons in the seventeenth-century by Richard Sibbes and in the eighteenth-century by Jonathan Edwards. The sermon by Sibbes examines 1 Peter 3:21, and particularly the phrase "an appeal to God for a good conscience." It also highlights the advantages of a pure conscience. The sermon by Edwards examines why we may live in sin without knowing it and suggests ways to search our conscience to identify and arrest sin. These two sermons are included for two reasons. First, they offer helpful advice to Christians who want to deal seriously with sin and sharpen their consciences. Second, they reveal in a graphic way how differently the church once regarded sin—and thus how far contemporary Christianity has sunk. The church desperately needs to recover some of our ancestor's holy dread of sin—or we will enter the twenty-first century severely crippled.

My prayer is that this book will help to prompt evangelicals to turn again with new appreciation to the biblical doctrines of human depravity, sin, and the role of the conscience, leading to personal holiness. My prayer also is that it will help stem the tide of spiritual apathy, carelessness, shamelessness, and self-centeredness that worldly thinking has begun to breed among Bible-believing Christians. My most earnest prayer is that individual Christians who read it will be encouraged to reject such worldly values, and instead nurture "love from a pure heart and a good conscience and a sincere faith" (1 Tim. 1:5).

Part I

A Sinful Society

Modern society is full of sin, decadence, and devastating spiritual catastrophe. It can be seen at every turn. Part I isolates the causes in a sinful world where consciences have been silenced by sin.

Chapter 1, "Whatever Happened to Sin?," singles out society's tolerant notions about guilt and sin. It shows numerous examples of how society has treated every human failing as some kind of disease and created a "disease-model therapy" that only compounds the problem. It shows how victimism has taken the place of traditional morality, even in the church.

Chapter 2, "The Soul's Automatic Warning System," introduces the book's key concept of the vanishing conscience, which warns the soul about the presence of sin. It discusses how the conscience can be cleansed and strengthened.

Chapter 3, "How Sin Silences the Conscience," examines society's continuing downward spiral into sin because of secularism, lack of common sense, corrupt religion, uncontrolled lust, and sexual perversion. It parallels the decadence of Rome with today's moral decline and highlights the desperate need for revival.

1
Whatever Happened to Sin?

In all of the laments and reproaches made by our seers and prophets, one misses any mention of "sin," a word which used to be a veritable watchword of prophets. It was a word once in everyone's mind, but now rarely if ever heard. Does that mean that no sin is involved in all our troubles—sin with an "I" in the middle? Is no one any longer guilty of anything? Guilty perhaps of a sin that could be repented and repaired or atoned for? Is it only that someone may be stupid or sick or criminal—or asleep? Wrong things are being done, we know; tares are being sown in the wheat field at night. But is no one responsible, no one answerable for these acts? Anxiety and depression we all acknowledge, and even vague guilt feelings; but has no one committed any sins?

Where, indeed, did sin go? What became of it?

Dr. Karl Menninger[1]

Katherine Power was a fugitive for more than twenty-three years. In 1970, during the heyday of student radicalism, she participated in a Boston bank robbery in which a city policeman, the father of nine children, was shot in the back and killed. Pursued by federal authorities for murder, Ms. Power went into hiding. For fourteen years she was one of the FBI's Ten Most Wanted Fugitives. Finally, in late 1993, she surrendered to authorities.

In a statement she read to the press, Katherine Power characterized her actions in the bank robbery as "naive and unthinking." What motivated her to surrender? "I know that I must answer this accusation from the past, in order to live with full authenticity in the present."

Power's husband explained further: "*She did not return out of guilt.* She wanted her life back. She wants to be whole."

In a perceptive piece about Katherine Power's surrender, commentator Charles Krauthammer wrote,

> Her surrender—for the sake of "full authenticity"—was a form of therapy, indeed the final therapeutic step toward regaining her sense of self.
>
> Allan Bloom once described a man who had just gotten out of prison, where he had undergone "therapy." "He said that he had found his identity and learned to like himself," writes Bloom. "A generation ago he would have found God and learned to despise himself as a sinner."
>
> In an age where the word sin has become quaint—reserved for such offenses against hygiene as smoking and drinking (which alone merit "sin taxes")—surrendering to the authorities for armed robbery and manslaughter is not an act of repentance but of personal growth. Explains Jane Alpert, another '60s radical who served time (for her part in a series of bombings that injured twenty-one people): "Ultimately, I spent many years in therapy, learning to understand, to tolerate and forgive both others and myself."
>
> Learning to forgive oneself. Very important nowadays for revolutionaries with a criminal bent.[2]

Indeed, it is not at all uncommon these days to hear all kinds of people talking about learning to forgive themselves. But the terminology is misleading. "Forgiveness" presupposes an acknowledgement of guilt. Most people nowadays who speak of forgiving themselves explicitly repudiate the notion of personal guilt. Katherine Power is a typical example. Her husband denied that guilt had been a factor in her surrender. She only wanted to feel better about herself, to "answer [an] accusation from the past"—to be whole.

An admission of guilt today clearly is considered incompatible with the popular notion of "wholeness" and the need to protect the fantasy of a good self.

Guilt Bashing

Our culture has declared war on guilt. The very concept is considered medieval, obsolete, unproductive. People who trouble themselves with feelings of personal guilt are usually referred to therapists, whose task it is to boost their self-image. No one, after all, is supposed to feel guilty. Guilt is not conducive to dignity and self-esteem. Society encourages sin, but it will not tolerate the guilt sin produces.

Dr. Wayne Dyer, author of the 1976 mega-bestseller, *Your Erroneous Zones*, seems to have been one of the first influential voices to decry guilt altogether. He named guilt as "the most useless of all erroneous zone behaviors." According to Dr. Dyer, guilt is nothing but a neurosis. "Guilt zones," he wrote, "must be exterminated, spray-cleaned and sterilized forever."[3]

Society encourages sin, but it will not tolerate the guilt sin produces.

How do we spray-clean and sterilize our guilt zones? By renouncing the sinful behavior that makes us feel guilty? By repenting and seeking forgiveness? Not according to Dr. Dyer. In fact, his remedy for guilt is about as far from the biblical concept of repentance as it is possible to get. Here is his advice to readers suffering from guilt: "Do something which you know is bound to result in feelings of guilt. . . . Take a week to be alone if you've always wanted to do so, despite the guilt-engendering protestations from other members of your family. These kinds of behavior will help you to tackle that omnipresent guilt."[4] In other words, defy your guilt. If necessary, spurn your own spouse and children. Attack that sense of self-disapproval head on. Do something that is sure to make you feel guilty, then refuse to heed the cries of conscience, the duties of family responsibility, or even the appeal of your own loved ones. You owe it to yourself.

Guilt is rarely treated seriously anymore. It is usually portrayed as a mere annoyance, a nuisance, one of life's little aggravations. Our local newspaper recently ran a feature article on guilt. It was a light-hearted piece, dealing mostly with small, secret indulgences like rich food and French fries, sleeping late, and other "guilty pleasures," as the article called them. It quoted several psychiatrists and other mind experts. All of them characterized guilt as a usually groundless emotion that has the potential of taking all the fun out of life.

The library's periodical catalog lists these recent magazine articles under the heading *Guilt*: "How to Stop Being So Tough on Yourself," "Guilt Can Drive You Crazy," "Guilt Mongering," "Getting Rid of the Guilts," "Stop Pleading Guilty," "Guilt: Letting Go," "Don't Feed the Guilt Monster"—and a host of similar titles.

The headline of an advice column caught my eye. It summed up the universal counsel of our generation: "IT'S NOT YOUR FAULT." A woman had written to say she had tried every form of therapy she knew and still could not break a self-destructive habit.

"The first step you must take," the columnist responded, "is to stop blaming yourself. Your compulsive behavior is *not* your fault; refuse to accept blame—and above all, do not blame yourself—for what you cannot control. Heaping guilt on yourself only adds to your stress, low self-esteem, worry, depression, feelings of inadequacy, and dependence on others. Let go of your guilt feelings."

Nearly every kind of guilt can now be off-loaded. We live in a no-fault society. Even Ann Landers has written,

> One of the most painful, self-mutilating, time- and energy-consuming exercises in the human experience is guilt. . . . It can ruin your day—or your week or your life—if you let it. It turns up like a bad penny when you do something dishonest, hurt-ful, tacky, selfish, or rotten. . . . Never mind that it was the re-sult of ignorance, stupidity, laziness, thoughtlessness, weak

flesh, or clay feet. You did wrong and the guilt is killing you. Too bad. But be assured, the agony you feel is normal. . . . Remember guilt is a pollutant and we don't need any more of it in the world.[5]

In other words, you shouldn't let yourself feel bad "when you do something dishonest, hurtful, tacky, selfish, or rotten." Think of yourself as good. Ignorant, stupid, lazy, thoughtless, or weak, perhaps— but *good*. Don't pollute your mind with the debilitating thought that you might actually be guilty of something.

No Guilt, No Sin

That kind of thinking has all but driven words like *sin, repentance, contrition, atonement, restitution*, and *redemption* out of public discourse. If no one is supposed to feel guilty, how could anyone be a sinner? Modern culture has the answer: people are *victims*. Victims are not responsible for what they do; they are casualties of what happens to them. So every human failing must be described in terms of how the perpetrator has been victimized. We are all supposed to be "sensitive" and "compassionate" enough to see that the very behaviors we used to label "sin" are actually evidence of victimization.

Victimism has gained so much influence that as far as society is concerned, there is practically no such thing as sin anymore. Anyone can escape responsibility for his or her wrongdoing simply by claiming the status of a victim. It has radically changed the way our society looks at human behavior.

Anyone can escape responsibility for his or her wrongdoing simply by claiming the status of a victim.

A man who was shot and paralyzed while committing a burglary in New York recovered damages from the store owner who shot him. His attorney told a jury the man was first of all a victim of society, driven to crime by economic disadvantages. Now, the lawyer said, he is a victim of the insensitivity of the man who shot him. Because of that man's callous disregard of the thief's plight as a victim, the poor criminal will be confined to a wheelchair for the rest of his life. He deserves some redress. The jury agreed. The store owner paid a large settlement. Several months later, the same man, still in his wheelchair, was arrested while committing another armed robbery.

Bernard McCummings parlayed a similar victimism into wealth. After mugging and brutally beating an elderly New York man in the subway, McCummings was shot while fleeing the scene. Permanently paralyzed, he sued and won $4.8 million in compensation from the New York Transit Authority. The man he mugged, a cancer patient, is still paying doctor bills. McCummings, the mugger—whom the courts deemed the greater victim—is now a multimillionaire.[6]

In two separate cases in England, a barmaid who stabbed another woman to death in a barroom brawl, and a woman who angrily drove her car into her lover were both acquitted of murder after they claimed acute pre-menstrual syndrome (PMS) addled their thinking and caused them to act in ways they could not control. Both received therapy rather than punishment.[7]

A San Francisco city supervisor claimed he murdered a fellow supervisor and Mayor George Moscone because too much junk food—especially Hostess Twinkies—made him act irrationally. Thus the famous "Twinkie" defense was born. "A lenient jury bought the line and produced a verdict of voluntary manslaughter rather than murder."[8] They ruled that the junk food resulted in "diminished mental capacity," which mitigated the killer's guilt. He was out of prison before the mayor's next term would have been complete.

Rioting gang members in Los Angeles beat truck driver Reginald Denny almost to death before live television cameras. A jury acquitted them of all but the most minor charges, deciding that they were caught up in the mayhem of the moment and therefore not responsible for their actions.

It is theoretically possible today in America to commit the most monstrous crimes and get off scot-free, simply by blaming some imaginative mental or emotional disorder, or by inventing some affliction to explain why you are not responsible for what you have done.

A drug dealer and cocaine addict from the Bronx was acquitted of murder after killing eight children and two women whom he shot in the head at point-blank range. His crime was the largest mass killing in the New York area since 1949. But jurors decided that drugs and stress "were a reasonable explanation for his actions." They said the man "had acted under extreme emotional distress and the influence of drugs"—so they found him guilty on a lesser charge that brought only a light sentence.[9]

But it isn't only career criminals who are using such excuses to shift blame for their wrongdoing. Millions of people from the top of society to the bottom are using similar tactics to excuse themselves for the evil things they do.

Michael Deaver, Ronald Reagan's deputy chief of staff, pleaded not guilty to perjury, claiming alcoholism and drug use had impaired his memory. He admitted "he was secretly drinking up to a quart of Scotch a day" while working in the White House.[10] The judge was at least partly swayed by the argument and gave Deaver a suspended sentence.[11]

Richard Berendzen, president of American University in Washington, D. C., was caught making obscene telephone calls to women. Claiming he was a victim of childhood abuse, Berendzen received a suspended sentence and negotiated a million-dollar severance package from the university. He has now written a book about his ordeal in which he explains that the obscene calls were his method of "data gathering." The book was given rave reviews in the *Washington Post* and *USA Today*. [12]

The Sin-as-Disease Model

Perhaps the most prevalent means of escaping blame is by classifying every human failing as some kind of disease. Drunkards and drug addicts can check into clinics for treatment of their "chemical dependencies." Children who habitually defy authority can escape condemnation by being labeled "hyperactive" or having ADD (attention deficiency disorder). Gluttons are no longer blameworthy; they suffer from an "eating disorder." Even the man who throws away his family's livelihood to pay for prostitutes is supposed to be an object of compassionate understanding; he is "addicted to sex."

An FBI agent was fired after he embezzled two thousand dollars, then gambled it away in a single afternoon at a casino. Later he sued, arguing that his gambling addiction was a disability, so his firing was an act of illegal discrimination. He won the case! Moreover, his therapy for the gambling addiction had to be funded under his employer's health-care insurance, just as if he had been suffering from appendicitis or an ingrown toenail.[13]

These days *everything* wrong with humanity is likely to be explained as an illness. What we used to call sin is more easily diagnosed as a whole array of disabilities. All kinds of immorality and evil conduct are now identified as symptoms of this or that psychological illness. Criminal behavior, various perverse passions, and every imaginable addiction have all been made excusable by the crusade to label them medical afflictions. Even commonplace problems, such as emotional weakness, depression, and anxiety are also almost universally defined as quasi-medical, rather than spiritual, afflictions.

The American Psychiatric Association publishes a thick book to help therapists in the diagnosis of these new diseases. *The Diagnostic and Statistical Manual of Mental Disorders* (Third Edition, Revised)—or DSM-III-R, as it is popularly labeled—lists the following "disorders":

- *Conduct Disorder*—"a persistent pattern of conduct in which the basic rights of others and major age-appropriate societal norms or rules are violated."
- *Oppositional Defiant Disorder*—"a pattern of negativistic, hostile, and defiant behavior."
- *Histrionic Personality Disorder*—"a pervasive pattern of excessive emotionality and attention-seeking."
- *Antisocial Personality Disorder*—"a pattern of irresponsible and antisocial behavior beginning in childhood or early adolescence and continuing into adulthood."

And there are dozens more like those. Multitudes of parents, influenced by such diagnoses, refuse to punish their children for misbehavior. Instead, they seek therapy for ODD, or HDP, or whatever new diagnosis fits the unruly child's behavior.

In the words of one author, the disease-model approach to human behavior has so overwhelmed us as a society that we have gone haywire. We want to pass laws to excuse compulsive gamblers when they embezzle money to gamble and to force insurance companies to pay to treat them. We want to treat people who can't find love and who instead (when they are women) go after dopey, superficial men or (when they are men) pursue endless sexual liaisons without finding true happiness. And we want to call all these things—and many, many more—addictions.

. . . .

> What is this new addiction industry meant to accomplish? More and more addictions are being discovered, and new addicts are being identified, until all of us will be locked into our own little addictive worlds with other addicts like ourselves, defined by the special interests of our neuroses. What a repugnant world to imagine, as well as a hopeless one. Meanwhile, *all of the addictions we define are increasing.*[14]

Worse yet, the number of people who suffer from such newly identified "sicknesses" is increasing even faster. The therapy industry is clearly *not* solving the problem of what Scripture calls sin. Instead it merely convinces multitudes that they are desperately sick and therefore not really responsible for their wrong behavior. It gives them permission to think of themselves as patients, not malefactors. And it encourages them to undergo extensive—and expensive— treatment that lasts for years, or better yet, for a lifetime. These new diseases, it seems, are ailments from which no one is ever expected to recover completely.

The sin-as-disease model has proved to be a boon to the multi- billion-dollar counseling industry, and the shift toward long-term or even permanent therapy promises a bright economic future for pro- fessional therapists. One psychologist who has analyzed this trend suggests there is a clear strategy to the way therapists market their services:

1. Continue the psychologization of life;
2. Make problems out of difficulties and spread the alarm;
3. Make it acceptable to have the problem and be unable to resolve it on one's own;
4. Offer salvation [psychological, not spiritual].[15]

He notes that many therapists purposely extend their treatments over periods of many years, even after the original problem that provoked the client to seek counseling has been solved or forgotten. "They go on for so long and the client becomes so dependent on the therapist that a special period of time—sometimes extending to six months or more—is required to get the client ready to leave."[16]

Even commonplace problems, such as emotional weakness, depression, and anxiety are also almost universally defined as quasi-medical, rather than spiritual, afflictions.

"Recovery," the code-word for programs modeled after Alcoholics Anonymous, is explicitly marketed as a lifelong program. We've grown accustomed to the image of a person who has been sober for forty years standing up in an AA meeting and saying, "I'm Bill, and I'm an alcoholic." Now all "addicts" are using the same approach—including sex addicts, gambling addicts, nicotine addicts, anger addicts, wife-beating addicts, child-molesting addicts, debt addicts, self-abuse addicts, envy addicts, failure addicts, overeating addicts, or whatever. People suffering from such maladies are taught to speak of themselves as "recovering," never "recovered." Those who dare to think of themselves as delivered from their affliction are told they are living in denial.

The Wrong Prescription

Disease-model therapy therefore feeds the very problem it is supposed to treat. It alleviates any sense of guilt, while making people feel they are victims, helplessly bound for life to their affliction. Is it any wonder that such a diagnosis so often becomes a self-fulfilling prophecy?

Misdiagnosis means *any* prescribed treatment will be utterly ineffective. The care indicated for conditions labeled pathological usually involves long-term therapy, self-acceptance, a recovery program, or all of the above—perhaps even with some other psychological gimmick such as self-hypnosis thrown in to complete the elixir. "In place of evil, therapeutic society has substituted 'illness'; in place of consequence, it urges therapy and understanding; in place of responsibility, it argues for a personality driven by impulses. The illness excuse has become almost routine in cases of public misconduct."[17]

But assume for the moment that the problem *is* sin rather than sickness. The only true remedy involves humble repentance, confession (the recognition that you deserve the chastening of God because you alone are responsible for your sin)—then restitution, and growth through the spiritual disciplines of prayer, Bible study, communion with God, fellowship with other believers, and dependence on Christ. In other words, if the problem is in fact spiritual, labeling it a clinical issue will only exacerbate the problem and will offer no real deliverance from the sin. That is precisely what we see happening everywhere.

The sad truth is that disease-model treatment is disastrously counterproductive. By casting the sinner in the role of a victim, it ignores or minimizes the personal guilt inherent in the misbehavior. "I am sick" is much easier to say than, "I have sinned." But it doesn't deal with the fact that one's transgression is a serious offense against a holy, omniscient, omnipotent God. Personal guilt is for that very reason at the heart of what must be confronted when dealing with one's sin. But the disease-model remedy cannot address the problem of guilt without explaining it away. And by explaining guilt away, disease-model therapy does untold violence to the human conscience. It is therefore no remedy at all, but a disastrous prescription for escalating wickedness and eternal damnation.

The Victimization of Society

The obvious ineffectiveness of disease-model therapy has been no obstacle to its acceptance by society. After all, people want sin without guilt, and this philosophy promises just that. The trend has resulted in what author Charles J. Sykes calls "A Nation of Victims." Sykes is troubled by the rush to embrace victimism, which he suggests is badly eroding the moral character of American society. "The politics of victimization has taken the place of more traditional expressions of morality and equity," he writes.[18]

Victimism has so infected our culture that one might even say the victim has become the very symbol—the mascot—of modern society. Sykes observes,

> Whatever the future of the American mind—and the omens are not propitious—the destiny of the American character is perhaps even more alarming. . . .
>
> The National Anthem has become The Whine.
>
> Increasingly, Americans act as if they had received a lifelong indemnification from misfortune and a contractual release from personal responsibility. The British *Economist* noted with bemusement that in the United States, "If you lose your job you can sue for the mental distress of being fired. If your bank goes broke, the government has insured your deposits. . . . If you drive drunk and crash you can sue somebody for failing to warn you to stop drinking. *There is always somebody else to blame.*" [Emphasis added.]
>
> Unfortunately, that is a formula for social gridlock: the irresistible search for someone or something to blame colliding with the unmovable unwillingness to accept responsibility. Now enshrined in law and jurisprudence, victimism is reshaping the fabric of society, including employment policies, criminal justice, education, urban politics, and, in an increasingly Orwellian emphasis on "sensitivity" in language. A community of interdependent citizens has been displaced by a society of resentful, competing, and self-interested individuals who have dressed their private annoyances in the garb of victimism.[19]

Those who define themselves as victims claim entitlements and shun responsibility. They thus jettison any obligation they might have toward others or toward society as a whole. Once upon a time, when society affirmed the concept of personal responsibility, citizens were expected to contribute to society. They were encouraged to ask not what their country could do for them but what they could do for their country. Now that everyone is a victim, however, people think they have every right to demand society's benevolence without giving anything in return.

---

*Victimism has so infected our culture
that one might even say the victim
has become the very symbol—
the mascot—of modern society.*

Moreover, if everyone is a victim, no one needs to accept personal responsibility for wrong behavior or toxic attitudes. After all, victims are entitled to self-pity; they shouldn't be saddled with guilt feelings. Thus victimism obviates the conscience.

And if nobody shoulders any blame for society's ills, where *does* the guilt lie? With God? That would be the implication—if our culture even acknowledged God's existence. But in a society of victims there is no room for the concept of a benevolent, holy God.

Disease-Model Therapy Invades the Church

One might think that victimism and disease-model therapy are so obviously contrary to biblical truth that Bible-believing Christians would rise up *en masse* and expose the error of such thinking. But tragically, that has not been the case. Victimism has become almost as influential within the evangelical church as it is in the unbelieving world, thanks to self-esteem theology and the church's fascination with worldly psychology.

These days, when sinners seek help from churches and other Christian agencies, they are likely to be told that their problem is some emotional disorder or psychological syndrome. They might be encouraged to forgive themselves and told they ought to have more self-love and self-esteem. They are not as likely to hear that they must repent and humbly seek God's forgiveness in Christ. That is such an extraordinary change of direction for the church that even secular observers have noticed it.

Wendy Kaminer, for example, does not purport to be a Christian. If anything, she seems hostile to the church. She describes herself as "a skeptical, secular humanist, Jewish, feminist, intellectual lawyer."[20] But she has seen the change of direction within evangelicalism, and she describes it with uncanny precision. She notes that religion and psychology have always more or less deemed one another incompatible. Now she sees "not just a truce but a remarkable accommodation."[21] Even from her perspective as an unbeliever, she can see that this accommodation has meant a wholesale alteration of the fundamental message about sin and salvation. She writes:

> Christian codependency books, like those produced by the Minirth-Meier clinic in Texas, are practically indistinguishable from codependency books published by secular writers. . . . Religious writers justify their reliance on psychology by praising it for "catching up" to some eternal truths, but they've also found a way to make the temporal truths of psychology palatable. Religious leaders once condemned psychoanalysis for its moral neutrality. . . . Now popular religious literature equates illness with sin.[22]

Some of the criticism Kaminer levels against evangelicals is unwarranted or misguided, but in this respect, she is right on target: the inevitable result of Christians' embracing secular psychology has been the abandonment of any coherent concept of sin. And that has inevitably clouded the message we proclaim.

Describing the prevailing spirit of our age, Kaminer writes, "No matter how bad you've been in the narcissistic 1970s and the acquisitive 1980s, no matter how many drugs you've ingested, or sex acts performed, or how much corruption enjoyed, you're still essentially innocent: the divine child inside you is always untouched by the worst of your sins."[23] Elsewhere, she says,

> Inner children are always good—innocent and pure—like the most sentimentalized Dickens characters, which means that people are essentially good. . . . Even Ted Bundy had a child within. Evil is merely a mask—a dysfunction.
>
> The therapeutic view of evil as sickness, not sin, is strong in co-dependency theory—it's not a fire and brimstone theology. "Shaming" children, calling them bad, is considered a primary form of abuse. Both guilt and shame "are not useful as a way of life," Melody Beattie writes earnestly in Codependent No More. "Guilt makes *everything* harder. . . . We need to forgive ourselves" [(New York: Harper & Row, 1989), pp. 114–115]. Someone should

remind Beattie that there's a name for people who lack guilt and shame: sociopaths. We ought to be grateful if guilt makes things like murder and moral corruption "harder."[24]

Victimism has become almost as influential within the evangelical church as it is in the unbelieving world.

Ms. Kaminer suggests that evangelicalism has been infiltrated by this new anthropology-psychology-theology, and that it is antithetical to what we ought to believe and teach about sin. In that regard she surely understands more than the horde of evangelical writers who continue to echo themes from the secular self-esteem cult.

This is a serious matter. Whether you deny sin overtly and openly and totally, or covertly and by implication, any tampering with the biblical concept of sin makes chaos of the Christian faith.

Those ubiquitous phone-in counseling programs on Christian radio may provide one of the best barometers of popular Christianity's trends. When was the last time you heard an on-the-air counselor tell someone suffering from conscience pangs, "Your guilt is valid; you are sinful and must seek full repentance before God"?

Recently I listened to a talk show on a local religious radio station. This daily program features a man who bills himself as a Christian psychologist. On the day I listened he was talking about the importance of overcoming our sense of guilt. Self-blame, he told his audience, is usually irrational and therefore potentially very harmful. He gave a long lecture about the importance of forgiving oneself. The whole discourse was an echo of the world's wisdom: Guilt is a virtual mental defect. Don't let it ruin your self-image. And so on. He never mentioned repentance or restitution as prerequisites for self-forgiveness, and he never cited a single passage of Scripture.

That kind of counsel is as deadly as it is unbiblical. Guilt feelings may not always be rational, but they are nearly always a reliable signal that something is wrong somewhere, and we had better come to grips with whatever it is and make it right. Guilt functions in the spiritual realm like pain in the material realm. Pain tells us there is a physical problem that must be dealt with or the body will suffer harm. Guilt is a spiritual pain in the soul that tells us something is evil and needs to be confronted and cleansed.

To deny personal guilt is to sacrifice the soul for the sake of the ego. Besides, disavowal doesn't really deal with guilt, as we all know intuitively. Far from having beneficial results, it destroys the conscience, and thereby weakens a person's ability to avoid destructive sin. Furthermore, it actually renders a healthy self-image altogether unattainable. "How can we have self-respect if we are not responsible for what we are?"[25] More important, how can we have true self-respect without hearty approval from a healthy conscience?

The Futility of Denying Our Guilt

Twenty years ago psychiatrist Karl Menninger wrote a landmark book titled *Whatever Became of Sin?* [26] Menninger, who is no evangelical, nevertheless saw clearly the folly of treating social and behavioral problems as if their causes were all utterly nonmoral. He pointed out that modern psychology's approach—making guilt an aberration and treating self-blame as a fallacy—in effect absolves people from any moral responsibility for their behavior. That, Menninger said, eats at the fabric of the soul and society. He added that we desperately need to recover the conviction that certain behavior is *sinful*. After twenty years, the book still has the ring of a voice crying in the wilderness. But the message is needed more urgently than ever today.

Some of Menninger's views we might not entirely agree with. But his central thesis is right on target. He clearly understands that *mental* health is contingent upon, if not synonymous with, *moral* health. He therefore sees that the first step to any truly effective remedy for all mental and emotional afflictions is an honest assessment of one's own sin and the acceptance of complete responsibility for one's own moral failings. Most important, he knows there is ultimately no help for those who deny responsibility for their own behavior.

That single premise, if appreciated and applied throughout the massive counseling industry, would have an immediate beneficial effect on all society.

But as we have seen, most of the counseling being dispensed today takes precisely the opposite tack. When guilt feelings are derided as useless and unproductive, when shame is thought to be unwholesome, and when professional counselors encourage people to forgive themselves without repenting, what do we expect to become of the conscience?

What is evident is that people in our culture are becoming very good at blame-shifting—making scapegoats of parents, childhood disappointments, and other dysfunctions beyond their control. No matter what problem you suffer from—whether you are a cannibalizing serial murderer or just someone struggling with emotional distress—you can easily find someone who will explain to you why your failing is not your fault, and teach you how to silence a troubled conscience.

But from a *practical* perspective alone, that approach clearly is not working. More people than ever feel they are in need of professional counseling. Many are even becoming addicted to such therapy. Unable to cope with their own feelings, they become dependent on a therapist who must continually stoke their sense of self-worth with counsel like, "Don't be so hard on yourself"; "You mustn't blame yourself"; "You need to pamper your inner child"; "Stop punishing yourself"; "Let go of your guilt"; "You're not such a bad person"; and so on.

No matter what problem you suffer from—whether you are a cannibalizing serial murderer or just someone struggling with emotional distress— you can easily find someone who will explain to you why your failing is not your fault, and teach you how to silence a troubled conscience.

From a *biblical* perspective, that kind of counsel can be spiritually destructive. It fails to address the real problem of human sinfulness. It feeds the worst tendencies of human nature. It engenders the most catastrophic form of denial—denial of one's own guilt. And for most, who can't really shake the guilt, it adds more guilt for blaming someone who isn't really to blame at all.

Disavowing our personal culpability can never free us from a sense of guilt. On the contrary, those who refuse to acknowledge their sinfulness actually place themselves in bondage to their own guilt. "He that covereth his sins shall not prosper: but whoso confesseth and forsaketh them shall have mercy" (Prov. 28:13, KJV). "If we say that we have no sin, we are deceiving ourselves, and the truth is not in us. [But] if we confess our sins, He is faithful and righteous to forgive us our sins and to cleanse us from all unrighteousness" (1 Jn. 1:8–9).

Jesus Christ came into the world to save sinners! Jesus specifically said He had *not* come to save those who want to exonerate themselves (Mk. 2:17). Where there is no recognition of sin and guilt, when the conscience has been abused into silence, there can be no salvation, no sanctification, and therefore no real emancipation from sin's ruthless power.

2

The Soul's Automatic Warning System

An educated, sensitive conscience is God's monitor. It alerts us to the moral quality of what we do or plan to do, forbids lawlessness and irresponsibility, and makes us feel guilt, shame, and fear of the future retribution that it tells us we deserve, when we have allowed ourselves to defy its restraints. Satan's strategy is to corrupt, desensitize, and if possible kill our consciences. The relativism, materialism, narcissism, secularism, and hedonism of today's western world help him mightily toward his goal. His task is made yet simpler by the way in which the world's moral weaknesses have been taken into the contemporary church.

J. I Packer[1]

In 1984 an Avianca Airlines jet crashed in Spain. Investigators studying the accident made an eerie discovery. The "black box" cockpit recorders revealed that several minutes before impact a shrill, computer-synthesized voice from the plane's automatic warning system told the crew repeatedly in English, "Pull up! Pull up!" The pilot, evidently thinking the system was malfunctioning, snapped, "Shut up, Gringo!" and switched the system off. Minutes later the plane plowed into the side of a mountain. Everyone on board died.

When I saw that tragic story on the news shortly after it happened, it struck me as a perfect parable of the way modern people treat the warning messages of their consciences.

As we noted in the previous chapter, the wisdom of our age says guilt feelings are nearly always erroneous or hurtful; therefore we should switch them off. But is that good advice? What, after all, is the conscience—this sense of guilt we all seem to feel? How much heed should we pay to the pangs of a grieved conscience? The conscience is not infallible, is it? So how do we know whether the guilt we feel is legitimate or whether we're simply burdened with an excess of angst? What role does the conscience play in the life of a Christian who wants to pursue sanctification according to biblical means?

What Is the Conscience?

The conscience is generally seen by the modern world as a defect that robs people of their self-esteem. Far from being a defect or a disorder, however, our ability to sense our own guilt is a tremendous gift from God. He designed the conscience into the very framework of the human soul. It is the automatic warning system that tells us, "Pull up! Pull up!" before we crash and burn.

The conscience, Puritan Richard Sibbes wrote in the seventeenth century, is *the soul reflecting upon itself.*[2] Conscience is at the heart of what distinguishes the human creature. People, unlike animals, can contemplate their own actions and make moral self-evaluations. That is the very function of conscience.

The conscience is an innate ability to sense right and wrong. Everyone, even the most unspiritual heathen, has a conscience: "When Gentiles who do not have the Law do instinctively the things of the Law, these, not having the Law, are a law to themselves, in that they show the work of the Law written in their hearts, *their conscience bearing witness*, and their thoughts alternately accusing or else defending them" (Rom. 2:14–15, emphasis added).

The conscience entreats us to do what we believe is right and restrains us from doing what we believe is wrong. The conscience is not to be equated with the voice of God or the law of God. It is a human faculty that judges our actions and thoughts by the light of the highest standard we perceive. When we violate our conscience, it condemns us, triggering feelings of shame, anguish, regret, consternation, anxiety, disgrace, and even fear. When we follow our conscience, it commends us, bringing joy, serenity, self-respect, well-being, and gladness.

The word *conscience* is a combination of the Latin words *scire* ("to know") and *con* ("together"). The Greek word for "conscience" is found more than thirty times in the New Testament—*suneidēsis*, which also literally means "co-knowledge." Conscience is knowledge together with oneself; that is, conscience knows our inner motives and true thoughts. Conscience is above reason and beyond intellect. We may rationalize, trying to justify ourselves in our own minds, but a violated conscience will not be easily convinced.

Multitudes today respond to their conscience by attempting to suppress it, overrule it, or silence it.

The Hebrew word for conscience is *leb*, usually translated "heart" in the Old Testament. The conscience is so much at the core of the human soul that the Hebrew mind did not draw a distinction between conscience and the rest of the inner person. Thus when Moses recorded that Pharaoh "hardened his heart" (Exod. 8:15), he was saying that Pharaoh had steeled his conscience against God's will. When Scripture speaks of a tender heart (cf. 2 Chr. 34:27), it refers to a sensitive conscience. The "upright in heart" (Ps. 7:10) are those with pure consciences. And when David prayed, "Create in me a clean heart, O God" (Ps. 51:10), he was seeking to have his life and his conscience cleansed.

As we noted in chapter 1, multitudes today respond to their conscience by attempting to suppress it, overrule it, or silence it. They conclude that the real blame for their wrong behavior lies in some childhood trauma, the way their parents raised them, societal pressures, or other causes beyond their control. Or they convince themselves that their sin is a clinical problem, not a moral one—and therefore define their alcoholism, sexual perversion, immorality, or other vices as "diseases." To respond to the conscience with such arguments is tantamount to telling the conscience, "Shut up, Gringo!"

It is possible virtually to nullify the conscience through repeated abuse. Paul spoke of people whose consciences were so convoluted that their "glory is in their shame" (Phil. 3:19; cf. Rom. 1:32). Both the mind and the conscience can become so defiled that they cease making distinctions between what is pure and what is impure (cf. Tit. 1:15). After so much violation, the conscience finally falls silent. Morally, those with defiled consciences are left flying blind. The annoying warning signals may be gone, but the danger certainly is not; *in fact, the danger is greater than ever*.

Furthermore, even the most defiled conscience will not remain silent forever. When we stand in judgment, every person's conscience will side with God, the righteous judge. The worst sin-hardened evildoer will discover before the throne of God that he has a conscience which testifies against him.

The conscience, however, is *not* infallible. Nor is it a source of revelation about right and wrong. Its role is not to teach us moral and ethical ideals, but to hold us accountable to the highest standards of right and wrong we know. The conscience is informed by tradition as well as by truth, so the standards it holds us to are not necessarily biblical ones (1 Cor. 8:6–9). The conscience can be needlessly condemning in areas where there is no biblical issue. In fact, it can try to hold us to the very thing the Lord is trying to release us from (Rom. 14:14, 20–23). The conscience, to operate fully and in accord with true holiness, must be informed by the Word of God. So even when guilt feelings don't have a biblical basis, they are an important spiritual distress sign. If they're only signaling a weak conscience, that should spur us to seek the spiritual growth that would bring our conscience more in harmony with God's Word.

The conscience reacts to the convictions of the mind and therefore can be encouraged and sharpened in accordance with God's Word. The wise Christian wants to master biblical truth so that the conscience is completely informed and judges right because it is responding to God's Word. A regular diet of Scripture will strengthen a weak conscience or restrain an overactive one. Conversely, error, human wisdom, and wrong moral influences filling the mind will corrupt or cripple the conscience.

In other words, the conscience functions like a skylight, not a light bulb. It lets light into the soul; it does not produce its own. Its effectiveness is determined by the amount of pure light we expose it to, and by how clean we keep it. Cover it or put it in total darkness and it ceases to function. That's why the apostle Paul spoke of the importance of a clear conscience (1 Tim. 3:9) and warned against anything that would defile or muddy the conscience (1 Cor. 8:7; Tit. 1:15).

Or, to switch metaphors, our conscience is like the nerve endings in our fingertips. Its sensitivity to external stimuli can be damaged by the buildup of callouses or even wounded so badly as to be virtually impervious to any feeling. Paul also wrote of the dangers of a calloused conscience (1 Cor. 8:10), a wounded conscience (v. 12), and a seared conscience (1 Tim. 4:2).

The conscience is privy to all our secret thoughts and motives. It is therefore a more accurate and more formidable witness in the soul's courtroom than any external observer.

Psychopaths, serial killers, pathological liars, and other people who seem to lack any moral sense are extreme examples of people who have ruined or desensitized their consciences. Can such people really sin without remorse or scruples? If so, it is only because they have ravaged their own consciences through relentless immorality and lawlessness. They certainly weren't born devoid of any conscience. The conscience is an inextricable part of the human soul. Though it may be hardened, cauterized, or numbed into apparent dormancy, the conscience continues to store up evidence that will one day be used as testimony to condemn the guilty soul.

The Conscience Holds Court

Richard Sibbes pictured the conscience as a court in the council of the human heart. In Sibbes's imagery, the conscience itself assumes every role in the courtroom drama. It is a *register* to record what we have done in exact detail (Jer. 17:1). It is the *accuser* that lodges a complaint against us when we are guilty, and a *defender* to side with us in our innocence (Rom. 2:15). It acts as a *witness*, giving testimony for or against us (2 Cor. 1:12). It is the *judge*, condemning or vindicating us (1 Jn. 3:20–21). And it is the *executioner*, smiting us with grief when our guilt is discovered (1 Sam. 24:5). Sibbes compared the chastisement of a violated conscience to "a flash of hell."[3]

The conscience is privy to all our secret thoughts and motives. It is therefore a more accurate and more formidable witness in the soul's courtroom than any external observer. Those who gloss over an accusing conscience in favor of a human counselor's reassurances are playing a deadly game. Ill thoughts and motives may escape the eye of a human counselor, but they will not escape the eye of conscience. Nor will they escape the eye of an all-knowing God. When such people are summoned to final judgment, their own conscience will be fully informed of every violation and will step forward as an eternally tormenting witness against them.

That, Sibbes wrote, ought to discourage us from secret sins:

> We should not sin in hope of concealment. What if thou conceal it from all others, canst thou conceal [it from] thy own conscience? As one saith well, What good is it for thee that none knows what is done, when thou knowest it thyself? What profit is it for him that hath a conscience that will accuse him, that he hath no man to accuse him but himself? He is a thousand witnesses to himself. *Conscience is not a private witness.* It is a thousand witnesses. Therefore, never sin in hope to have it concealed. It were better that all men should know it than that

thyself should know it. All will be one day written in thy forehead. *Conscience will be a blab.* If it cannot speak the truth now, though it be bribed in this life, it will have power and efficacy in the life to come. . . . We have the witness in us; and, as Isaiah saith, 'Our sins witness against us.' It is in vain to look for secrecy. Conscience will discover all.[4]

How the Conscience Is Cleansed

One aspect of the miracle of salvation is the cleansing and rejuvenating effect the new birth has on the conscience. At salvation, the believer's heart is "sprinkled clean from an evil conscience" (Heb. 10:22). The means through which the conscience is cleansed is the blood of Christ (Heb. 9:14). That does not mean, of course, that Jesus' actual blood has some mystical or magical potency as a conscience-cleansing agent. What does it mean?

The theological concepts involved here are simple but quite profound. The Old Testament Law required blood sacrifices to atone for sin. But Old Testament sacrifices could do nothing for the conscience. Hebrews 9:9–10 says, "Gifts and sacrifices [under the Levitical system] could not make the worshiper perfect in conscience, since they relate only to food and drink and various washings, regulations for the body imposed until a time of reformation." Those sacrifices had no actual efficacy in atoning for sin, "for it is impossible for the blood of bulls and goats to take away sins" (Heb. 10:4). They simply demonstrated the faith and obedience of the worshiper while foreshadowing the death of Christ, who would shed His blood as the once for-all perfect sacrifice for sin.

Christ's atonement fully satisfied
the demands of God's righteousness,
so forgiveness and mercy are guaranteed
to those who receive
Christ in humble, repentant faith.

Christ's sacrifice on the cross therefore accomplished what the blood of goats and bulls and the ashes of heifers could only symbolize: "He Himself bore our sins in His body on the cross" (1 Pet. 2:24). Our sins were imputed to Him, and He paid the penalty for them. Conversely, His perfect righteousness is imputed to us who believe (Rom. 4:22–24; Phil. 3:9). Since the guilt of all our sins was entirely erased by His death, and since His unblemished righteousness is credited to our account, God declares us not guilty and receives us as fully righteous. That is the doctrine known as *justification*.

When God's own verdict is "Not guilty; wholly righteous" how can anyone else accuse us? "Who will bring a charge against God's elect? God is the one who justifies; who is the one who condemns? Christ Jesus is He who died, yes, rather who was raised, who is at the right hand of God, who also intercedes for us" (Rom. 8:33–34). In other words, when Satan, "the accuser of our brethren . . . , who accuses them before our God day and night" (Rev. 12:10), brings an allegation against us, the blood of Christ speaks of mercy. When our own sins cry out against us, the blood of Christ speaks on our behalf. Thus the blood of Christ "speaks better than the blood of Abel" (Heb. 12:24).

Most important, whenever our own conscience would mercilessly condemn us, the blood of Christ cries for forgiveness. Christ's atonement fully satisfied the demands of God's righteousness, so forgiveness and mercy are guaranteed to those who receive Christ in humble, repentant faith. We accept the responsibility for our sin, and also believe God that in the death of Christ sin is forgiven. We confess our sin so that the Lord can cleanse our conscience and give us joy (1 Jn. 1:9). That is how "the blood of Christ, who through the eternal Spirit offered Himself without blemish to God, cleanse[s] your conscience from dead works to serve the living God" (Heb. 9:14). In other words, our faith communicates to our conscience that we are pardoned through the precious blood of Christ.

Does that mean believers can persist in sinning and yet enjoy a clear conscience? Certainly not. "How shall we who died to sin still live in it?" (Rom. 6:2). The new birth entails a complete overhaul of the human soul (2 Cor. 5:17). A washed and rejuvenated conscience is only one evidence that such a transformation has taken place (cf. 1 Pet. 3:21). Love of righteousness and hatred of sin is another evidence (1 Jn. 3:3, 8). Believers whose behavior contradicts their faith cause their consciences to be defiled (1 Cor. 8:7). And those who profess Christ but ultimately reject faith and a good conscience suffer shipwreck spiritually (1 Tim. 1:19)—that is, they prove they never truly believed in the first place (cf. 1 Jn. 2:19).

A sound conscience therefore goes hand in hand with assurance of salvation (Heb. 10:22). The steadfast believer must maintain the proper focus of faith in order to have a conscience that is perpetually being cleansed from guilt: "If we confess our sins, He is faithful and righteous to forgive us our sins and to [keep on cleansing] us from all unrighteousness" (1 Jn. 1:9).

What a gift it is to be cleansed from a defiled conscience! In the same way that a grieved conscience is a flash of hell, so a pure conscience is a foretaste of glory.

It is the Christian's high and holy duty to guard the purity of his regenerated conscience. Paul had much to say about this. Note how he spoke of the conscience in the following verses (emphasis added):

- "Paul, looking intently at the Council, said, 'Brethren, I have lived my life with *a perfectly good conscience* before God up to this day'" (Acts 23:1).
- "In view of this, I also do my best to maintain always *a blameless conscience* both before God and before men" (Acts 24:16).
- "The goal of our instruction is love from a pure heart and *a good conscience* and a sincere faith" (1 Tim. 1:5).
- "Fight the good fight, keeping faith and *a good conscience*" (1 Tim. 1:18–19).
- "I serve [God] with *a clear conscience* the way my forefathers did" (2 Tim. 1:3).

One of the basic qualifications for deacons, Paul told Timothy, is "holding to the mystery of the faith with *a clear conscience*" (1 Tim. 3:9).

Ironically, a weak conscience is more likely to accuse than a strong conscience. Scripture calls this a weak conscience because it is too easily wounded.

A pure conscience is essential not only for what it does for one-self, but for what it says to others. A sound conscience marks the life that is a strong testimony for Christ. Paul frequently pointed to his conscience as a witness: "For our proud confidence is this, the testimony of our conscience, that in holiness and godly sincerity, not in fleshly wisdom but in the grace of God, we have conducted ourselves in the world, and especially toward you" (2 Cor. 1:12). "We have renounced the things hidden because of shame, not walking in craftiness or adulterating the word of God, but by the manifestation of truth commending ourselves to every man's conscience in the sight of God" (2 Cor. 4:2). Peter wrote, "Keep a good conscience so that in the thing in which you are slandered, those who revile your good behavior in Christ may be put to shame" (1 Pet. 3:16).

Overcoming a Weak Conscience

As we noted briefly earlier, Scripture indicates that some Christians have weak consciences. A weak conscience is not the same as a seared conscience. A seared conscience becomes inactive, silent, rarely accusing, insensitive to sin. But the weakened conscience usually is hypersensitive and overactive about issues that are not sins. Ironically, a weak conscience is more likely to accuse than a strong conscience. Scripture calls this a weak conscience because it is *too easily wounded*. People with weak consciences tend to fret about things that should provoke no guilt in a mature Christian who knows God's truth.

A weak conscience results from an immature or fragile faith not yet weaned from worldly influences and not yet saturated in the Word of God. Weak believers are to be accepted with love and not judged because their consciences are too tender. Paul instructed the Romans, "Now accept the one who is weak in faith, but not for the purpose of passing judgment on his opinions. One man has faith that he may eat all things, but he who is weak eats vegetables only" (Rom. 14:1–2). We see from Paul's comment that the weak believer is likely to be overscrupulous, legalistic, troubled by his conscience in an unhealthy way. And as we shall note, a weak conscience is often the companion of legalism.

Repeatedly Paul admonished the early church that those with strong consciences were not to be judgmental (Rom. 14:3), and above all they must not encourage those who are weak to violate their consciences. Weak believers must not learn to overrule conscience. If that becomes a habit—if they condition themselves to reject all the promptings of conscience—they will thus forfeit one of the most important means of sanctification.

In fact, Paul instructed those who were strong to defer whenever possible to the qualms of the weaker brother's conscience. To encourage an immature believer to wound his own conscience is to lead him into sin: "He who doubts [on account of a weak conscience] is condemned if he eats, because his eating is not from faith; and whatever is not from faith is sin" (Rom. 14:23).

The Corinthian church was torn by a disagreement over whether it was sinful to eat food offered to idols. Corinth, a pagan city, was filled with temples where food was sacrificed to heathen gods and goddesses. Food would be prepared, then laid on the altar by a worshiper. Obviously, the idol could not consume the food, so the pagan priests and priestesses would take whatever was offered and sell it at a discount. That was how such people earned their livelihood. Food offered to idols could therefore be obtained in Corinth at prices considerably cheaper than in the regular food shops.

Some Christians believed such food was defiled and therefore sinful to eat. Others, knowing that idols are nothing, could eat the food without qualms. Corinthian believers were beginning to split into factions over the issue, so they asked Paul to instruct them.

Paul's advice illuminates the question of how Christians should respond to their consciences. First of all, he told them, an idol is nothing. "There is no such thing as an idol in the world, and . . . there is no God but one" (1 Cor. 8:4). "For us there is but one God" (v. 6). Idols are imaginary gods. They do not exist. As believers we do not even acknowledge them. How can a non-existent god defile otherwise edible food? Therefore to eat food offered to idols is *not* inherently sinful. The question of what foods are edible is a matter of complete liberty for a Christian. "Food will not commend us to God; we are neither the worse if we do not eat, nor the better if we do eat" (v. 8).

But, Paul pointed out, not everyone's faith was strong enough to embrace that truth. Many of the Corinthians had recently been saved out of idolatry. They had spent their whole lives developing a mindset of fear and worship directed toward these false gods. The associations and memories of the old life of darkness were too strong. Food offered on a heathen altar was more than their consciences could bear (1 Cor. 8:7).

No believer, Paul told the Corinthians, has a right to violate his or her conscience. More significant, no believer has a right to urge fellow Christians to sin by violating their consciences—even if their consciences are merely weak and condemning them for something they are legally and morally free to do. Liberty in Christ is thus accompanied by an uncompromising accountability to our own consciences, and by a still higher responsibility to the whole body of believers:

> Take care lest this liberty of yours somehow become a stumbling block to the weak. For if someone sees you, who have knowledge, dining in an idol's temple, will not his conscience, if he is weak, be strengthened to eat things sacrificed to idols? For through your knowledge he who is weak is ruined, the brother for whose sake Christ died. And thus, by sinning against the brethren and wounding their conscience when it is weak, you sin against Christ (vv. 9–12).

A weak and constantly accusing conscience is a spiritual liability, not a strength. Many people with especially tender consciences tend to display their overscrupulousness as if it were proof of deep spirituality. It is precisely the opposite.

The point is this: If your faith is strong and your conscience healthy, you may enjoy your own freedom in Christ without making any effort to arouse more intense scrutiny from your own conscience: "Eat anything that is sold in the meat market, without asking questions for conscience' sake" (1 Cor. 10:25). But if you have reason to think that someone watching you might be wounded in conscience by your exercise of freedom, abstain. Guard the other person's tender conscience. Paul gave this example: "If anyone should say to you, 'This is meat sacrificed to idols,' do not eat it, for the sake of the one who informed you, and *for conscience' sake; I mean not your own conscience, but the other man's*" (vv. 28–29, emphasis added). Don't put a stumbling block or an occasion to fall in someone else's way (Rom. 14:13).

A weak and constantly accusing conscience is a spiritual liability, not a strength. Many people with especially tender consciences tend to display their overscrupulousness as if it were proof of deep spirituality. It is precisely the opposite. Those with weak consciences tend to be too easily offended and stumble frequently (cf. 1 Cor. 8:13). They are often overly critical of others (Rom. 14:3–4). They are too susceptible to the lure of legalism (Rom. 14:20; cf. Gal. 3:2–5). Their thoughts and hearts are soon defiled (Tit. 1:15).

Throughout Paul's discussion of those with weak consciences (Rom. 14; 1 Cor. 8–10), he treats the condition as a state of spiritual immaturity—a lack of knowledge (1 Cor. 8:7) and a lack of faith (Rom. 14:1, 23). Paul clearly expected that those with weak consciences would grow out of that immature state, like children inevitably outgrow their fear of the dark. Those who choose instead to live in such a state—particularly those who point to a too-tender conscience as something to boast about—have a warped sense of what it means to be mature in the faith. True spiritual growth enlightens the mind and strengthens the heart in faith. It is ultimately the only way to overcome a weak conscience.

Keeping a Pure Conscience

How can we keep our consciences pure? What is the proper response to guilt feelings? Those questions will be the focus of much of this book, but for now here are some simple principles to remember involving confession, forgiveness, restitution, procrastination, and education.

Confess and forsake known sin. Examine your guilt feelings in light of Scripture. Deal with the sin God's Word reveals. Proverbs 28:13 says, "He who conceals his transgressions will not prosper, but he who confesses and forsakes them will find compassion." First John 1 speaks of confession of sin as an ongoing characteristic of the Christian life: "If we confess our sins, He is faithful and righteous to forgive us our sins and to cleanse us from all unrighteousness" (v. 9). We should certainly confess to those we have wronged: "Therefore, confess your sins to one another, and pray for one another, so that you may be healed" (Jas. 5:16). But above all, we should confess to the One whom sin offends most. As David wrote, "I acknowledged my sin to Thee, and my iniquity I did not hide; I said, 'I will confess my transgressions to the Lord'; and Thou didst forgive the guilt of my sin" (Ps. 32:5).

Ask forgiveness and be reconciled to anyone you have wronged. Jesus instructed us, "If therefore you are presenting your offering at the altar, and there remember that your brother has something against you, leave your offering there before the altar, and go your way; first be reconciled to your brother, and then come and present your offering" (Matt. 5:23–24). "If you forgive men for their transgressions, your heavenly Father will also forgive you. But if you do not forgive men, then your Father will not forgive your transgressions" (Matt. 6:14–15).

Make restitution. God told Moses: "Speak to the sons of Israel, 'When a man or woman commits any of the sins of mankind, acting unfaithfully against the Lord, and that person is guilty, then he shall confess his sins which he has committed, and he shall make restitution in full for his wrong, and add to it one-fifth of it, and give it to him whom he has wronged'" (Num. 5:6–7). The principle behind this law is binding on believers living in the New Testament era as well (cf. Philem. 19; Lk. 19:8).

Don't procrastinate in clearing your wounded conscience. Paul said he did his best "to maintain always a blameless conscience both before God and before men" (Acts 24:16). Some people put off dealing with their guilt, thinking their conscience will clear itself in time. It won't. Procrastination allows the guilt feelings to fester. That in turn generates depression, anxiety, and other emotional problems. Guilt feelings may persist long after the offense is forgotten, often spilling over to other areas of our lives. That's one reason people often feel guilty and are not sure why. Such confused guilt may be a symptom that something is terribly wrong spiritually. Paul may have had that in mind when he wrote, "To those who are defiled and unbelieving, nothing is pure, but both their mind and their conscience are defiled" (Tit. 1:15).

Dealing with a wounded conscience immediately by heart-searching prayer before God is the only way to keep it clear and sensitive. Putting off dealing with guilt inevitably compounds the problems.

Educate your conscience. As we saw earlier, a weak, easily grieved conscience results from a lack of spiritual knowledge (1 Cor. 8:7). If your conscience is too easily wounded, don't violate it; to do so is to train yourself to override conviction, and that will lead to overriding true conviction about real sin. Moreover, violating the conscience is a sin in itself (v. 12, cf. Rom. 14:23). Instead, immerse your conscience in God's Word so it can begin to function with reliable data.

An important aspect of educating the conscience is teaching it to focus on the right object—divinely revealed truth. If the conscience looks only to personal feelings, it can accuse us wrongfully. We are certainly not to order our lives according to our feelings. A conscience fixed on feelings becomes unreliable. Individuals subject to depression and melancholy especially should not allow their conscience to be informed by their feelings. Despondent feelings will provoke unnecessary doubts and fears in the soul when not kept in check by a well-advised conscience. The conscience must be persuaded by God's Word, not by our feelings.

Furthermore, conscience errs when the mind focuses wholly on our faltering in sin and ignores the triumphs of God's grace in us. True Christians experience both realities. Conscience must be allowed to weigh the fruit of the Spirit in our lives as well as the remnants of our sinful flesh. It must see our faith as well as our failings. Otherwise the conscience will become overly accusing, prone to unwholesome doubts about our standing before God.

We must subject our conscience to the truth of God and the teaching of Scripture. As we do that, the conscience will be more clearly focused and better able to give us reliable feedback. A trustworthy conscience becomes a powerful aid to spiritual growth and stability.

Recovering the Doctrine of the Conscience

The conscience may be the most underappreciated and least understood attribute of humanity. Psychology, as we have noted, is usually less concerned with understanding the conscience than with attempting to silence it. The influx of popular psychology into evangelicalism has had the disastrous effect of undermining a biblical appreciation of the role of the conscience. It is bad enough that secular society's collective conscience has been vanishing for years. But now the don't-blame-yourself philosophy is having a similar effect in the church.

But as we have seen, Scripture never suggests that we should respond to our conscience by repudiating guilt. On the contrary, the Bible reveals that most of us are far more guilty than our own hearts tell us. Paul wrote, "I am conscious of nothing against myself, yet I am not by this acquitted; but the one who examines me is the Lord" (1 Cor. 4:4).

Rather than discarding or silencing a condemning conscience, we who know Christ must educate our consciences carefully with the pure Word of God, listen to them, and learn to understand them. Above all, we must keep our consciences undefiled. That is crucial to our testimony before an ungodly world.

We must not permit the message we proclaim to become infected with worldly notions that minimize guilt and seek only to make people feel good about themselves. The popular gospel of our generation usually leaves the impression that Jesus is a Savior from trouble, sadness, loneliness, despair, pain, and suffering. Scripture says He came to save people from *sin*. Therefore one of the fundamental truths of the gospel is that all of us are contemptible sinners (Rom. 3:10–23). The only way to find real forgiveness and freedom from our sin is through humble, contrite repentance. We can't escape guilt by telling ourselves we are really not that bad. We must come face to face with the exceeding sinfulness of our sin. Isn't that the whole point of this familiar parable?

> Two men went up into the temple to pray, one a Pharisee, and the other a tax-gatherer. The Pharisee stood and was praying thus to himself, "God, I thank Thee that I am not like other people: swindlers, unjust, adulterers, or even like this tax-gatherer. I fast twice a week; I pay tithes of all that I get." But the tax-

gatherer, standing some distance away, was even unwilling to lift up his eyes to heaven, but was beating his breast, saying, "God, be merciful to me, the sinner!" I tell you, this man went down to his house justified rather than the other; for everyone who exalts himself shall be humbled, but he who humbles himself shall be exalted (Lk. 18:10–14).

The gospel thus speaks directly through the Holy Spirit to the human conscience. Before it ever offers salvation, it must bring the sinner face to face with his or her own desperate sinfulness. Those who are conditioned to disavow their consciences in small matters certainly will not respond to a message that convicts them of sin so heinous as to warrant eternal condemnation. The attack on the conscience is therefore hardening people against the truth of the gospel.

Some Christians, sensing this effect, have concluded that the gospel message needs updating. They have removed the idea of sin altogether from the message. They offer Christ as a Savior from meaninglessness, as a means to personal fulfillment, as a solution to self-image problems, or as an answer to emotional needs. The gospel they extend to unbelievers makes no appeal to the conscience, no mention of sin. It is therefore an impotent and spurious message.

How can anyone genuinely repent who has no sense of personal responsibility for sin? Thus the contemporary tendency to devalue the conscience actually undermines the gospel itself.

Others, instead of eliminating sin from the message completely, treat the subject as briefly or as mildly as possible. They might stress the universality of sin but never explain the seriousness of it: "Of course you've sinned. We all have!"—as if it were sufficient to concede the notion of universal sinfulness without really feeling any personal guilt in one's own conscience. But how can anyone genuinely repent who has no sense of personal responsibility for sin? Thus the contemporary tendency to devalue the conscience actually undermines the gospel itself.

The vanishing conscience has a detrimental effect on Christian living as well. The conscience is an important key to joy and victory in the Christian life. The benefits of a pure conscience comprise some of the greatest blessings of the Christian life. As we have noted, the apostle Paul frequently appealed to his blameless conscience in the midst of the afflictions and persecutions he suffered (e.g., Acts 23:1; 24:16; 2 Cor. 1:12). Through those trials the knowledge that his heart was unimpeachable supplied him with the strength and confidence to endure. Paul carefully guarded his heart and conscience lest he lose that source of assurance. He also treasured his pure conscience as a thing of joy in and of itself.

A pure conscience is more to be sought than the world's approval. The very process of spiritual maturity is learning to subject one's conscience to Scripture, then live accordingly, regardless of popular opinion.

Charles Wesley wrote this hymn about the conscience:

> I want a principle within
> Of watchful, godly fear,
> A sensibility of sin,
> A pain to feel it near.
> Help me the first approach to feel
> Of pride or wrong desire;
> To catch the wandering of my will,
> And quench the kindling fire.
>
> From Thee that I no more may stray,
> No more Thy goodness grieve,
> Grant me the filial awe, I pray,
> The tender conscience give.
> Quick as the apple of an eye,
> O God, my conscience make!
> Awake my soul when sin is nigh,
> And keep it still awake.

That hymn is rarely sung these days. The church as a whole seems to have forgotten the spiritual importance of a sound conscience. I am convinced that is one of the chief reasons so many Christians seem to live in sorrow and defeat. They are not taught to respond correctly to their consciences. They treat their consciences flippantly. They have not learned the importance of keeping the conscience clear and healthy. Instead they dispute what their own conscience tells them. They treat any sense of guilt or self-blame as a liability or a threat. They expend too much of their spiritual energy in a vain attempt to deal with feelings spawned by an accusing conscience—without a corresponding willingness to deal with the sin that offended the conscience in the first place.

That is spiritual suicide. Paul wrote of those who by rejecting their consciences "suffered shipwreck in regard to their faith" (1 Tim. 1:19). They are like a pilot who turns off his warning system.

We *must* pay attention to our consciences. The cost of switching them off is frightfully high. It will inevitably result in a devastating spiritual catastrophe. Of all people, we who are committed to the truth of Scripture cannot relinquish the importance of a sound conscience. We must recover and apply the biblical truth about the conscience, or we will be left with nothing whatsoever to say to a sinful world.

3

How Sin Silences the Conscience

This myth [that mankind is basically good] deludes people into thinking that they are always victims, never villains; always deprived, never depraved. It dismisses responsibility as the teaching of a darker age. It can excuse any crime, because it can always blame something else—a sickness of our society or a sickness of the mind.

One writer called the modern age "the golden age of exoneration." When guilt is dismissed as the illusion of narrow minds, then no one is accountable, even to his conscience.

The irony is that this should come alive in this century, of all centuries, with its gulags and death camps and killing fields. As G. K. Chesterton once said, the doctrine of original sin is the only philosophy empirically validated by centuries of recorded human history.

Charles W. Colson[1]

The legacy of the age of psychology is disastrous, pervasive wickedness. Sin has hardly ever been as heinous as it is in our age. Drugs, prostitution, pornography, sexual perversion, and crime are rampant in our cities. Gang violence has turned our streets into war zones. Criminals are getting younger and bolder all the time. The prison system is overcrowded and ineffective.

Such problems are not new, someone will say. Similar evils have plagued mankind since the earliest times. And indeed they have. But unlike previous generations, ours fails to see even the grossest wickedness for what it is—a transgression against the immutable moral law of a supremely holy God. Modern society seems to miss the point that such behavior is actually *sinful.*

Bob Vernon, former Assistant Chief of the Los Angeles Police Department, warns of the increasing number of what he terms "moral flatliners"—young people who choose crime as a career and who can commit the most heinous acts with no apparent remorse. He describes one such youth, a gang member known as "Cool Aid." Cool Aid unleashed a barrage of gunshots on a float carrying the queen's court in a high-school homecoming parade. Several young girls were wounded, one critically. The crime was carried out in broad daylight, and scores of eyewitnesses immediately fingered Cool Aid as the perpetrator. In the interrogation room after his arrest, Cool Aid explained to Chief Vernon his motives for the shooting. He needed to do some prison time because he knew he would get free medical treatment behind bars. He had a case of venereal disease that required treatment and some teeth that needed filling. He also planned to spend the time in prison getting "buffed out" by lifting weights. But before he went in, he had to acquire a "rep"—a reputation. "I'll be known as the enforcer," he proudly told police officers.[2]

Vernon writes,

> What we see so clearly in Cool Aid's case is [one of the root problems] destroying our society and families: the loss of conscience. The trend is to no longer be ashamed of our darker side. This shocking trend is ravaging our culture. It's becoming a badge of honor to not only violate social norms, but even to flaunt that behavior. . . . The behaviors have always been there, even those we've recognized as harmful to society. The significant change is in how we react to those actions.

Today it's not uncommon to literally applaud a person who discloses what in the past has been looked upon as a weakness [or a sin]. The "Phil Donahue" show is an obvious example of this trend. People get on nationwide TV, admit to breaking their marriage vows, and boast of a determination to continue the practice. Others talk of purposely bringing a baby into the world with no family to support it. Some flaunt the lies and deception that have brought them wealth, and many brag about cheating the government on their tax returns. Usually the audience cheers the speaker's "courage" in publicly going against the social norms.[3]

Today it's not uncommon to literally applaud a person who discloses what in the past has been looked upon as a weakness [or a sin]. (Bob Vernon)

Is society becoming incapable of even thinking in terms of good and evil? Has the relativism of a humanistic culture rendered modern society wholly amoral?

Hardened by the Deceitfulness of Sin

The most ominous aspect of our culture's moral slide is that the problem tends to feed itself. Sin denied dulls the conscience. The writer of Hebrews warned about the danger of being "hardened by the deceitfulness of sin" (3:13). Sin defies and deceives the human conscience, and thereby hardens the human heart. A sin-hardened heart grows ever more susceptible to temptation, pride, and every kind of evil. Unconfessed sin therefore becomes a cycle that desensitizes and corrupts the conscience and drags people deeper and deeper into bondage.

On the cultural level, for example, we can see that as conviction of sin is silenced and the community conscience vanishes, society becomes more corrupt and more tolerant of worse debauchery.

The rapid erosion of social standards regarding obscenity and moral propriety provides abundant evidence of this phenomenon. What was shocking and unacceptable only a decade ago is now standard fare on network television. Lewd humor that would have been judged inappropriate outside the locker room not so long ago is now the main attraction in children's entertainment. And things are steadily growing worse. Just when "The Simpsons" seemed to be plumbing the depths of moral nihilism in animated cartoons, MTV introduced a couple of characters who make Bart Simpson look like a choirboy. Beavis, and his friend whose name is too crude to mention, epitomize the degeneracy of modern culture. Everything that is vulgar, disrespectful, or illegal, they consider "cool"—and all that is good or sacred, they ridicule.

Beavis and his buddy are the heroes of the next generation. That is an appalling thought. How low can the culture sink?

Evidence of serious moral decline is all around. Look at the tabloids lining the supermarket checkout stands. The headlines scream news of people's perversions, adultery, gluttony, extravagance, arrogance, selfishness, drunkenness, immorality, anger, and all kinds of vice. Worst of all, as Chief Vernon pointed out, these vices are brandished almost like badges of honor! Have you noticed the proliferation of T-shirts and bumper stickers that are printed with the most unspeakable profanities to be displayed shamelessly in public? Our society takes pleasure in its own wickedness. People are not ashamed of their sin; they boast about it. They go on televised talk shows just to glory in their own depravity. And the audiences love it. As the apostle Paul wrote, "Although they know the ordinance of God, that those who practice such things are worthy of death, they not only do the same, but also give hearty approval to those who practice them" (Rom. 1:32).

Paul made that comment at the end of Romans 1, concluding a discourse about the downward spiral of sin. His words throughout the second half of that chapter are strikingly applicable to the predicament of contemporary society. Here the apostle shows how and why the human conscience vanishes. He reveals that those who ignore or suppress their conscience risk a dreadful judgment: God ultimately abandons such people to the devastating effects of their own sin. That is exactly what we see happening in our nation. It is also the record of human history—nation after nation being abandoned by God after they first abandoned Him and became hopelessly enthralled with their own sin.

First the Bad News . . .

Romans 1:16 begins an extended, systematic treatment of the gospel that continues throughout the epistle. Paul crowned his introduction and greeting to the Roman believers with these words: "I am not ashamed of the gospel, for it is the power of God for salvation to everyone who believes, to the Jew first and also to the Greek. For in it the righteousness of God is revealed from faith to faith; as it is written, 'But the righteous man shall live by faith'" (Rom. 1:16–17).

There can be no salvation for those who aren't convinced of the seriousness of their sin.

Right there, just when it seemed Paul was going to begin talking about the *good news* and the power of God unto salvation, he unleashed this thunderbolt: "For the wrath of God is revealed from heaven against all ungodliness and unrighteousness of men, who suppress the truth in unrighteousness" (1:18). About this verse and the passage that follows, D. Martyn Lloyd-Jones wrote, "It is a terrible [terrifying] passage. Melancthon described the eighteenth verse as 'an exordium terrible as lightning.' And it has not only the terrifying quality of lightning, but also its illuminating power."[4]

It turns out that the good news about salvation starts with the bad news about sin. As Jesus said, "It is not those who are healthy who need a physician, but those who are sick; I did not come to call the righteous, but sinners" (Mk. 2:17). Paul knew that those who underestimate the enormity and gravity of human sinfulness—especially those who do not see their own depravity—cannot apply the only effective remedy to their problems. That, after all, is precisely the issue we are addressing in this book.

There can be no salvation for those who aren't convinced of the seriousness of their sin. There can be no word of reconciliation for sinners who remain oblivious to their estrangement from God. True fear of God cannot grip those who are blind to the depth of their sinfulness. And no mercy is available for those who do not tremble at God's holy threats.

In other words, to attempt to eradicate the human conscience is one of the most spiritually destructive pursuits any individual or society can engage in. It results in God's wrath—not yet ultimate wrath (hell) or eschatalogical wrath (the Day of the Lord), but temporal wrath. That is, He removes restraining grace and turns a person or a society over to the cycle of sin without the mitigating deterrent of conscience. This is the very judgment Paul spoke of at Lystra, when he said that God "in the generations gone by . . . permitted all the nations to go their own ways" (Acts 14:16).

That is Paul's main point in Romans 1:18–32. There he describes the judgment of God that results in humanity's decline into wanton sin. Notice that the most dramatic feature of his narrative is not the ghastly sins he names—although he chronicles some pretty gross practices. But the singular feature that marks each step of mankind's descent under God's wrath involves the hardening and decimation of the conscience.

The Conscience Evident Within

Paul says God's wrath is revealed because people "suppress the truth in unrighteousness" (Rom. 1:18). He is referring to sinners who have successfully hushed their own consciences. "The truth" they suppress is innately-known truth about the character of God, a sense of good and bad, and a basic knowledge of right and wrong. These things are universally known to all, "evident within them, for God made it evident to them" (v. 19). In other words, God manifests Himself in the most basic sense within every human conscience.

That internal knowledge about God is further augmented by evidences of His power and deity in the natural order of creation— "His invisible attributes, His eternal power and divine nature have been clearly seen, being understood through what has been made" (v. 20). The truth thus revealed is not cryptic or ambiguous—it is "clearly seen." Nor is it observable only by a few specially gifted souls. "The heavens are telling of the glory of God; and their expanse is declaring the work of His hands" (Ps. 19:1). They testify to a universal audience.

In other words, these truths—that God exists, that He is powerful, that He is good, and that He is glorious—are evident to believers and non-believers, Christians and pagans, Jews and Gentiles. No one can plead ignorance. Even the most unenlightened pagan knows more truth than he is willing to accept. Those who suppress that truth—those who abrogate their consciences—"are without excuse" (v. 20).

The Downward Spiral

Paul traces the wrath of God through humanity's descent into deeper and more pervasive sin. He outlines the steps of that descent, and they read as if they had been taken from the front pages of our newspapers. The more modern society reaches into the abyss of unbelief and wantonness, the more the truth of Scripture is fulfilled. Notice how the issues Paul outlined nearly two-thousand years ago describe precisely the sins most popular today. They appear in the following areas: secularism, lack of common sense, corrupt religion, uncontrolled lust, and sexual perversion.

Notice how the issues Paul outlined nearly two-thousand years ago describe precisely the sins most popular today.

Foolish speculations. "Even though they knew God, they did not honor Him as God, or give thanks; but they became futile in their speculations, and their foolish heart was darkened" (Rom. 1:21).

Once a person begins to suppress the truth in unrighteousness, that person looses all spiritual moorings. Reject the light, and you are left in darkness. That is precisely what has happened to the human race throughout history.

Modern society is no exception to the rule. If anything, we have greater access to truth than any other previous generation. Yet unbelief may be more widespread now than ever before.

As science advances, we learn more and more about the intricacy and complexities of the universe. Modern science has discovered, for example, that the molecular world is far more elaborate than anyone imagined a hundred years ago. We are able to identify subatomic particles. We know that a single drop of water contains innumerable billions of particles. A single drop of pond water also contains a whole community of tiny, marvelous living creatures unimaginable before the advent of microscopes. At the opposite end of the spectrum, we now realize that the edges of our own galaxy are far broader and the universe more complex than our grandparents ever could have realized. We understand more than ever about how it all fits together, about how nature is delicately balanced.

We ought to be more certain than any of our forebears about the infinite power and wisdom of the Creator. Science has uncovered whole wondrous worlds in nature that previous generations never knew existed. The more we see of creation, the more it reveals the order and the wisdom and the goodness of the One who designed it all and spoke it into existence. Yet at the same time science is learning all of this, scientific theory is becoming increasingly atheistic. Incredibly, as the power, sophistication, and harmony of the universe come more and more to light, many modern scientists try all the more desperately to explain away the notion of a divine Creator who rules the universe.

Could such an ordered, systematic creation be the result of mere chance? No more than shaking a paper bag filled with watch parts might produce an accurate timepiece. But evolutionary atheism is nothing more than "futile speculation," explanations devised by people who want to suppress the truth about God from their own consciences. Thus, their foolish hearts are darkened (v. 21).

The human race is devolving, not evolving. Instead of ascending into freedom and enlightenment, mankind, having rejected the true God, is receding into the bondage and gloom of its own sin and unbelief. When men and women refuse God, they become enslaved to sin, enveloped in darkness, entrapped by futility. Forsaking God, they forsake truth, light, and eternal life. They spurn the basis of all morality and start on the downward spiral Paul describes in these verses.

Spiritual darkness inevitably accompanies moral corruption. People who reject God necessarily forfeit righteousness. Godlessness inescapably leads to moral perversion—and vice versa. Unbelief and immorality are thus inextricably woven together.

The death of common sense. "Professing to be wise, they became fools" (Rom. 1:22). Those who refuse to honor God lack spiritual understanding. Even their rational faculties are corrupted by their unbelief. Their thinking is especially twisted with regard to spiritual matters, because their sin is spiritual rebellion. They have no means of discerning between truth and falsehood, right and wrong. Having rejected God, they have no hope of reasoning their way to spiritual truth. They are fools in the most profound sense of the word: "The fool has said in his heart, 'There is no God.' They are corrupt, they have committed abominable deeds; there is no one who does good" (Ps. 14:1; cf. 53:1).

The foolishness that verse describes is a comprehensive spiritual blindness. It is the worst foolishness of all. It corrupts the conscience and leaves the unbeliever incapable of right thinking about any spiritual matters.

Our society is shot through with spiritual foolishness. It seems moral judgment has been completely overturned. Public schools cannot teach the Bible or even morality but are encouraged to instruct children in sexual technique, then supply them with free condoms. School nurses are not supposed to dispense aspirin without parental consent, but they may send young girls to abortion clinics without informing anyone in authority. Baby whales and baby seals have more legal rights than unborn infants. Courts are more concerned to protect criminals' rights than victims' rights.

Common sense rarely figures into public policy or society's sense of morality. Professing wisdom, our culture has enshrined its foolishness proudly for all to see.

Corrupt religion. Moral foolishness inevitably corrupts spirituality. In fact, all the religions humanity has ever devised are the fruit of blind spiritual foolishness. They "[exchange] the glory of the incorruptible God for an image in the form of corruptible man and of birds and four-footed animals and crawling creatures" (Rom. 1:23).

Contrary to the notions of modern anthropology, human religion has not followed an upward evolutionary path. Religion did not begin with paganism and mature over time into monotheism. The exact opposite is true. All human religion, according to Scripture, moves in a direction away from the truth, away from the true God, tending always toward idolatry ("an image in the form of corruptible man"), then animism ("of birds and four-footed animals and crawling creatures").

Contrary to the notions of modern anthropology, human religion has not followed an upward evolutionary path.

After the Fall, Scripture says, "men began to call upon the name of the Lord" (Gen. 4:26). From the Fall to the Flood, there is no record of any idolatry. God destroyed the world in the Flood because "the wickedness of man was great on the earth, and . . . every intent of the thoughts of his heart was only evil continually" (Gen. 6:5). But nothing in Scripture states that people had devised false gods to worship.

Sometime after the Flood, idolatry began to predominate. Abraham was called out of an idolatrous family (Josh. 24:2). Egypt was overrun with idolatry by the time of Moses. And when Israel returned to the Promised Land, they discovered forms of idolatry among the Canaanites that were even more hideous than anything they had seen in Egypt. When they failed to wipe out all the Canaanites, those people's false religions became a perpetual snare to the succeeding generations of Israelites.

Ancient history confirms that religion has *devolved* and descended into polytheism and animism. Herodotus, writing in the fifth century B.C., said early Persia had no pagan temples or idols.[5] Augustine cites a first-century Roman historian, Varro, who said "the old Romans were a hundred threescore and ten years without idols."[6] That means it was not until 170 years *after* Rome was founded that the Romans adopted polytheism and idolatry. Lucian, a second-century Greek writer, made a similar observation about ancient Greece and Egypt.[7]

People are by nature inclined to turn from the glory of God to idols, to "[exchange] the truth of God for a lie, and [worship and serve] the creature rather than the Creator" (Rom. 1:25). The human conscience demands God, but people tend to choose a diety of their own making. That is why the First Commandment is, "You shall have no other gods before Me. You shall not make for yourself an idol, or any likeness of what is in heaven above or on the earth beneath or in the water under the earth. You shall not worship them or serve them" (Ex. 20:3–5). But even while Moses was receiving that commandment from the Lord, Aaron and the Israelites were making a golden calf to worship (32:1–6).

Is our society any different from the Romans 1 description? Certainly not. People in modern culture tend to have materialistic idols—money, prestige, success, philosophy, health, pleasure, sports, entertainment, possessions, and other such things. Those things become idols when we give them the love and dedication we owe to God. The problem is the same—worshiping the creation rather than the Creator.

But don't get the idea that the idolatry in our society is somehow more sophisticated than the idolatry of primitive paganism. Consider the changes that have taken place in religion in America in the past fifty years or so. The New Age movement has popularized Hinduism. Astrology, spiritism, and other occult religions have enjoyed unprecedented popularity. Native American religions, Voodoo, Santeria, Druidism, Wicca (witchcraft), and other ancient pagan beliefs have been revived. Now Satan worship, a thing unheard of in our nation two generations ago, is one of the fastest growing cults in the nation—and is especially conspicuous in the youth culture. I recently heard a news report that in Orange County, California, alone more than five hundred cases of ritual animal sacrifice involving stolen pets have been recorded over the past decade.

Now people in our culture are worshiping the elements, spotted owls, or dolphins and whales. Earth- and creature- worship seem at their apex in this society, which has no place for the Creator God. Mother Earth is preferred to Father God.

Far from being humanity's highest attainment, religion is one of the most obvious manifestations of the debauchery of our race.

The vilest sin of all is blaspheming God by having other gods before Him. So sinners who reject the true God are often extremely religious. Manmade religion is not evidence of human nobility; it is proof of human depravity. False religion is humanity at its lowest. It is not humanity ascended to the heights, but people lost and groping in the muck of godlessness. All the trends in modern religion and modern materialism underscore that fact.

Uncontrolled lust. Another step in humanity's downward spiral occurs when people become enslaved to their own passions: "God gave them over in the lusts of their hearts to impurity, that their bodies might be dishonored among them" (Rom. 1:24).

Nothing characterizes contemporary Western society more than lust. The size and power of the modern entertainment industry testifies eloquently to how thoroughly given over to lust our society is. Greed, gluttony, and sexual desire are the primary tools of the advertizing industry. Lust is big business in our culture.

A dozen or so daily televised talk shows appeal shamelessly to people's prurient interests.

As people's lusts are fed and encouraged, society grows more and more tolerant of immorality, indecency, obscenity, pornography, profanity, and other forms of smut. We noted earlier how standards in the entertainment industry have declined dramatically in the past few years. Gratuitous obscenities and sex scenes are routinely included even in films promoted as children's fare. Music videos thrive on sex and sleaze. What the television networks are willing to broadcast into our living rooms becomes more explicit each season.

A dozen or so daily televised talk shows appeal shamelessly to people's prurient interests. Every conceivable lewd and perverted practice is paraded before daytime audiences. The only moral values viewers are expected to maintain, it seems, are tolerance and an open mind toward any kind of behavior.

Sinful lust comes in various forms. The Greek word for lust is *epithumia*, which simply means "desire." Sinful desires include an insatiable hunger for pleasure, profits, power, prestige, and sex. In short, lust is a desire for anything God forbids. Such sinful cravings Scripture calls fleshly lusts (cf. Rom. 13:14; Eph. 2:3; 2 Pet. 2:18; 1 Jn. 2:16). We are explicitly commanded to "abstain from fleshly lusts, which wage war against the soul" (1 Pet. 2:11).

Those who feed their lusts are judged accordingly: "God gave them over . . . to impurity" (Rom. 1:24). The expression "gave them over" (Gk., *paradidōmi*) is a word sometimes used of putting someone in prison (Mk. 1:14; Acts 8:3). It speaks of a judicial act of God whereby He withdraws His restraining hand from an individual whose conscience is hardened. That person becomes enslaved to his or her own lusts. In other words, God allows the consequences of that person's sin to run their catastrophic course. That course, driven by uncontrolled lust, inevitably reverts to the worst forms of sexual promiscuity: "Their bodies [are] dishonored among them" (Rom. 1:24).

Sexual perversion. Free from the deterrent of a healthy conscience and without God's gracious restraint, runaway lusts inevitably lead to the most debased and perverted kinds of sexual sin. Fleshly desires deteriorate to become "degrading passions": "For this reason God gave them over to degrading passions; for their women exchanged the natural function for that which is unnatural, and in the same way also the men abandoned the natural function of the woman and burned in their desire toward one another, men with men committing indecent acts and receiving in their own persons the due penalty of their error" (Rom. 1:26–27).

That is precisely the course our society has taken. Sexual practices that were almost universally viewed as hideously perverted a few decades ago are now flaunted and celebrated in our streets. Homosexuals have become bold—even arrogant—in demanding society's approval for their wickedness. Nonbiblical thinking has so corrupted society's collective conscience that the consensus is fast growing sympathetic with the homosexual movement. Having abandoned Scripture as a standard, our culture has no authority to declare homosexuality immoral. A few consciences are still struck with horror at the thought of such iniquity. But extreme pressure is brought to bear upon such people to try to make them feel they should be broad-minded, accepting, permissive, and even supportive of such perversions. Those who are not fully committed to Scripture have no line of defense against the tide of public opinion. And so society's collective conscience erodes even further, hastening the downward spiral.

How tolerant has our society become of homosexual practices? Many large cities now sponsor annual "Gay Pride" celebrations, featuring parades with floats and marching groups that exalt the homosexual lifestyle. The news reports you see about "Gay Pride" parades do not tell the full story. They couldn't. Much of what goes on in those parades is so explicit and so debauched that to capture the images and put them on television news would constitute the grossest kind of pornography. Such parades have become rallying points for the homosexual community in their bid to gain political influence and thereby impose their deviant and deadly value system on the rest of society. In that pursuit they have had remarkable success over the past few years.

New York City, for example, opened the nation's first high school for homosexuals—Harvey Milk School, named for a murdered San Francisco city supervisor who was also a homosexual rights activist.[8] The school meets, incongruously enough, in the parish house of a Methodist church. Some of the school's students are transvestites, and some are male prostitutes.

Gay advocacy groups abound and have grown more militant in recent years. With names such as Queer Nation, GLAAD ("Gay and Lesbian Alliance Against Defamation"), ACT-UP ("AIDS Coalition To Unleash Power"), SQUISH ("Strong Queers United In Stopping Heterosexism"), Dykes on Bikes, and Fighting Fairies, these groups practice a kind of in-your-face activism designed to shock, defy, and intimidate anyone who dares suggest that their lifestyle is sinful.

Politically, the gay rights movement has made substantial gains. In his first year as president, Bill Clinton appointed at least seventeen homosexuals and lesbians to public office—then invited them all to a breakfast reception to celebrate. "For the first time in the history of mankind a president has sought to break this barrier, this taboo," one of the appointees said triumphantly. "For that, Bill Clinton is going to go down in history."[9]

Government agencies and the courts are now adding their clout to the effort to recognize homosexuality as a legitimate lifestyle. In

Wisconsin, two young female students advertised for a third room-mate to share their private residence. Because they rejected an applicant who had told them she was a lesbian, they were forced by the state Human Rights Commission to pay the lesbian applicant $1,500 for having caused her distress. The Commission also demanded a public letter of apology and required the two girls to attend a "re-education class" taught by homosexuals.

Such government-sponsored moral indoctrination is becoming more and more common. Homosexual rights laws have forced groups such as Big Brothers to advertize in homosexual newspapers for men whom they match up with fatherless boys for companionship and role modeling. The organization once excluded homosexual applicants, but they have changed their policy under government pressure. The same kind of pressure has been levied against the Boy Scouts to accept homosexuals as scoutmasters.

The rhetoric of gay-rights activism portrays homosexuality in wholly non-moral terms: it is an "alternate lifestyle," a matter of one's "sexual orientation." At the heart of the argument is the notion that one's sexual behavior is not a matter of choice. Homosexual tendencies are determined by genetic, not environmental causes—or so the argument goes—and therefore homosexuality cannot be inherently immoral. But in the first place, researchers have not been able to establish that homosexual tendencies have any genetic causes. Even if such a cause could be established, however, would that alter the fact that God's Word declares homosexuality to be immoral? Humanistic psychopathology has been attempting for years to blame all sorts of sinful behavior—alcoholism, drug addiction, habitual criminality, and sexual perversion—on genetic causes. That whole line of argument misses the obvious point that Scripture clearly teaches we are all born utterly sinful. Everyone has an inborn tendency to sin. That does not release us from the guilt of sinful actions.

And what is the next "alternate lifestyle" or "sexual orientation" to be legitimized? Sadomasochism—sex mixed with brutality? Bestiality—sex with animals? Necrophilia—sex with corpses? Or perhaps pedophilia—sex with children?

You might be shocked to know that homosexual pedophiles already have an advocacy group: NAMBLA—"National American Man Boy Love Association." NAMBLA's slogan is "Sex by eight, before it's too late." The organization, which operates openly under constitutional protection, even publishes a newsletter for members all across the country. The publisher of that paper is a school-teacher!

Others believe incest should be legalized and encouraged. The Sex Information and Education Council of the United States (SEICUS) has circulated a paper suggesting that "moral and religious pronouncements with respect to incest" are all wrong. Guilt about breaking the taboo is actually more harmful than the practice itself, the paper says. It complains that the incest taboo "has prevented scientific investigation," and calls for those with "the guts to find out what is really happening" to launch an aggressive program of incest research.[10] SEICUS, by the way, is the same group that has been so influential in setting the sex-education agenda for public schools nationwide.

---

*What is most distressing is that
many churches and denominations
are now ordaining practicing
homosexuals to the ministry.*

Society has become so tolerant that no behavior, it seems, is too perverted to be openly advocated. All of this is frightening evidence that God has abandoned our sinful society to its own degrading passions. Humanism has dehumanized our culture.

What is most distressing is that many churches and denominations are now ordaining practicing homosexuals to the ministry. The homosexual community even has its own denominations, some of which profess to be evangelical. More and more people within the evangelical community are voicing the opinion that homosexuality may not really be sinful after all. Many church leaders seem reluctant to take an uncompromising biblical stand.

But Scripture is clear. The Bible condemns homosexuality in explicit and undeniable terms. The Old Testament law grouped homosexuality with incest, bestiality, and other perversions, and the penalty for its practice was death (Lev. 20:13, cf. vv. 11–16). In Romans 1, Paul clearly teaches that homosexual practices are "indecent acts" (v. 27), driven by "degrading passions" (v. 26). The apostle listed homosexuality with the lowest forms of human degradation: "those who are lawless and rebellious . . . , the ungodly and sinners . . . , the unholy and profane . . . , those who kill their fathers or mothers . . . , murderers and immoral men and *homosexuals* and kidnappers and liars and perjurers, and whatever else is contrary to sound teaching" (1 Tim. 1:9–10, emphasis added). He wrote, "Do you not know that the unrighteous shall not inherit the kingdom of God? Do not be deceived; neither fornicators, nor idolaters, nor adulterers, nor effeminate, nor *homosexuals*, nor thieves, nor the covetous, nor drunkards, nor revilers, nor swindlers, shall inherit the kingdom of God" (1 Cor. 6:9–10, emphasis added).

Is there no hope for homosexuals? Thankfully, there *is* hope. Those who repent and are reborn in Christ can be freed from the sins that would otherwise destroy them. Immediately after giving that long list of the kinds of people who will not inherit the kingdom, Paul wrote to the Corinthian believers, "*Such were some of you;* but you were washed, but you were sanctified, but you were justified in the name of the Lord Jesus Christ, and in the Spirit of our God" (v. 11, emphasis added).

Unrepentant homosexuals, according to Scripture, "receiv[e] in their own persons the due penalty of their error" (Rom. 1:27). And the society that tolerates such sins is judged as well. What is "the due penalty of their error"? The consequences of their sin. AIDS is certainly one aspect of that. But an even worse judgment, the final temporal blow from the hand of a righteous God, is when He "[gives] them over to a depraved mind" (v. 28). They bottom out spiritually as well as morally. The conscience seems to vanish completely. They can indulge themselves in the evil acts they so love—"those things which are not proper"—until they fill themselves up with unrighteousness.

The Death of the Conscience

It is unsettling to see how precisely the decline of our society parallels Paul's description of the downward spiral of sin. Maurice Roberts has written,

The wheel of history has come full-circle. We are, as a civilization, rotating back to the state of affairs depicted by the apostle Paul in the first chapter of the Epistle to the Romans. . . .

The time was when Bible commentators expounded Romans chapter 1 more or less from the standpoint of the first century of the Roman world only. But that day has gone forever. The modern Christian in the West can now see himself as much in the arena of a reprobate society as did the apostles. The state of modern religion and morals exactly parallels that of the apostolic age and it is summed up in the one word: *Decadence*. Pagan Rome could teach modern man very little that he does not know already about sophisticated wickedness. Pagan Greece, pagan Egypt, and pagan Babylon might even learn a thing or two from this generation about how to shun gospel-light and add to the mountains of man's provocation.

What makes the Bible-reader saddest of all is to see that society today has learnt nothing from the past or from two thousand years of Bible production and printing, but is repeating the very vices which always provoke God to give the world over to its own sensuality and self-destruction.[11]

Perhaps even more distressing is the realization that we have already reached that final stage. Conscience has been silenced. Nothing is left to instruct people's behavior but their own depraved minds. The mind becomes a tool of lust unrestrained:

Just as they did not see fit to acknowledge God any longer, God gave them over to a depraved mind, to do those things which are not proper, being filled with all unrighteousness, wickedness, greed, evil; full of envy, murder, strife, deceit, malice; they are gossips, slanderers, haters of God, insolent, arrogant, boastful, inventors of evil, disobedient to parents, without understanding, untrustworthy, unloving, unmerciful; and, although they know the ordinance of God, that those who practice such things are worthy of death, they not only do the same, but also give hearty approval to those who practice them (Rom. 1:28–32).

For the third time in the space of five verses, Paul has used the word *paradidōmi*, "gave them over." First he said, "God gave them over . . . to impurity" (v. 24); then, "God gave them over to degrading passions" (v. 26); and now, "God gave them over to a depraved mind" (v. 28). Notice the downward progression. Again, it exactly parallels the decline of contemporary society over the past three or four decades. Who can read those verses and deny that they describe our own society right now with an uncanny precision? The mind is morally useless. It cannot discern right from wrong, good from evil. We might assume that someone would figure out that a biblical moral standard would correct much that is wrong with our society, but that simple, rational idea escapes the reprobate mind. Confirmed sinners cannot think logically about moral issues. The conscience itself is victimized!

In a final act of temporal judgment, God has utterly abandoned people to the wickedness they love so much: "unrighteousness, wickedness, greed, evil; full of envy, murder, strife, deceit, [and] malice," so that society is filled with "gossips, slanderers, haters of God, insolent, arrogant, boastful, inventors of evil, disobedient to parents, without understanding, untrustworthy, unloving, unmerciful" (vv. 29–31).

The word translated "unloving" in that list is *astorgos*, literally meaning "without natural affection"—and it is so translated in the King James Version. It speaks of those who lack instinctive love for their own families—such as mothers who abandon their children, husbands who beat their wives, children who despise their parents, fathers who molest their children, or brothers and sisters who loathe one another. Our society is rife with such wrongdoing; perhaps no other description would better characterize contemporary culture than to say people lack natural affection.

The other items in Paul's list—such as greed, envy, murder, strife, deceit, gossip, slander, insolence, arrogance, pride, inventive evildoing, disobedience to parents, mercilessness, and hatred of God—perfectly catalog the most visible traits of modern society. Not that previous generations have been free of such evils. But unlike our ancestors, people in our day openly exhibit such sins with a shameless arrogance. "They not only do [those things], but also give hearty approval to those who practice them" (v. 32). Something is seriously, desperately wrong with our culture.

People who follow the culture rather than obey God's Word are utterly without excuse. "They know the ordinance of God, that those who practice such things are worthy of death," Paul writes (v. 32). Their own consciences witness against them. They may suppress their sense of guilt now, but when they must give account to God, their own consciences will stand against them.

Civilization as we know it has reached the deepest level of corruption and abides under a sentence of divine condemnation.

Those who deal falsely with their own consciences place themselves under God's holy wrath even in this life. "God [gives] them over to a depraved mind" (v. 28). In other words, it turns out that the damage they do to their own consciences *is* God's immediate judgment against them. "This is the judgment," Jesus said, "that the light is come into the world, and men loved the darkness rather than the light; for their deeds were evil" (Jn. 3:19). Those who reject the light are condemned to live in darkness. God gives them over to their own depravity, and their conscience ceases to function correctly.

It is a wretched and horrifying state of affairs. Our society openly condones and defends the worst kinds of evil. Civilization as we know it has reached the deepest level of corruption and abides under a sentence of divine condemnation. People's consciences have been seared, debased, obstructed, repressed, and overturned. Without a functioning conscience, people are destined only to sink deeper and deeper into wickedness. Humanity is merely storing up wrath against the day of wrath (cf. Rom. 2:5).

Is there hope? For those willing to repent and follow Christ, there is. They can "be saved from this perverse generation" (Acts 2:40). Their consciences can be renewed and cleansed (Heb. 9:14). They can become new creatures (2 Cor. 5:17).

Can society itself be saved? Certainly not without full-scale revival. Unless multitudes turn to Christ, the downward spiral is certain to continue. With so many dampened consciences and hardened hearts, it would take a revival of unprecedented proportions to reverse the downward direction of our culture. The problems are spiritual and cannot be solved through politics or education. Christians who believe political activism can reverse the trends in our society do not understand the nature of the problem. True believers must realize that the state of our society is the result of the righteous judgment of God. God has not commissioned His people to reconstruct society. We are not called to expend our energies for moral reform. We are salt—a preservative for a decaying generation (Matt. 5:13). And we are lights designed to shine in a way that enables people who see our good works to glorify our heavenly Father (vv. 14–16). In other words, our primary task is to preach the truth of God's Word, live in obedience to that truth, and to keep ourselves unstained by the world (Jas. 1:27). Our influence on society must be the fruit of that kind of living, not the product of fleshly energy or political clout.

What we can do, and *must* do, is keep our own consciences pure. We must saturate our minds and hearts with the truth of Scripture, and refuse to yield to the spirit of our age. To do that, we must understand our own sinfulness and know how to deal with our sins. That will be the focus of the following chapters.

Part II
The Nature of Sin

We must understand the nature of sin—specifically our own sinfulness—before we can know how to deal with it, without and within. If we are to rejuvenate our vanishing consciences, we must first understand the nature of sin. Once we understand the enemy, we will be able to employ the biblical strategy to gain real victory over sin (the focus of Part III). Part II specifically provides this understanding by showing how and why the conscience is silenced by sin.

Chapter 4, "What Do You Mean, Totally Depraved?" explains the doctrine of total depravity as explained by Paul in Romans 1–3. It also introduces the self-esteem credo of modern psychology as a major stumbling block to people's understanding the depth of their own sinfulness. It shows society's focus on self, not God.

Chapter 5, "Sin and Its Cure," examines the character of sin and how we attempt to justify it. It explores the theological problem of where sin and evil come from and how they fit in God's providence. It then turns to the liberation from sin through union with Christ and the new birth.

Chapter 6, "The Conquered Enemy Within," examines some misguided religious attempts to deal with sin. It exposes the dangers of perfectionism and examines several perfectionist groups in church history. It shows the importance of keeping the proper relationship between sanctification and justification. It treats what it means to be "freed from sin."

4
What Do You Mean, "Totally Depraved"?

The blind man can see no difference between a master-piece of Titian or Raphael and the queen's head on a vil-lage signboard. The deaf man cannot distinguish between a penny whistle and a cathedral organ. The very animals whose smell is most offensive to us have no idea that they are offensive and are not offensive to one another. And man, fallen man, I believe, can have no just idea what a vile thing sin is in the sight of that God whose handiwork is absolutely perfect.

J. C. Ryle[1]

No concept is more important to the gurus of modern psychology than self-esteem. According to the self-esteem credo, there are no bad people—only people who think badly of themselves.

For years, educational experts, psychologists, and a growing number of Christian leaders have championed self-esteem as a panacea for all sorts of human miseries. According to the purveyors of this doctrine, if people feel good about themselves, they will behave better, have fewer emotional problems, and achieve more. People with high self-esteem, we are told, are less likely to commit crimes, act immorally, fail academically, or have problems in their relationships with others.

The Blind Faith of Self-Esteem

Advocates of self-esteem have been remarkably successful in convincing people that self-esteem is the solution to whatever ails anyone. One survey revealed that a majority of people view self-esteem as the single most important motivator for hard work and success. In fact, self-esteem ranked several points higher than a sense of responsibility or fear of failure.[2]

But does self-esteem really work? Does it, for example, promote higher achievement? There is plenty of evidence to suggest it does not. In a recent study, a standardized math test was given to teenagers from six different nations. Besides the math questions, the test asked the youngsters to respond yes or no to the question, "I am good at mathematics." American students scored lowest on the math questions, far behind Korean students, who had the top scores. Ironically, more than three-fourths of the Korean students had answered *no* to the "I am good at math" question. In stark contrast, however, 68 percent of the American students believed their math skills were just fine.[3] Our kids may be failing math, but they obviously feel pretty good about how they are doing.

Morally, our culture is in precisely the same boat. Empirical evidence strongly suggests, as we have seen, that society is at an all-time moral low. We might expect people's self-esteem to be suffering as well. But statistics show Americans are feeling better about themselves than ever. In a survey conducted in 1940, 11 percent of women and 20 percent of men agreed with the statement, "I am an important person." In the 1990s, those figures jumped to 66 percent of women and 62 percent of men.[4] Ninety percent of people surveyed in a recent Gallup Poll say their own sense of self-esteem is robust and healthy.[5] Incredibly, while the moral fabric of society continues to unravel, self-esteem is thriving. All the positive thinking about ourselves seems not to be doing anything to elevate the culture or motivate people to live better lives.

Can it really be that low self-esteem is what is wrong with people today? Does anyone seriously believe that making people feel better about themselves has helped the problems of crime, moral decay, divorce, child abuse, juvenile delinquency, drug addiction, and all the other evils that have dragged society down? Could so much still be wrong in our culture if the assumptions of self-esteem theory were true? Do we really imagine that more self-esteem will finally solve society's problems? Is there even a shred of evidence that would support such a belief?

Absolutely none. A report in *Newsweek* suggested that "the case for self-esteem . . . is a matter less of scientific pedagogy than of faith—faith that positive thoughts can make manifest the inherent goodness in anyone."[6] In other words, the notion that self-esteem makes people better is simply a matter of blind religious faith. Not only that, it is a religion that is antithetical to Christianity, because it is predicated on the unbiblical presupposition that people are basically good and need to recognize their own goodness.

The Church and the Self-Esteem Cult

Nevertheless, the most persuasive proponents of self-esteem religion have always included clergymen. Norman Vincent Peale's "positive thinking" doctrine, which was popular a generation ago, was simply an early self-esteem model. Peale wrote *The Power of Positive Thinking* in 1952.[7] The book opened with these words: "Believe in yourself! Have faith in your abilities!" In the introduction, Peale called the book a "personal-improvement manual . . . written with the sole objective of helping the reader achieve a happy, satisfying, and worthwhile life."[8] The book was marketed as motivational therapy, not theology. But in Peale's estimation the whole system was merely "applied Christianity; a simple yet scientific system of practical techniques of successful living that works."[9]

Evangelicals for the most part were slow to embrace a system that called people to faith in themselves rather than faith in Jesus Christ. Self-esteem as Norman Vincent Peale outlined it was the off-spring of theological liberalism married to neo-orthodoxy.

The most persuasive proponents of self-esteem religion have always included clergymen.

Time has evidently worn away evangelicals' resistance to such doctrine. Now many of the hottest-selling books in evangelical book-stores promote self-esteem and positive thinking. Even *Newsweek* has commented on the trend. Noting that self-esteem is considered "religiously correct" nowadays, the magazine observed:

> The notion [of self-esteem] may put off anyone old enough to re-member when "Christian" as an adjective was often followed by "humility." But American churches, which once did not shrink from calling their congregants wretches, have moved toward a more congenial view of human nature . . . . Chastising sinners is considered counterproductive: it makes them feel worse about themselves.[10]

Surely the most influential voice selling self-esteem to evangelicals is Norman Vincent Peale's best-known disciple, Dr. Robert Schuller. Broadcasting weekly to millions of people world-wide, Schuller's "Hour of Power" telecast relentlessly promotes the "theology" of self-esteem. More than any other source, this weekly media exposure has advocated and normalized self-esteem for the church in our day. It has bred an effective movement by creating an appetite to receive this teaching. Indeed, that is its intent.

Unlike Peale, who until recent years made no pretense of being evangelical, Schuller has always framed his teaching in the termi-nology of traditional, conservative, Reformed theology. He speaks of conversion, calls unbelievers to be born again, and affirms the need for a personal relationship with Jesus Christ. But Schuller's actual teaching owes far more to neo-orthodoxy than to evangelicalism. In fact, his self-esteem doctrines reflect *secular humanism*, a non-religious system of thought that places human beings, their values, and their needs above the glory of God.

If this teaching is seriously in error, as I am convinced it is, it must be refuted and the church needs to be warned of the danger (Tit. 1:9, ff.).

J. C. Ryle decried the tendency of his own age to tolerate seriously aberrant theology under the rubric of magnanimity and charity:

> The tendency of modern thought is to reject dogmas, creeds and every kind of bounds in religion. It is thought grand and wise to condemn no opinion whatsoever, and to pronounce all earnest and clever teachers to be trustworthy, however heterogeneous and mutually destructive their opinions may be. Everything, forsooth, is true and nothing is false! Everybody is right and nobody is wrong! Everybody is likely to be saved and nobody is to be lost![11]

Christian love demands that we walk in truth (2 Jn. 6), and that we not turn a blind eye to error. Because I preach and publish, I must be held accountable to the Word of God for what I teach. So must all preachers. Please understand that my criticism of Dr. Schuller's teaching is by no means an attack on his personal character. My concerns are altogether doctrinal, not personal. Because of the aggressive influence of his teaching on the contemporary church worldwide, it is imperative that we let him speak for himself, then measure what he says by the pure Word of God.

The Sanctification of Human Pride?

Robert Schuller says "the 'will to self-love' is the deepest of all human desires."[12] Far from being a sin, he says, people's lust for self-love is a good thing that should be encouraged, fostered, and fed. He labels the church's historic aversion to pride "neurotic"; and he contends that people should be taught not to fear human pride.[13] *"The cross sanctifies the ego trip,"* he has written.[14] Amplifying that statement on a televised talk show, he declared, "Jesus had an ego. He said, 'I, if I be lifted up, will draw all men unto me.' *Wow, what an ego trip He was on!*"[15]

According to Schuller, "sin is psychological self-abuse."[16] More specifically, "Sin is any act or thought that robs myself or another human being of his or her self-esteem," and hell is simply the loss of pride that follows such an act.[17]

Can such statements be reconciled with the biblical teaching that pride itself was the first sin, which resulted in Satan's fall (cf. Isa. 14:12–14) as well as Adam's (Gen. 3)? Can they be harmonized with Jesus' words about the publican who lamented his own unworthiness? Jesus held that man up as an example of true repentance (Lk. 18:13–14).

Far from being a sin, he says, people's lust for self-love is a good thing that should be encouraged, fostered, and fed.

In self-esteem theology, however, "a profoundly deep sense of unworthiness" is no virtue; it is unbelief.[18] Moreover, according to this doctrine, "The most serious sin is the one that causes me to say, 'I am unworthy. I may have no claim to divine sonship if you examine me at my worst.' For once a person believes he is an 'unworthy sinner,' it is doubtful if he can really honestly accept the saving grace God offers in Jesus Christ."[19] Dr. Schuller even suggests that "too many prayers of confession of sin and repentance have been destructive to the emotional health of Christians by feeding their sense of nonworth."[20]

Those who take the whole Bible at face value are likely to surmise differently. David prayed, "The sacrifices of God are a broken spirit; a broken and a contrite heart, O God, Thou wilt not despise" (Ps. 51:17). In the first of His beatitudes Jesus said, "Blessed are the poor in spirit: for theirs is the kingdom of heaven" (Matt. 5:3). James wrote, "Cleanse your hands, you sinners; and purify your hearts, you double-minded. Be miserable and mourn and weep; let your laughter be turned into mourning, and your joy to gloom. Humble yourselves in the presence of the Lord, and He will exalt you" (Jas. 4:8–10). Scripture also says, "Before destruction the heart of man is haughty, but humility goes before honor" (Prov. 18:12; cf. Prov. 15:33). "God is opposed to the proud, but gives grace to the humble. Humble yourselves, therefore, under the mighty hand of God, that He may exalt you at the proper time" (1 Pet. 5:5–6). "Whosoever shall exalt himself shall be abased; and he that shall humble himself shall be exalted" (Matt. 23:12, KJV).

On a recent radio interview Dr. Schuller was asked how he reconciles his teaching with Scriptures like those. In his reply he stated, "Just because it's in the Bible doesn't mean you should preach it."[21] Borrowing a rudimentary error from neo-orthodoxy, he downplays the authority of Scripture, setting up a false dichotomy between Christ's authority and the authority of His Word ("Christ is the Lord over the Scriptures; the Scriptures are not Lord over Christ. . . . The Bible must not compete with the Lord for the seat of glory").[22] He echoes the common neo-orthodox notion that Jesus' words are "safer ground" on which to build one's ministry than the writings of the apostle Paul.[23] Schuller is particularly averse to expressions like "the wrath of God": "I'll *never* use that language," he told a talk-show host. "I'm interested in attracting people, not driving them farther away. . . . There are times when if we are wise, there's language we will not use."[24] Why? Because according to Dr. Schuller, "the gospel message is not only faulty but potentially dangerous if it has to put a person down before it attempts to lift him up."[25]

In fact, Schuller states that the "basic defect" of contemporary Christianity is our "failure to proclaim the gospel in a way that can satisfy every person's deepest need—one's spiritual hunger for glory."[26] He says the church should glorify the human being and reinterpret sin in a way that does not assault a person's self-esteem.[27] "What we need," he declares, "is a theology of salvation that begins and ends with a recognition of every person's hunger for glory."[28]

What about *God's* glory? According to the new self-esteem theology, that is the wrong starting point: "Classical theology has erred in its insistence that theology be 'God-centered,' not 'man-centered.'"[29] "This is part of the reason the church is in the predicament it is in today," Dr. Schuller alleges.[30] In his estimation "Reformation theology [also] failed to make clear that the core of sin is a lack of self-esteem."[31] Thus he calls for a fresh starting point for our faith—other than Scripture, other than the doctrine of God. That new starting point, he suggests, must be an emphasis on the glory of humanity. "The 'Dignity of the Person,'" Schuller writes, "will then be the new theological bench mark!"[32] "And the result will be a faith that will bring glory to the human race."[33]

What Is Man, That Thou Art Mindful of Him?

But is human glory a worthy goal? God says, "I am the Lord, that is My name; I will not give My glory to another" (Isa. 42:8). God has said, "For the sake of My name I delay My wrath, and for My praise I restrain it for you, in order not to cut you off. Behold, I have refined you, but not as silver; I have tested you in the furnace of affliction. For My own sake, for My own sake, I will act; for how can My name be profaned? And *My glory I will not give to another*" (Isa. 48:9–11, emphasis added). In other words, God extends His longsuffering, grace, and mercy to mankind not because we are worthy of it, but for His own name's sake—for His own glory, not ours. "O Lord, *what is man*, that Thou dost take knowledge of him? Or the son of man, that Thou dost think of him? Man is like a mere breath; His days are like a passing shadow" (Ps. 144:3–4, emphasis added; cf. Job 7:17; 15:14; Ps. 8:4; Heb. 2:6).

In other words, God extends His longsuffering, grace, and mercy to mankind not because we are worthy of it, but for His own name's sake— for His own glory, not ours.

On the other hand, the gospel according to self-esteem theology says, "We must tell people everywhere that God wants them to feel good about themselves!"[34]

Does God really want all people to feel good about themselves? Or does He first call sinners to recognize the utter helplessness of their own estate? The answer is obvious to those who let Scripture speak for itself.

Self-esteem theology is forced to redefine sin in a way that minimizes the offense to God: "The core of sin is a negative self-image."[35] In other words, sin—according to the self-esteem gospel—is an offense against *human* glory. It is a transgression against ourselves, our own dignity—not necessarily an offense against God or His law. In fact, classical theology's definition of sin as rebellion against God is now deemed "shallow and insulting."[36]

Robert Schuller goes so far as to deny that fallen human nature is truly evil: "By nature we are fearful, not bad. . . . Label it a 'negative self-image,' but do not say that the central core of the human soul is wickedness. If this were so, then truly, the human being is totally depraved."[37]

Understanding the Doctrine of Total Depravity

Scripture, of course, teaches from beginning to end that all humanity *is* totally depraved. Paul says unredeemed people are "dead in . . . trespasses and sins" (Eph. 2:1). Apart from salvation, all people walk in worldliness and disobedience (v. 2). We who know and love the Lord once "lived in the lusts of our flesh, indulging the desires of the flesh and of the mind, and were by nature children of wrath, even as the rest" (v. 3). We were "separate from Christ, excluded from the commonwealth of Israel, and strangers to the covenants of promise, having no hope and without God in the world" (v. 12).

Scripture, of course, teaches from beginning to end that all humanity is totally depraved.

In those passages Paul describes the state of unbelievers as estrangement from God. Paul's words cannot be twisted to support Dr. Schuller's assertion that the human problem is fearfulness rather than depravity. In fact, Paul says, "There is no fear of God" in the unregenerate person (Rom. 3:18). Before our salvation, we were actually God's enemies (Rom. 5:8, 10). We were "alienated and hostile in mind, engaged in evil deeds" (Col. 1:21). Sinful passions, inflamed by our hatred of God's law, motivated all our living (Rom. 7:5). We were tainted by sin in every part of our being. We were corrupt, evil, thoroughly sinful.

Theologians refer to this doctrine as "total depravity." It does not mean that unbelieving sinners are always as bad as they could be (cf. Lk. 6:33; Rom. 2:14). It does not mean that the expression of sinful human nature is always lived out to the fullest. It does not mean that unbelievers are incapable of acts of kindness, benevolence, goodwill, or human altruism. It certainly does not mean that non-Christians cannot appreciate goodness, beauty, honesty, decency, or excellence. It *does* mean that none of this has any merit with God.

Depravity also means that evil has contaminated every aspect of our humanity—our heart, mind, personality, emotions, conscience, motives, and will (cf. Jer. 17:9; Jn. 8:44). Unredeemed sinners are therefore incapable of doing anything to please God (Isa. 64:6). They are incapable of truly loving the God who reveals Himself in Scripture. They are incapable of obedience from the heart, with righteous motives. They are incapable of understanding spiritual truth. They are incapable of genuine faith. And that means they are incapable of pleasing God or truly seeking Him (Heb. 11:1).

Total depravity means sinners have no ability to do spiritual good or work for their own salvation from sin. They are so completely disinclined to love righteousness, so thoroughly dead in sin, that they are not able to save themselves or even to fit themselves for God's salvation. Unbelieving humanity has no capacity to desire, understand, believe, or apply spiritual truth: "A natural man does not accept the things of the Spirit of God; for they are foolishness to him, and he cannot understand them, because they are spiritually appraised" (1 Cor. 2:14). In spite of all this, people are *proud* of themselves! Lack of self-esteem is not the issue.

Because of Adam's sin, this state of spiritual death called total depravity has passed to all mankind. Another term for this is "original sin." Scripture explains it this way: "Through one man sin entered into the world, and death through sin, and so death spread to all men, because all sinned (Rom. 5:12). When, as head of the human race, Adam sinned, the whole race was corrupted. "Through the one man's disobedience the many were made sinners" (Rom. 5:19). How such a thing could happen has been the subject of much theological discussion for centuries. For our purposes, however, it is sufficient to affirm that Scripture clearly teaches that Adam's sin brought guilt upon the entire race. We were "in Adam" when he sinned, and therefore the guilt of sin and the sentence of death passed upon all of us: "In Adam all die" (1 Cor. 15:22).

We might be tempted to think, *If I'm sinful by birth and never had a morally neutral nature, how can I be held responsible for being a sinner?* But our corrupt nature is precisely why our guilt is such a serious matter. Sin flows from the very soul of our being. It is because of our sinful nature that we commit sinful acts: "For from within, out of the heart of men, proceed the evil thoughts, fornications, thefts, murders, adulteries, deeds of coveting and wickedness, as well as deceit, sensuality, envy, slander, pride and foolishness. All these evil things proceed from within and defile the man" (Mk. 7:21–23). We are "by nature children of wrath" (Eph. 2:3). Original sin—including all the corrupt tendencies and sinful passions of the soul —is as deserving of punishment as all our voluntary acts of sin. What is sin, after all, but *anomia*—"lawlessness" (1 Jn. 3:4)? Or as the Westminster Shorter Catechism says, "Sin is any want of conformity to, or transgression of, the law of God" (q. 14). Far from being an excuse, original sin itself is at the heart of *why* we are guilty. And original sin itself is sufficient grounds for our condemnation before God.

Moreover, original sin with its resulting depravity is the *reason* we commit voluntary acts of sin. D. Martyn Lloyd-Jones wrote,

> Why is it that man ever chooses to sin? The answer is that man has fallen away from God, and as a result, his whole nature has become perverted and sinful. Man's whole bias is away from God. By nature he hates God and feels that God is opposed to him. His god is himself, his own abilities and powers, his own desires. He objects to the whole idea of God and the demands which God makes upon him. . . . Furthermore, man likes and covets the things which God prohibits, and dislikes the things and the kind of life to which God calls him. These are no mere dogmatic statements. They are facts. . . . They alone explain the moral muddle and the ugliness that characterise life to such an extent to-day.[38]

Salvation from original sin is only through the cross of Christ: "As through the one man's disobedience [Adam's sin] the many were made sinners, even so through the obedience of the One [Jesus Christ] the many will be made righteous" (Rom. 5:19). We are born in sin (Ps. 51:5), and if we are to become children of God and enter God's kingdom, we must be born again by God's Spirit (Jn. 3:3–8).

In other words, contrary to what most people think—contrary to the presuppositions of self-esteem doctrine—men and women are not naturally good. Just the opposite is true. We are by nature enemies of God, sinners, lovers of ourselves, and in bondage to our own sin. We are blind, deaf, and dead to spiritual matters, unable even to believe apart from God's gracious intervention. Yet we are relentlessly proud! In fact, nothing is more illustrative of human wickedness than the desire for self-esteem. And the first step to a proper self-image is a recognition that these things are true.

We are by nature enemies of God, sinners, lovers of ourselves, and in bondage to our own sin.

That's why Jesus *commended* the tax-gatherer—rather than rebuking him for his low self-esteem—when the man pounded his chest and pleaded, "God, be merciful to me, the sinner!" (Lk. 18:13). The man had finally come to the point where he saw himself for what he was and he was so overcome that his emotion released in acts of self-condemnation. The truth is, his self-image had never been more sound than at that moment. Rid of pride and pretense, he now saw there was nothing he could ever do to earn God's favor. Instead, he pleaded with God for mercy. And therefore he "went down to his house justified"—exalted by God because he had humbled himself (v. 14). For the first time ever he was in a position to realize true joy, peace with God, and a new sense of self-worth that is granted by God's grace to those He adopts as His children (Rom. 8:15).

All Have Sinned and Fall Short

Deep in our hearts, we all know something is desperately wrong with us. Our conscience constantly confronts us with our own sinfulness. Try as we might to blame others or seek psychological explanations for how we feel, we cannot escape reality. We cannot ultimately deny our own consciences. We all feel our guilt, and we all know the horrible truth about who we are on the inside.

We *feel* guilty because we *are* guilty. Only the cross of Christ can answer sin in a way that frees us from our own shame. Psychology might mask some of the pain of our guilt. Self-esteem might sweep it under the rug for a time. Other things—such as seeking comfort in relationships, or blaming our problems on someone else—might make us feel better, but the relief is only superficial. And it is dangerous. In fact, it often intensifies the guilt, because it adds dishonesty and pride to the sin that originally wounded the conscience.

We feel guilty because we are guilty. Only the cross of Christ can answer sin in a way that frees us from our own shame.

True guilt has only one cause, and that is sin. Until sin is dealt with, the conscience will fight to accuse. And sin—not low self-esteem—is the very thing the gospel is given to conquer. That is why, as we saw in chapter 3, the apostle Paul began his presentation of the gospel to the Romans with a lengthy discourse about sin. Total depravity is the first gospel truth he introduced, and he spent nearly three full chapters on the subject. Romans 1:18–32 demonstrates the guilt of the pagans. Romans 2:1–16 proves the guilt of the moralist, who violates the very standard by which he judges others. And Romans 2:17–3:8 establishes the guilt of the Jews, who had access to all the benefits of divine grace but as a whole rejected God's righteousness nonetheless.

Since Romans 1 Paul has argued eloquently, citing evidence from nature, history, sound reason, and conscience to prove utter sinfulness of all humanity. And in verses 9–20 of chapter 3, he sums it all up. Paul reasons like an attorney giving his final summation. He reviews his arguments like a prosecutor who has made an iron-clad case against all humanity. It is a powerful and compelling presentation, replete with a charge, convincing proof, and the inexcapable verdict.

The charge. "What then? Are we better than they? Not at all; for we have already charged that both Jews and Greeks are all under sin" (Rom. 3:9). Paul's indictment thus begins with two questions: What then? or, "Is there any need of further testimony?" And, Are we better than they? or, "Can anyone honestly claim to live above the level of human nature I have been describing?"

"*Not at all*," he answers. Everyone from the most degenerate, perverted sinners (Rom. 1:28–32) to the most rigidly legalistic Jews falls into the same category of total depravity. In other words, the entire human race, without exception, is arraigned in the divine courtroom and charged with being "under sin"—wholly subjugated to the power of sin. All unredeemed people, Paul is saying, are subservient to sin, in thrall to it, taken captive to sin's authority.

Paul's Jewish readers would have found this truth every bit as shocking and unbelievable as it must be to those weaned on modern self-esteem doctrine. His Jewish readers believed they were acceptable to God by birth and that only Gentiles were sinners by nature. Jews were, after all, God's chosen people. The idea that all Jews were sinners was contrary to the beliefs of the Pharisees. They taught that only derelicts, beggars, and Gentiles were born in sin (cf. Jn. 9:34). But Scripture clearly pronounces otherwise. Even David said, "I was brought forth in iniquity, and in sin my mother conceived me" (Ps. 51:5) "The whole world lies in the power of the evil one" (1 Jn. 5:19). Modern humanity, weaned on self-esteem psychology, also finds it shocking to learn that all of us are by nature sinful and unworthy creatures.

The proof. Paul, continuing his courtroom summation, goes on to prove from the Old Testament Scriptures the universality of human depravity:

> As it is written, "There is none righteous, not even one; there is
> none who understands, there is none who seeks for God; all
> have turned aside, together they have become useless; there is
> none who does good, there is not even one." "Their throat is an
> open grave, with their tongues they keep deceiving," "The poi-
> son of asps is under their lips"; "Whose mouth is full of cursing
> and bitterness"; "Their feet are swift to shed blood, destruction
> and misery are in their paths, and the path of peace have they
> not known" (Rom. 3:10–17).

Notice how Paul underscores the universality of sin. In those few verses, he says "none" or "not even one" six times. No person escapes the accusation. "The Scripture has shut up all men under sin" (Gal. 3:22).

Paul's argument is constructed in three parts: how sin corrupts the character (Rom. 3:10–12), how sin defiles the conversation (vv. 13–14), and how sin perverts the conduct (vv. 15–17). First he proves *how sin corrupts the character*: "There is none righteous . . . there is none who does good, there is not even one" (Rom. 3:10–12). Here Paul makes six charges. He says that because of their innate depravity, people are universally evil ("none righteous"), spiritually ignorant ("none who understands"), rebellious ("none who seeks for God"), wayward ("all have turned aside"), spiritually useless ("to-gether they have become useless"), and morally corrupt ("there is none who does good").

The verse Paul is quoting is Psalm 14:1: "The fool has said in his heart, 'There is no God.' They are corrupt, they have committed abominable deeds; there is no one who does good." The words at the end of Romans 3:12, "not even one," are an editorial comment from Paul, added to make the truth inescapable for someone who might otherwise think of himself as an exception to the rule—as is the common attitude of self-justifying sinners.

Notice Paul does not suggest that some sinners might be prone to think worse of themselves than they ought to. The very opposite is true: "I say to every man among you not to think more highly of himself than he ought to think" (Rom. 12:3). Undue pride is the typi-cal and expected response of sinners. Modern self-esteem teaching, in fact, is the expression of that very pride. Making a savage feel good about himself only increases his deadliness.

Again, the utter depravity Paul is describing certainly does not

mean that all people play out the expression of their sin to the ultimate degree. There are certainly some people who are "good" in a
relative sense. They may have characteristics of compassion, gener-
osity, kindness, integrity, decency, thoughtfulness, and so on. But
even those characteristics are imperfect and sullied with human sin
and weakness. No one—"not even one"—comes close to true righteousness. God's standard, after all, is absolute perfection: "You are
to be perfect, as your heavenly Father is perfect" (Matt. 5:48). In
other words, no one who falls short of the touchstone of perfection
is acceptable to God! What does that do to self-esteem theology?
How does one feel good about oneself when God Himself declares
us worthy of His wrath?

There *is* an answer to the dilemma, of course. God justifies the
ungodly by faith (Rom. 4:5). Christ's own perfect righteousness is
imputed to our account, so by faith we can stand before God clothed
in a perfect righteousness that is not our own (Phil. 3:9). This does
not speak of external works we do. It is a superior righteousness, the
totality of Christ's own righteousness, credited to our account. Christ
on our behalf has already fulfilled the requirement of being as perfect as our heavenly Father is perfect. His virtue is assigned to our
account, so God regards us as fully righteous.

But we're jumping ahead of the apostle's carefully arranged
evidence. He adds a paraphrase also from Psalm 14: "The Lord has
looked down from heaven upon the sons of men, to see if there are
any who understand, who seek after God" (v. 2; cf. 53:3). Ignorance
and depravity go hand in hand. But people are not sinful and enemies of God because of their spiritual ignorance; rather they are
spiritually ignorant because of their sinfulness and their adversarial
disposition toward God. They are "darkened in their understanding,
excluded from the life of God, because of the ignorance that is in
them, *because of the hardness of their heart*" (Eph. 4:18, emphasis
added). In other words, because of their hatred of God and their love
for their own sin, they reject the witness of God in creation and the
testimony of their conscience (Rom. 1:19–20). That, as we noted in
chapter 3, hardens the heart and darkens the mind.

The hard heart and darkened mind refuse to seek for God:
"There is *none* who seeks for God." That again echoes Psalm 14:2.
God invites the seeker, and promises that those who seek Him with
all their hearts will find Him (Jer. 29:13). Jesus also promised that

everyone who seeks Him will find Him (Matt. 7:8). But the sinful heart is inclined away from God and does not seek Him. Without God's gracious, sovereign intervention, seeking and drawing sinners to Himself first, no one would seek and be saved. Jesus Himself said, "No one can come to Me, unless the Father who sent Me draws him" (Jn. 6:44).

Without God's gracious, sovereign
intervention, seeking and
drawing sinners to Himself first,
no one would be saved.

Rather than seeking God, sinners inevitably go their own way. Still using the 14th Psalm, Paul cites verse 3: "They have all turned aside"—or as Romans 3:12 has it, "All have turned aside." This is reminiscent of Isaiah 53:6: "All of us like sheep have gone astray, each of us has turned to his own way." Sinners are naturally wayward. Inherent in human depravity is an inescapable drift away from truth and righteousness. Sinners always lose their way: "There is a way which seems right to a man, but its end is the way of death" (Prov. 14:12).

The taint of sin further renders the sinner "useless" (v. 12)— translating a Greek word used to describe spoiled milk or contaminated food to be thrown out. Unredeemed people are unfit for any spiritual good, useless for righteousness, fit only to be thrown into the fire and burned (Jn. 15:6). Their great need is not self-esteem or positive thinking, but redemption from their prideful sin.

In the next few verses Paul presents his second proof concerning *how sin defiles the conversation*: "Their throat is an open grave, with their tongues they keep deceiving, the poison of asps is under their lips; whose mouth is full of cursing and bitterness" (3:13–14). One's true character inevitably becomes apparent in conversation. Scripture is filled with affirmation of this truth:

- "The mouth speaks out of that which fills the heart. The good man out of his good treasure brings forth what is good; and the evil man out of his evil treasure brings forth what is evil" (Matt. 12:34–35).
- "The things that proceed out of the mouth come from the heart" (15:18).
- "The mouth of the righteous flows with wisdom, but the perverted tongue will be cut out. The lips of the righteous bring forth what is acceptable, but the mouth of the wicked, what is perverted" (Prov. 10:31–32).
- "The tongue of the wise makes knowledge acceptable, but the mouth of fools spouts folly. . . . The heart of the righteous ponders how to answer, but the mouth of the wicked pours out evil things" (Prov. 15:2, 28).
- "Your iniquities have made a separation between you and your God, and your sins have hidden His face from you, so that He does not hear. For your hands are defiled with blood, and your fingers with iniquity; your lips have spoken falsehood, your tongue mutters wickedness" (Isa. 59:2–3).
- "They bend their tongue like their bow; lies and not truth prevail in the land. . . . Every neighbor goes about as a slanderer. And everyone deceives his neighbor, and does not speak the truth; they have taught their tongue to speak lies" (Jer. 9:3–5).

Paul chooses more passages from the psalms to underscore the point:

- "Poison of a viper is under their lips" (Ps. 140:3).
- "There is nothing reliable in what they say; their inward part is destruction itself; their throat is an open grave; they flatter with their tongue" (Ps. 5:9).
- "His mouth is full of curses and deceit and oppression; under his tongue is mischief and wickedness" (Ps. 10:7).

Those verses, all written to condemn "the wicked," Paul applies to everyone. He is making the point that human depravity is universal. *All* are wicked. *Everyone* is guilty. *No one* can claim exemption from the charges Paul levels.

Moreover, he is illustrating how thoroughly sin pervades and permeates every aspect of our humanity. Note how completely sin contaminates the conversation: it defiles the "throat," corrupts the "tongue," poisons the "lips," and pollutes the "mouth." Evil speech, an expression of the wickedness of the heart, thus defiles every organ it touches as it "proceeds out of the mouth," defiling the whole person (Matt. 15:11).

Third, Paul concludes his proof by quoting several verses to show *how sin perverts the conduct*: "Their feet are swift to shed blood, destruction and misery are in their paths, and the path of peace have they not known" (Rom. 3:15–17). Here Paul is quoting a passage from Isaiah. This is significant, because in these verses Isaiah was excoriating Israel for their sins against Jehovah. This was no denunciation of wicked pagans, but an indictment of religious people who believed in God: "Their feet run to evil, and they hasten to shed innocent blood; their thoughts are thoughts of iniquity; devastation and destruction are in their highways. They do not know the way of peace, and there is no justice in their tracks; they have made their paths crooked; whoever treads on them does not know peace" (Isa. 59:7–8).

In some of our larger cities, as many as two hundred murders will occur in a typical week.

The phrase "their feet are swift to shed blood" describes sinful humanity's penchant for murder. Remember, Jesus taught that hatred is the moral equivalent of murder (Matt. 5:21–22). The seed of hatred ripens and matures, and the fruit it bears is the shedding of blood. Sinners are naturally attracted to hatred and its violent offspring. People are "swift" in their advance toward such acts. We see this very clearly in our own society. An article in *Newsweek*, for example, recently reported that "a twelve-year-old boy turn[ed] without a word and [shot] dead a seven-year-old girl because she 'diss'ed' him by standing on his shadow."[39]

In some of our larger cities, as many as two hundred murders will occur in a typical week. Drive-by shootings, drunken brawls, gang violence, family strife, and other crimes all contribute to the body count. If lack of self-esteem is the problem of the human heart, why, we must ask, is the murder rate on the rise so dramatically in a society where self-esteem is also growing? The answer is that low self-esteem is not the problem. On the contrary, pride itself is the very problem that leads to all sin, including hate, hostility, and killing. A love for bloodshed festers in the heart of sinful humanity. Remove the moral restraints from society, and the inevitable result will be an escalation of murder and violence—no matter how good people feel about themselves.

"Destruction and misery" further characterize the tendencies of depraved humanity. Again, no one familiar with the trends of modern society can deny the truth of Scripture on this point. The lid is off, and we can see clearly the true nature of the human heart. What else could explain our culture—where people are robbed, beaten, raped, or murdered for no reason other than sheer enjoyment? Wanton destruction is so much a part of society that we have become inured to much of it.

"Gangsta rap"—music that glorifies murder, rape, and drug use—now accounts for many of the hottest-selling albums on the record charts. The lyrics of most gangsta rap are indescribably vile. They mix violence, sexual imagery, and unimaginable profanity in a way that is repulsive and purposely offensive. Worse, they openly incite young people to join gangs, kill policemen, rape women, riot, and commit other acts of wanton destruction. Gangsta rap is big business. These recordings are not sold secretly out of the back of some hoodlum's car, but marketed openly in retail stores everywhere—with slick ad campaigns designed by executives in companies like Capitol Records. And the prime target for such products are kids younger than eighteen. A whole generation is being indoctrinated with these vices. Destruction and misery *are* in their path. And woe to those unfortunate enough to cross their path! In recent months several nationally-known rap artists have been charged with violent crimes, including murder and gang rape.

Why is it that misery and despair are so characteristic of this modern age, even though humanity has made such remarkable advances in technology, psychology, and medicine? It is because depravity is at the very heart of the human soul. All these problems are so bound up in the human heart that no amount of learning and no measure of self-esteem will ever erase them. As science advances, people only become more sophisticated in their use of evil means. The destruction and misery wrought by human sin does not diminish; it accelerates. The history of this century, filled with world wars, holocausts, serial killers, escalating crime, and bloody revolutions, is graphic proof of that. Depravity is bound up in the human heart.

In other words, "the path of peace" is unknown to sinful humanity (Rom. 3:17). Though we hear much talk these days of "peace, peace," there is no peace (cf. Jer. 6:14).

Paul sums up the evidence for human depravity: "There is no fear of God before their eyes" (Rom. 3:18). There he returns to the psalms for a final quotation. Psalm 36:1 says, "Transgression speaks to the ungodly within his heart; there is no fear of God before his eyes." Human sinfulness is a defect of the human heart itself. Evil commands the heart of man. People's hearts are naturally attuned to wickedness. They have no native fear of God.

We don't hear much about fearing God these days. Even many Christians seem to feel the language of fear is somehow too harsh or too negative.

Fear of the Lord, of course, is the primary prerequisite to spiritual wisdom (Prov. 9:10). Moses commanded Israel, "You shall fear only the Lord your God; and you shall worship Him, and swear by His name" (Deut. 6:13). In fact, as Moses summed up the responsibilities of the Israelites, this is what he said: "And now, Israel, what does the Lord your God require from you, but to *fear* the Lord your God, to walk in all His ways and love Him, and to serve the Lord your God with all your heart and with all your soul, and to keep the Lord's commandments and His statutes which I am commanding you today for your good?" (Deut. 10:12–13, emphasis added). We in the New Testament era are likewise commanded to "cleanse ourselves from all defilement of flesh and spirit, perfecting holiness in the fear of God" (2 Cor. 7:1). We are to "honor all men; love the brotherhood, *fear God*, honor the king" (1 Pet. 2:17, emphasis added; cf. Rev. 14:7).

"The fear of the Lord is the instruction for wisdom" (Prov. 15:33). "By the fear of the Lord one keeps away from evil" (Prov. 16:6). "The fear of the Lord is a fountain of life, that one may avoid the snares of death" (Prov. 14:27).

We don't hear much about fearing God these days. Even many Christians seem to feel the language of fear is somehow too harsh or too negative. How much easier it is to speak of God's love and infinite mercy. But longsuffering, kindness, and such attributes aren't the truths that are missing from most people's concept of God. The problem is that most people don't think of God as Someone to be *feared*. They don't realize that He hates the proud and punishes evildoers. They presume on His grace. They fear what people think more than they care what God thinks. They seek their own pleasure, unmindful of God's displeasure. Their conscience is defiled and in danger of vanishing. "There is no fear of God before their eyes."

The fear of God, by the way, is a concept diametrically opposed to the doctrine of self-esteem. How can we encourage fear of the Lord in people and at the same time be obsessed with boosting their self-esteem? Which is the more biblical pursuit? The Scriptures speak for themselves.

The verdict. Having presented a convincing case for total depravity, Paul makes the verdict clear: "Now we know that what things soever the law saith, it saith to them who are under the law: *that every mouth may be stopped, and all the world may become guilty before God*" (Rom. 3:19, KJV, emphasis added).

Here Paul blasts the assumption of those who believed that merely *having* the law of God somehow made the Jews morally superior to pagan Gentiles. The law carried its own condemnation against those who did not keep it perfectly: "Cursed is he who does not confirm the words of this law by doing them" (Deut. 27:26; cf. Gal. 3:10). "Whoever keeps the whole law and yet stumbles in one point, he has become guilty of all" (Jas. 2:10). Merely having the law did not make the Jews any better than the rest of humanity.

The Gentiles, on the other hand, were accountable to the law written on their own consciences (Rom. 2:11–15). Both groups are proven in violation of the law they possessed. The prosecution rests. There can be no defense. Every mouth must be stopped. The case is closed. Unredeemed humanity is guilty of all charges. There are no grounds for acquittal. The whole world stands guilty before God.

Self-esteem is no solution to human depravity. It aggravates it! The problems of our culture—especially the anguish that wracks individual human hearts—will not be solved by the deception of getting people to think better of themselves. People really *are* sinful to the core. The guilt and shame we all feel as sinners is legitimate, natural, and even appropriate. It has the beneficial purpose of letting us know the depth of our own sinfulness. We dare not whisk it aside for the faulty teachings of humanistic self-esteem.

Self-esteem is no solution to human depravity.

I recently read an unusually clear-sighted article dealing with the myth of human goodness from a non-Christian perspective. The author, a Jewish social critic, writes,

> To believe that people are basically good after Auschwitz, the Gulag and the other horrors of our century, is a statement of irrational faith, as irrational as any [fanatical] religious belief. Whenever I meet people—especially Jews, victims of the most concentrated evil in history—who persist in believing in the essential goodness of people, I know that I have met people for whom evidence is irrelevant. How many evils would human beings have to commit in order to shake a Jew's faith in humanity? How many more innocent people have to be murdered and tortured? How many more women need to be raped?[40]

This article lists five consequences of the people-are-basically-good myth. Notice how they all contribute to the destruction of the conscience:

The first such consequence is, quite logically, the attribution of all evil to causes outside of people. Since people are basically good, the bad that they do must be caused by some external force. Depending on who is doing the blaming, that outside force could be the social environment, economic circumstances, parents, schools, television violence, handguns, racism, the devil, government cutbacks, or even corrupt politicians (as expressed by this frequently heard foolishness: "How can we expect our children to be honest when the government isn't?").

People are therefore not responsible for the evil they commit. It's not my fault that I mug old women, or that I cheat much of the time—something (chosen from the previous list) made me do it.

A second terrible consequence is the denial of evil. If good is natural, then bad must be unnatural, or "sick." Moral categories have been replaced by psychological ones. There is no longer good and evil, only "normal" and "sick."

Third, neither parents nor schools take the need to teach children goodness seriously—why teach what comes naturally? Only those who recognize that people are not basically good recognize the need to teach goodness.

Fourth, since much of society believes that evil comes from outside of people, it has ceased trying to change people's values and concentrates instead on changing outside forces. People commit crimes? It is not values and character development that we need to be concerned with; we need to change the socioeconomic environment that "produces" rapists and murderers. Irresponsible men impregnate irresponsible women? It is not better values they need, but better sex education and better access to condoms and abortions.

Fifth, and most destructive of all, those who believe that people are basically good conclude that people do not need to feel accountable of their behavior to God and to a religion, only to themselves.[41]

That author, oddly enough, denies human depravity as well as human goodness. He believes people are neither good *nor* bad but choose their way in life. (At the outset of his article, however, he quotes Genesis 8:21: "The intent of man's heart is evil from his youth.")

Despite this inconsistency in the author's position, the article shows very clearly the dangers of the myth of human goodness. The church must safeguard sound doctrine by recovering the doctrine of human depravity. As J. C. Ryle wrote nearly a century ago,

> A scriptural view of sin is one of the best antidotes to that vague, dim, misty, hazy kind of theology which is so painfully current in the present age. It is vain to shut our eyes to the fact that there is a vast quantity of so-called Christianity nowadays which you cannot declare positively unsound, but which, nevertheless, is not full measure, good weight and sixteen ounces to the pound. It is a Christianity in which there is undeniably "something about Christ and something about grace and something about faith and something about repentance and something about holiness," but it is not the real "thing as it is" in the Bible. Things are out of place and out of proportion. As old Latimer would have said, it is a kind of "mingle-mangle," and does no good. It neither exercises influence on daily conduct, nor comforts in life, nor gives peace in death; and those who hold it often wake too late to find that they have got nothing solid under their feet. Now I believe that the likeliest way to cure and mend this defective kind of religion is to bring forward more prominently the old scriptural truth about the sinfulness of sin.[42]

"To believe that people are basically good after Auschwitz, the Gulag and the other horrors of our century, is a statement of irrational faith, as irrational as any [fanatical] religious belief." (Dennis Prager)

You may be asking, on the other hand, *Does God want us to wallow in shame and self-condemnation permanently?* Not at all. God offers freedom from sin and shame through faith in Jesus Christ. If we are willing to acknowledge our sinfulness and seek His grace, He will wonderfully deliver us from our sin and all its effects. "There is therefore now no condemnation for those who are in Christ Jesus. For the law of the Spirit of life in Christ Jesus has set you free from the law of sin and of death" (Rom. 8:1–2). The liberation from sin those verses describe is the only basis on which we can really feel good about ourselves. And it is to that process that we now turn our attention.

5

Sin and Its Cure

Man's very nature is fallen. Man is wrong at the centre of his being, and therefore everything is wrong. He cannot be improved, for, finally, nothing will suffice but a radical change, a new nature. Man loves the darkness and hates the light. What can be done for him? Can he change himself? Can he renew his nature? "Can the Ethiopian change his skin or the leopard his spots?" Can man change the whole bias of his life? Give him new clothing, provide him with a new house in new surroundings, entertain him with all that is best and most elevating, educate him and train his mind, enrich his soul with frequent doses of the finest culture ever known, do all and more, but still he will remain the same essential man, and his desires and innermost life will be unchanged.

D. Martyn Lloyd-Jones[1]

Tom Wolfe's 1987 blockbuster novel *The Bonfire of the Vanities*[2] told the story of a fictional young Wall Street tycoon, Sherman McCoy, who is caught in the vortex of a scandal after he and his mistress inadvertently take a wrong exit on a Bronx expressway. Lost in the wrong part of town, they are threatened by some thugs who try to block their car. One of the young attackers is seriously injured when the car strikes him as McCoy and his lover are fleeing the scene. The boy lies in a coma for more than a year before dying. Meanwhile, the case becomes a political *cause célèbre*, with McCoy at the mercy of a ruthless press and inept criminal justice system. The book tells the story of how his world slowly and painfully unravels.

Though innocent of most of the charges against him, McCoy is by no means guiltless. His troubles begin because he is trying to conceal his adultery. He compounds his own guilt with a series of lies in an attempt to cover up. His own duplicity ultimately draws him deeper and deeper into trouble. In the end, he loses his career, his family, his fortune, and all his friends—and seems headed for a lengthy trial probably followed by a prison term.

Wolfe's book anticipated with remarkable accuracy a string of celebrity scandals that characterized the second half of the 1980s. Jim and Tammy Bakker, Gary Hart, Jimmy Swaggart, Michael Milken, and a host of others all saw their lives disintegrate in a manner reminiscent of Sherman McCoy. What all these cases demonstrate so graphically is the destructive, catastrophic effects of sin. Sin once begun will eat like gangrene at the human soul. It will dishonor the sinner, expose him, scandalize him, and ultimately destroy his life. "Be sure your sin will find you out" (Num. 32:23).

The Scandal of Sin

Sin rules every human heart, and if it had its way, it would damn every human soul. If we do not understand our own sinfulness or see our sin as God sees it, we cannot understand or make use of sin's remedy. Those who want to deny their guilt or hide their own sinfulness cannot discover sin's cure. Those who try to justify their sin forfeit the justification of God. Until we understand what an utterly abhorrent thing our sin is, we can never even know God.

If we do not understand our own sinfulness or see our sin as God sees it, we cannot understand or make use of sin's remedy.

Sin is abominable to God. He hates it (cf. Deut. 12:31). His eyes "are too pure to approve evil, and [He cannot] look on wickedness with favor" (Hab. 1:13). Sin is contrary to His very nature (Isa. 6:3; 1 Jn. 1:5). The ultimate penalty—death—is exacted for every infraction against the divine law (Ezek. 18:4, 20; Rom. 6:23). Even the very smallest transgression is worthy of the same severe penalty: "For whoever keeps the whole law and yet stumbles in one point, he has become guilty of all" (Jas. 2:10).

Sin stains the soul. It degrades a person's nobility. It darkens the mind. It makes us worse than animals, for animals cannot sin. Sin pollutes, defiles, stains. All sin is gross, disgusting, loathsome, revolting in God's sight. Scripture calls it "filthiness" (Prov. 30:12; Ezek. 24:13; Jas. 1:21). Sin is compared to vomit, and sinners are the dogs who lick it up (Prov. 26:11; 2 Pet. 2:22). Sin is called mire, and sinners are the swine who love to wallow in it (Ps. 69:2; 2 Pet. 2:22). Sin is likened to a putrefying corpse, and sinners are the tombs that contain the stench and foulness (Matt. 23:27). Sin has turned humanity into a polluted, befouled race.

The terrifying consequences of sin include hell, of which Jesus said, "If your right eye makes you stumble, tear it out, and throw it from you; for it is better for you that one of the parts of your body perish, than for your whole body to be thrown into hell" (Matt. 5:30). Scripture describes hell as a dreadful, hideous place where sinners are "tormented with fire and brimstone. . . . And the smoke of their torment goes up forever and ever; and they have no rest day and night" (Rev. 14:10–11). Those truths become all the more alarming when we realize that they are part of the inspired Word of an infinitely merciful and gracious God.

God wants us to understand the exceeding sinfulness of sin (Rom. 7:13). We dare not take it lightly or dismiss our own guilt frivolously. When we really see sin for what it is, we must hate it.

Scripture goes even further than that: "You will remember your ways and all your deeds, with which you have defiled yourselves; and *you will loathe yourselves* in your own sight for all the evil things that you have done" (Ezek. 20:43, emphasis added). In other words, when we truly see what sin is, far from achieving self-esteem, we will despise ourselves.

Nature of Human Depravity

Sin pervades our innermost beings. As we saw in the previous chapter, sin is at the very core of the human soul. "Out of the heart come evil thoughts, murders, adulteries, fornications, thefts, false witness, slanders. These are the things which defile the man" (Matt. 15:19–20). "The evil man out of the evil treasure [of his heart] brings forth what is evil; for his mouth speaks from that which fills his heart" (Lk. 6:45).

Yet sin is not a weakness or flaw for which we cannot be held responsible. It is an energetic, purposeful antagonism to God. Sinners freely and gladly choose sin. It is human nature to love sin and hate God. "The carnal mind is enmity against God" (Rom. 8:7, KJV).

Yet sin is not a weakness or flaw for which we cannot be held responsible. It is an energetic, purposeful antagonism to God.

In other words, sin is rebellion against God. Sinners reason in their hearts, "With our tongue we will prevail; our lips are our own; *who is lord over us?*" (Ps. 12:4, emphasis added). Isaiah 57:4 characterizes sinners as rebellious children who open wide their mouths and stick out their tongues against God. Sin would dethrone God, depose Him, usurp Him, and set self in His rightful place. All sin is ultimately an act of pride, which says, "Move over, God; I'm in charge." That's why all sin at its core is blasphemy.

We initially love our sin; we delight in it; we seek opportunities to act it out. Yet because we know instinctively that we are guilty before God, we inevitably attempt to camouflage or disavow our own sinfulness. There are many ways we do this, as we have noted in previous chapters. They can be summarized in roughly three categories: covering up, justifying ourselves, and being oblivious to our own sins.

First, *we try to cover up*. Adam and Eve did this in the Garden, after the first sin: "The eyes of both of them were opened, and they knew that they were naked; and they sewed fig leaves together and made themselves loin coverings" (Gen. 3:7)—then they hid themselves from the presence of the Lord (v. 8). King David tried in futility to cover his guilt when he sinned against Uriah. He had committed adultery with Uriah's wife, Bathsheba. When she became pregnant, David first plotted to try to make it seem as if Uriah was the father of the baby (2 Sam. 11:5–13). When that didn't work, he schemed to have Uriah killed (vv. 14–17). That only compounded his sin. For all the months of Bathsheba's pregnancy, David continued to cover his sin (2 Sam. 11:27). Later, when David was confronted with his sin and repented, he confessed, "When I kept silent about my sin, my body wasted away through my groaning all day long. For day and night Thy hand was heavy upon me; my vitality was drained away as with the fever heat of summer" (Ps. 32:3–4).

Second, *we attempt to justify ourselves*. Sin is always someone else's fault. Adam blamed Eve, whom he described as "the woman whom *Thou* gavest to be with me" (Gen. 3:12, emphasis added). That shows he was blaming God as well. He didn't even know what a woman was, until he woke up married to one! God, he reasoned, was responsible for the woman who victimized him. We likewise try to excuse our wrongdoing because we think it is someone else's fault. Or we argue that we think we have a valid reason. We convince ourselves that it is OK to return evil for evil (cf. Prov. 24:29; 1 Thess. 5:15; 1 Pet. 3:9). Or we reason that if our ultimate motives are good, evil can be justified—the perversion of thinking the end justifies any means (cf. Rom. 3:8). We call sin sickness, label ourselves victims, or deny that what we have done is really wrong. The human mind is endlessly creative when it comes to finding ways to justify evil.

Third, *we are oblivious to our own sin*. We do often sin in ignorance or presumption. That's why David prayed, "Who can discern his errors? Acquit me of hidden faults. Also keep back Thy servant from presumptuous sins" (Ps. 19:12–13). Jesus warned against the folly of tolerating a log in our own eye while being concerned about a tiny speck in someone else's (Matt. 7:3). Because sin is so pervasive, we naturally tend to be insensitive to our own sin, just as a skunk is impervious to its own odor. Even a highly sensitive conscience can't know everything (cf. 1 Cor. 4:4).

Sin does not necessarily express itself in overt acts. Sinful attitudes, sinful dispositions, sinful desires, and a sinful state of heart are just as reprehensible as the actions they produce. Jesus said anger is as sinful as murder, and lust is tantamount to adultery (Matt. 5:21–28).

Sin is deceitful in a way that hardens the sinner against its own enormity (Heb. 3:13). We naturally want to minimize our sin, as if it were not really any big deal. After all, we tell ourselves, God is merciful and loving, is He not? He understands our sin and can't be so hard on us, can He? But to reason that way is to be deceived by sin's cunning.

Sin, according to Scripture, "is the transgression of the law" (1 Jn. 3:4, KJV). In other words, "Everyone who practices sin also practices lawlessness; and sin is lawlessness" (NASB). Sin, therefore, is any lack of conformity to the perfect moral standard of God. The central demand of God's law is that we love Him: "You shall love the Lord your God with all your heart, and with all your soul, and with all your strength, and with all your mind" (Lk. 10:27). Hence, lack of love for God is the epitome of all sin.

But "the carnal mind . . . is not subject to the law of God, neither indeed can be" (Rom. 8:7, KJV). Our natural hatred of the law is such that even knowing what the law demands stirs up in us an urge to disobey. Paul wrote, "The sinful passions [are] aroused by the Law. . . . I would not have come to know sin except through the Law; for I would not have known about coveting if the Law had not said, 'You shall not covet.' But sin, taking opportunity through the commandment, produced in me coveting of every kind" (Rom. 7:5, 7). Such is the sinner's penchant for sin that it controls him. He is in bondage to it. But he nevertheless pursues it with an insatiable appetite, and with all the passion in his heart.

The Theological Problem Posed by Evil

Where did sin come from? We know that God created everything in the universe and saw that it was very good (Gen. 1:31). "All things came into being by Him, and apart from Him nothing came into being that has come into being" (Jn. 1:3). That raises the obvious question of whether God is responsible for evil. If He isn't, who is? Didn't God have the power to keep sin from spoiling His perfect creation?

It is helpful to see that sin is not a separate substance that exists independently of moral agents. Evil is not a created thing. It is not an element. Sin is an ethical and moral reality, not a physical one. Sin is a defect in something good. Nobody *created* it; it is a loss of perfection in beings whom God created perfectly.

Nobody created it; sin is a loss of perfection in beings whom God created perfectly.

But that doesn't really resolve the question of how sin happened. How could perfect beings rebel? How could angels who were made perfect turn against God? How could humans, created in God's own image, choose to sin? And if God could have stopped it, why didn't He? Is He somehow to blame for the existence of evil?

Attempts to resolve the problem of sin's origin in a way that vindicates God's goodness are called "theodicies". The theodicy of Christian Scientists is simple; they flatly deny the reality of evil. According to their system, all sin, badness, disease, and other negative effects of evil are simply figments of the imagination, or as they would say, the errors of mortal thinking. Jay Adams answers the Christian Science theodicy: "They implode their own belief by this internally-inconsistent, self-contradictory explanation. If there is no such thing as evil, if God is all, and all is God (as they also teach), then, this all-knowing god of which every human being is a part, cannot err, and there is no such thing as a mortal mind."[3] The Christian Science theodicy is no answer to the problem of evil.

Another theodicy suggests that God was not able to control

the entrance of evil into the world. Having created creatures who enjoyed free will, He could not control their use of their moral freedom or overrule their choices. God, according to this view, has no command over circumstances that occur in His universe. He is at the mercy of circumstances. God, like people, is a "victim" of sin and evil. That is essentially the view expressed in Rabbi Harold Kushner's bestselling book, *When Bad Things Happen to Good People*.[4]

The problem with that view is that it denies God's sovereignty. Scripture clearly teaches that God is utterly sovereign over all things. Or, as the Westminster Confession says, "God from all eternity did, by the most wise and holy Counsel of His own will, freely and unchangeably ordain whatsoever comes to pass" (Chap. 3, sec. 1). He "works all things after the counsel of His will" (Eph. 1:11). "From Him and through Him and to Him are all things" (Rom. 11:36). His purposes are unchangeable (Heb. 6:17). His plan is eternal (Eph. 3:11). And with God "there is no variation, or shifting shadow" (Jas. 1:17). All His works were determined according to His purposes in eternity past.

In fact, Scripture clearly teaches that God is sovereign over every circumstance, situation, and event:

He controls so-called random happenings. "The lot is cast into the lap, but its every decision is from the Lord" (Prov. 16:33). "Are not two sparrows sold for a cent? And yet not one of them will fall to the ground apart from your Father" (Matt. 10:29).

He is sovereign over the free actions of all moral agents. "The king's heart is like channels of water in the hand of the Lord; He turns it wherever He wishes" (Prov. 21:1). "We are His workmanship, created in Christ Jesus for good works, which God prepared beforehand, that we should walk in them" (Eph. 2:10). "It is God who is at work in you, both to will and to work for His good pleasure" (Phil. 2:13).

He determines even the most evil acts of sinners. Peter told the crowd who had demanded Christ's crucifixion, "This Man, delivered up *by the predetermined plan and foreknowledge of God*, you nailed to a cross by the hands of godless men and put Him to death. And God raised Him up again, putting an end to the agony of death, since it was impossible for Him to be held in its power" (Acts 2:23–24, emphasis added). The companions of Peter and John prayed, "Truly in this city there were gathered together against Thy holy servant Jesus, whom Thou didst anoint, both Herod and Pontius Pilate, along with the Gentiles and the peoples of Israel, *to do whatever Thy hand and Thy purpose predestined to occur*" (Acts 4:27–28, emphasis added). Joseph told his brothers, "Now do not be grieved or angry with yourselves, because you sold me here; for God sent me before you to preserve life" (Gen. 45:5). And Isaiah 10:5 says God used the wicked nation of Assyria as the rod of His anger.

He appoints the powers that oversee the evil world system. Pontius Pilate said to Jesus, "Do You not know that I have authority to release You, and I have authority to crucify You?" Jesus replied, "You would have no authority over Me, unless it had been given you from above" (Jn. 19:10–11). Truly "there is no authority except from God, and those which exist are established by God" (Rom. 13:1).

Indeed, the whole course of all events and circumstances is ordained in the divine decree, from the most profound milestone of the divine plan to the most trivial detail. God even determines the number of hairs on our heads (Matt. 10:30).

Ultimately, we must concede that sin is something God *meant* to happen. He planned for it, ordained it—or, in the words of the Westminster Confession, He decreed it. Sin is not something that sneaked in and took Him by surprise, caught Him off guard, or spoiled His plans. The reality of sin figured into His changeless purposes from eternity past. Thus evil and all its consequences were included in God's eternal decree before the foundation of the world.

Ultimately, we must concede that sin is something God meant to happen.

Yet by the same token God cannot be considered the author, or originator, of sin. "God cannot be tempted by evil, and He Himself does not tempt anyone" (Jas. 1:13). "God is light, and in Him there is no darkness at all" (1 Jn. 1:5).

God in no sense *causes* sin, *incites* it, *condones* it, *authorizes* it, *approves* it, or otherwise *consents to* it. God is never the cause or the agent of sin. He only *permits* evil agents to do their deeds, then over-rules the evil for His own wise and holy ends. God's purposes in permitting evil are always good. That is why Joseph could say to his brothers, who had sold him into slavery, "You meant evil against me, but God meant it for good in order to bring about this present result, to preserve many people alive" (Gen. 50:20).

Scripture also tells us that God permitted evil so that He could "demonstrate His wrath and . . . make His power known" (Rom. 9:22). In other words, He allowed sin to enter His perfect creation so that He could display His hatred of evil and destroy it forever. Why did He not wipe out all evil immediately the moment it first appeared? Scrip-ture suggests an answer for that as well. He "endured [it] with pa-tience . . . in order that He might make known the riches of His glory upon vessels of mercy, which He prepared beforehand for glory" (Rom. 9:22–23). That means He allows evil to continue even now so that He can display His mercy and grace fully through the redemp-tion of sinners. Sin thus allows God to reveal His glory in forgiveness.

Ultimately, however, Scripture does not undertake any elabo-rate philosophical argument to vindicate God for the existence of evil. It simply declares that He is "holy, holy, holy" (Isa. 6:3; Rev. 4:8). It reveals that He hates evil (Ps. 11:5; Zech. 8:17; Lk. 16:15). And it makes clear that the existence of sin does not in any way dampen God's glory or taint His impeccable character: "Far be it from God to do wickedness, and from the Almighty to do wrong" (Job 34:10). "Ascribe greatness to our God! The Rock! His work is perfect, for all His ways are just; a God of faithfulness and without injustice, righteous and upright is He" (Deut. 32:3–4). "The Lord is upright; He is my rock, and there is no unrighteousness in Him" (Ps. 92:15). "Thou art not a God who takes pleasure in wickedness; no evil dwells with Thee" (Ps. 5:4).

The most satisfying theodicy is implied in the cross of Christ. As R. L. Dabney wrote, "The doctrine of Christ's sacrifice, coupled with His proper divinity, enables us to complete our 'theodicy' of the permission of evil. . . . For had there been in God the least defect of [holiness or benevolence], He certainly would never have found it in His heart to send His infinite Son, more great and important than all worlds, to redeem anyone."[5]

Sin and the Cross of Christ

In fact, the cross is proof of both the immense love of God and the profound wickedness of sin. Do you want to see God's love at its pinnacle and sin's vileness at its nadir? Look at the passion of our Lord Jesus Christ. See Him hanging on the cross—the sinless, spotless, Lamb of God, bearing the sins of the world (cf. Jn. 1:29). Hear Him cry in agony, "Eli, Eli, lama sabachthani?"—that is, "My God, My God, why hast Thou forsaken Me?" (Matt. 27:46). Realize that nothing short of the shed blood of the eternal, beloved Son of God Himself could have atoned for sin. The weight of our guilt must have been infinitely heavy and the heinousness of our sin indescribably black to require such a sacrifice! And God's love must have been inexpressibly rich to allow it!

---

*The cross is proof of both
the immense love of God and
the profound wickedness of sin.*

Sin is a horrible malignancy for which there is no other cure. "Weighed down with iniquity, offspring of evildoers, sons who act corruptly! They have abandoned the Lord, they have despised the Holy One of Israel, they have turned away from Him. . . . The whole head is sick, and the whole heart is faint. From the sole of the foot even to the head there is nothing sound in it, only bruises, welts, and raw wounds, not pressed out or bandaged, nor softened with oil" (Isa. 1:4–6). That pictures sin as an incurable leprosy of the soul. We are sick with sin from top to bottom, within and without.

Sinners cannot improve their own condition. Jeremiah 13:23 says, "Can the Ethiopian change his skin or the leopard his spots? Then you also can do good who are accustomed to doing evil." Sin is so much a part of our nature and we love it so much that we are unable to break away from its domination over our lives. We love darkness rather than light (Jn. 3:19). The unregenerate mind is naturally "hostile toward God; for it does not subject itself to the law of God, for *it is not even able to do so*; and those who are in the flesh *cannot please God*" (Rom. 8:7–8, emphasis added). Unredeemed sinners are slaves of their sin (Jn. 8:34; Rom. 6:20). As Job asked, "Who can make the clean out of the unclean? No one!" (Job 14:4). "The bad tree bears bad fruit . . . nor can a bad tree produce good fruit" (Matt. 7:17–18).

No amount of tears can atone for sin. No number of good deeds can make amends for wrong we have done against God. No quantity of prayer or personal devotion can extenuate our guilt or cover it in any way. Even everlasting burning in hell will not purify the soul from sin. In the human realm there is nothing in time or eternity that can free us from the guilt of our sin. Those who seek a do-it-yourself solution to the problem of sin only shackle themselves all the more securely to their guilt.

Moreover, the smallest sin is so exceedingly vile that God—despite His infinite mercy, grace, and forgiveness—will not and cannot overlook even one sin without exacting its full penalty.

There has to be a solution. There must be a way God can satisfy His perfect righteousness yet enable Him to display His rich mercy toward sinners. The cross of Christ provided the way by enabling the only Perfect Sacrifice to atone for human sin once for all.

The offering for sin had to be perfect, spotless, untainted by sin. Jesus lived a sinless, holy life in perfect obedience to God's law. "We do not have a high priest who cannot sympathize with our weaknesses, but One who has been tempted in all things as we are, yet without sin" (Heb. 4:15). He is "holy, innocent, undefiled, separated from sinners and exalted above the heavens" (Heb. 7:26).

Our Lord, the sinless One, was the Lamb of God to be offered up as a sacrifice for our sin (Jn. 1:29). That is the very purpose for which He came. "You know that He appeared in order to take away sins; and in Him there is no sin" (1 Jn. 3:5). As He hung on the cross, He carried the guilt of *our* sin. "Surely *our* griefs He Himself bore, and *our* sorrows He carried. . . . He was pierced through for *our* transgressions, He was crushed for *our* iniquities; the chastening for *our* well-being fell upon Him" (Isa. 53:4–5, emphasis added). He "offered Himself without blemish to God" to cleanse *our* consciences (Heb. 9:14). He paid the penalty to the fullest on *our* behalf. And in the same way that our sins were imputed to Him, so His righteousness is reckoned to us who believe: "[God] made Him who knew no sin to be sin on our behalf, that we might become the righteousness of God in Him" (2 Cor. 5:21). He rose from the dead to declare His victory over sin. "[He] was delivered up because of our transgressions, and was raised because of our justification" (Rom. 4:25).

Our Lord, the sinless One, was the Lamb of God to be offered up as a sacrifice for our sin (Jn. 1:29).

"He Himself bore our sins in His body on the cross, that we might die to sin and live to righteousness; for *by His wounds you were healed*" (1 Pet. 2:24, emphasis added). That is the only possible remedy for our sin. It is the only way God can be both "just and the justifier of the one who has faith in Jesus" (Rom. 3:26).

God's healing for sin involves more than forgiveness and justification. God transforms the very nature of the sinner. He makes us partakers of His own nature (2 Pet. 1:4). Martyn Lloyd-Jones wrote,

> Man needs a new nature. Whence can he obtain it? Again, there is but one answer, in Jesus Christ the Son of God. He came from Heaven and took upon Him human nature perfect and whole. He is God and man. In Him alone are the divine and the human united. And He offers to give us His own nature. He desires to make of us new men. He is "the first-born among many brethren." All who believe on Him, and receive Him, obtain this new nature, and as the result all things become different. Those who hated God now love Him and desire to know more and more about Him. Their supreme desire now is to please Him and to honour and to glorify Him. The things which formerly delighted them they now hate and detest, and the ways of God are the ways they desire.[6]

That is God's gracious answer to our sin. He redeems those who believe and makes them new creatures (2 Cor. 5:17). He gives them an entirely new nature, including a love for righteousness and an aversion to sin. As we shall see in subsequent chapters, the residue of sin still remains in believers until they are finally glorified, but they are no longer enslaved to sin or incapable of pleasing God.

God So Loved the World

As much as God hates sin, He loves sinners. Set against the dark background of our sin, the grace of God becomes all the more wondrous. The most familiar passage in all Scripture is John 3:16. Without an understanding of the wickedness of sin, however, we cannot grasp the tremendous significance of this verse: "For God so loved the world, that He gave His only begotten Son, that whoever believes in Him should not perish, but have eternal life."

"For God so loved the world, that He gave His only begotten Son, that whoever believes in Him should not perish, but have eternal life." (John 3:16)

"God so loved . . ." Why would God love me despite my sin?

"God so loved the world . . ." Why would God love a whole world of sinners?

"God so loved the world, that He gave His only begotten Son . . ." Why would God's love for sinners be so compelling as to make Him sacrifice His beloved Son in such agony and humiliation?

"God so loved the world, that He gave His only begotten Son, that whoever believes in Him . . ." Why would God make salvation so simple for sinners, requiring only faith of us, and having done all the necessary expiatory work Himself?

"God so loved the world, that He gave His only begotten Son, that whoever believes in Him should not perish . . ." Why would God want to exempt sinners from the judgment they themselves deserve, even to the point of allowing His only begotten Son to accept that judgment on behalf of those who do not deserve His mercy?

"God so loved the world, that He gave His only begotten Son, that whoever believes in Him should not perish, but have eternal life." Why would God want to give everlasting life in His presence to sinners who have done nothing but oppose Him and hate Him?

The answer is found in *God's grace.* "God, being rich in mercy, because of His great love with which He loved us, even when we were dead in our transgressions, made us alive together with Christ (by grace you have been saved)" (Eph. 2:4–5). "The wages of sin is death, but the free gift of God is eternal life in Christ Jesus our Lord" (Rom. 6:23). "Blessed are those whose lawless deeds have been forgiven, and whose sins have been covered. Blessed is the man whose sin the Lord will not take into account" (Rom. 4:7–8).

You Must Be Born Again

How does a sinner obtain forgiveness and acquire the perfect righteousness of Christ? How can someone who is sinful by nature become a partaker in the divine nature?

As Jesus told a Pharisee named Nicodemus, "You must be born again" (Jn. 3:3). Nicodemus saw that as an impossible demand: "How can a man be born when he is old?" (v. 4). Jesus simply reiterated, "Truly, truly, I say to you, unless one is born of water and the Spirit, he cannot enter into the kingdom of God. That which is born of the flesh is flesh, and that which is born of the Spirit is spirit. Do not marvel that I said to you, 'You must be born again'" (vv. 5–7).

Jesus was talking about a spiritual rebirth, a regenerative act of God. Nicodemus was right in suggesting that the new birth is not something a sinner can accomplish for himself. It is a sovereign work of the Spirit of God, which cannot be controlled by human means: "The wind blows where it wishes and you hear the sound of it, but do not know where it comes from and where it is going; so is everyone who is born of the Spirit" (v. 8). Salvation is wholly God's work.

If you're reading this as an unbeliever or as someone who is unsure whether you have ever been born again, you might be tempted to despair. If the Spirit works sovereignly when and where and in whom He will, aren't we in an impossible dilemma? You might ask with the people who heard Peter at Pentecost, "What shall we do?" (Acts 2:37)—or like the Philippian jailer, "What must I do to be saved?" (Acts 16:30). If that is the plea of your own heart, the Spirit of God is *already* working within. God has established a time for you, and *now* is that time: "Behold, now is 'the acceptable time,' behold, now is 'the day of salvation'" (2 Cor. 6:2). "The Holy Spirit says, 'Today if you hear His voice, do not harden your hearts'" (Heb. 3:7–8).

Nicodemus was right in suggesting that the new birth is not something a sinner can accomplish for himself. It is a sovereign work of the Spirit of God, which cannot be controlled by human means.

The Spirit was working in Nicodemus's heart too. And Jesus told him what God required of him: "As Moses lifted up the serpent in the wilderness, even so must the Son of Man be lifted up; that whoever believes may in Him have eternal life" (Jn. 3:14–15). Our Lord was recalling an incident from the Old Testament, when the Israelites had sinned against God by grumbling about Moses, complaining that the journey through the wilderness was too difficult, and protesting that food and water were too scarce (Num. 21:5). God punished them by sending a plague of poisonous serpents among them. Many were bitten and dying, and Moses interceded with God on their behalf. The Lord instructed Moses, "Make a fiery serpent, and set it on a standard; and it shall come about, that everyone who is bitten, when he looks at it, he shall live" (Num. 21:8). Moses made a bronze serpent and put it on a pole as God had commanded. The sinning Israelites only had to look at the snake and they were instantly healed. Jesus would also be lifted up, He told Nicodemus, and whoever believed in Him would be saved.

Nicodemus could not have understood every aspect of what Jesus was telling him. Surely it did not occur to him that the way Jesus would be "lifted up" would be on a cross of crucifixion. But Nicodemus, as an Old Testament scholar, was entirely familiar with Moses' account of the bronze serpent. He knew this much: that the ones who had to look at the snake were the rebellious Israelites who had sinned, and that those who looked were healed solely by God's miraculous grace—not because of any medicine they took, not because of anything they did to earn God's favor, but simply because they had enough faith to look and trust God for the cure.

As a spiritual leader over all Israel, Nicodemus undoubtedly identified with Moses whenever he read the account of the bronze serpent. Jesus was suggesting that he should take his place with the sinning Israelites instead. In other words, he was confronting Nicodemus with his sinfulness. He was urging Nicodemus to repent. And He was calling Nicodemus to believe in Him as the Savior who would be lifted up so that whoever believes might be saved.

In other words, "Repent and believe in the gospel" (Mk. 1:15) was Jesus' appeal to Nicodemus. That is God's message to all sinners, and He graciously makes the invitation broad enough so that "*whoever* believes in Him should not perish, but have eternal life" (Jn. 3:16, emphasis added). As you read this, if you are unsure of your spiritual condition, or longing to be free from your sin, this is also the Lord's message to you: "There is no God else beside me; a just God and a Saviour; there is none beside me. *Look unto me, and be ye saved*, all the ends of the earth: for I am God, and there is none else" (Isa. 45:21–22, KJV, emphasis added). Or as contemporary translations render the verse, "Turn to Me, and be saved" (NASB).

Repent. The turning that passage calls for is *repentance* toward Christlikeness. It is not merely a positive "decision for Christ." We cannot simply add Christ to a sin-laden life, then go on loving sin, as if giving lip-service to Him somehow sanctifies all our wickedness. Repentance means turning from our love of sin, and turning to Jesus Christ for salvation: "Repent ye therefore, and be converted" (Acts 3:19).

Specifically, repentance means "turn[ing] away from all your transgressions" (Ezek. 18:30). It means confessing and forsaking your iniquities (Prov. 28:13). It means abhorring your sin, being full of indignation against it (2 Cor. 7:11).

Repentance certainly does not mean you must do works of penance or correct your behavior *before* you can turn to Christ. Turn to the Savior *now*, and in turning to Him, you will turn your heart from all that dishonors him (cf. 1 Thess. 1:9). *He* will begin a good work in you that He Himself will see through to completion (Phil. 1:6).

"Repent and turn to God," and you will discover that changed behavior is the inevitable fruit (Acts 26:20; Lk. 3:8; Matt. 7:20).

Turn to Him today, while it is still today (Heb. 3:13). "Seek the Lord while He may be found; call upon Him while He is near. Let the wicked forsake his way, and the unrighteous man his thoughts; and let him return to the Lord, and He will have compassion on him; and to our God, for He will abundantly pardon" (Isa. 55:7). Do not despise or take for granted the riches of His kindness, forbearance, and patience, for "the kindness of God leads you to repentance" (Rom. 2:4). God does not delight in the death of the wicked, "but rather that the wicked turn from his way and live" (Ezek. 33:11).

These truths apply to *you*. The call to repent is universal: "God is now declaring to men that all everywhere should repent" (Acts 17:30). "The Lord . . . is patient toward you, not wishing for any to perish but for all to come to repentance" (2 Pet. 3:9). "Therefore, repent and live" (Ezek. 18:32).

Repentance means you turn now and follow Jesus. Jesus issued this open invitation: "If anyone wishes to come after Me, let him . . . follow Me" (Matt. 16:24). "If anyone serves Me, let him follow Me" (Jn. 12:26).

But you cannot follow Him halfheartedly. The full invitation is this: "If anyone wishes to come after Me, let him *deny himself, and take up his cross daily*, and follow Me" (Lk. 9:23, emphasis added). "No one, after putting his hand to the plow and looking back, is fit for the kingdom of God" (v. 62). "He who loves father or mother more than Me is not worthy of Me; and he who loves son or daughter more than Me is not worthy of Me. And he who does not take his cross and follow after Me is not worthy of Me" (Matt. 10:37–38). "If anyone comes to Me, and does not hate his own father and mother and wife and children and brothers and sisters, yes, and even his own life, he cannot be My disciple. Whoever does not carry his own cross and come after Me cannot be My disciple" (Lk. 14:26–27).

Jesus cautions you to count the cost carefully (Lk. 14:28–33). "For whoever wishes to save his life shall lose it; but whoever loses his life for My sake and the gospel's shall save it. For what does it profit a man to gain the whole world, and forfeit his soul? For what shall a man give in exchange for his soul?" (Mk. 8:35–37).

Our Lord even pictured repentance as a kind of death: "Unless a grain of wheat falls into the earth and dies, it remains by itself alone; but if it dies, it bears much fruit" (Jn. 12:24).

Believe. Repentance and faith go hand in hand. If repentance stresses our turning *away from* sin and self, believing emphasizes what our hearts turn *toward*. "Believe in the Lord Jesus, and you shall be saved" (Acts 16:31). "If you confess with your mouth Jesus as Lord, and believe in your heart that God raised Him from the dead, you shall be saved" (Rom. 10:9). Repentance without faith would be no good, for righteousness comes not by sorrowing over sin. "Righteousness . . . comes from God on the basis of faith" (Phil. 3:9). Our penitence does not save us; only Christ can do that. Good resolutions cannot win God's favor; we must lay hold of Christ by faith. "There is salvation in no one else; for there is no other name under heaven that has been given among men, by which we must be saved" (Acts 4:12).

Repentance and faith go hand in hand. If repentance stresses our turning away from sin and self, believing emphasizes what our hearts turn toward.

You must believe in the Christ of Scripture. He is both Savior and Lord (cf. Lk. 2:11). "I, even I, am the Lord; and there is no savior besides Me" (Isa. 43:11). You must welcome Him as your Lord, not as Savior only (Col. 2:6). You must receive Him on His own terms; you cannot have His pardon without also accepting His right to rule over you.

And you cannot lay hold of Christ while still clinging to your sin. He came to save His people from their sins (Matt. 1:21)—not to offer heaven to sinners still revelling in their wickedness. The salvation He offers is not merely an escape from the flames of hell, but it is first of all a glorious liberation from the dominion of sin.

Having seen the awful reality of sin, why would anyone want a salvation that stops short of delivering the sinner from sin's bondage? When you understand the exceeding sinfulness of sin, when you realize its power over you, and when you know the dreadful hazards it poses to your soul, you should be driven to Christ as your refuge.

What is truly wonderful is that He promises to receive those who come to Him (Jn. 6:37).

What is truly wonderful is that He promises to receive those who come to Him (Jn. 6:37). More than that, He bids them come: "Come to Me, all who are weary and heavy-laden, and I will give you rest. Take My yoke upon you, and learn from Me, for I am gentle and humble in heart; and you shall find rest for your souls. For My yoke is easy, and My load is light" (Matt. 11:28–30).

Recognition of sin is the necessary first step on the only path to Christ and the salvation He offers.

6

The Conquered Enemy Within

Let me put it very plainly in this way: there is no point in our saying that we believe that Christ has died for us, and that we believe our sins are forgiven, unless we can also say that for us old things are passed away and that all things are become new; that our outlook towards the world and its method of living is entirely changed. It is not that we are sinless, nor that we are perfect, but that we have finished with that way of life. We have seen it for what it is, and we are new creatures for whom everything has become new.

D. Martyn Lloyd-Jones[1]

Nobody's perfect. That truth, which ought to make us tremble before a God who is holy, holy, holy, is usually invoked instead to excuse sinful behavior, to make us feel better. How often do we hear people brush aside their own wrongdoing with the casual words, "Well, after all, nobody's perfect"? People claim they're not perfect to boost their self-esteem, but it is another evidence of a vanishing conscience. There is accuracy in the claim, but it should be a timid confession, not a flippant means of justifying sin.

Scripture recognizes that we are not perfect. Even the apostle Paul wrote, "*Not that I have already obtained it, or have already become perfect,* but I press on in order that I may lay hold of that for which also I was laid hold of by Christ Jesus. Brethren, *I do not regard myself as having laid hold of it yet;* but one thing I do: forgetting what lies behind and reaching forward to what lies ahead, I press on toward the goal for the prize of the upward call of God in Christ Jesus" (Phil. 3:12–14, emphasis added).

It is folly to think that being imperfect somehow provides us with a legitimate excuse to exempt us from God's perfect standard.

We all fall short of perfection—way short. Paul teaches us that our own imperfection should only spur us on toward the goal of complete Christlikeness. When we begin to use our human frailty as an excuse from guilt, we are walking on dangerous ground. We must continue to press on toward the goal: "Therefore you are to be perfect, as your heavenly Father is perfect" (Matt. 5:48). "You shall be holy, for I am holy" (1 Pet. 1:16). It is folly to think that being imperfect somehow provides us with a legitimate excuse to exempt us from God's perfect standard.

The Danger of Perfectionism

Ironic as it may seem, however, it is equally dangerous—or

surely even more so—to think spiritual perfection is something at-
tainable by Christians in this lifetime. Church history is littered
with examples of sects and factions who taught various versions of
Christian perfectionism. Nearly all these groups have either made
utter shipwreck of the faith or been forced to modify their perfectionism to accommodate human imperfection. Every perfectionist
inevitably comes face-to-face with clear and abundant empirical
evidence that the residue of sin remains in the flesh and troubles
even the most spiritual Christians throughout their earthly lives.
In order to hang onto perfectionist doctrine, they must redefine
sin or diminish the standard of holiness. Too often they do this at
the expense of their own consciences.

One perfectionist group, the Oneida Community, founded by
John Humphrey Noyes, flourished in New York from 1849 to 1879.
Based on a notion of perfectionism that had much in common with
the teaching of Charles Finney (Noyes was a convert of Finney's),
the Oneida Community was the best known of about fifty utopian
communes that operated in New York state in the second half of the
nineteenth century. Oneida members (about three hundred of them)
lived in a commune whose centerpiece was a huge stone mansion.
They started a tableware company that still thrives today. They
worked together, worshiped together, and fashioned a communal
lifestyle that was widely hailed in its day as a model of Christian
brotherhood and holiness.

What the outside world did not fully understand until after the
commune was dissolved in 1879 is that the Oneida Community also
practiced communal marriage. Every woman was considered married to every man, and all were at liberty to have sex with anyone
else in the community they chose. Worse, children were expected to
be sexually active as soon as they were old enough. Noyes himself
usually initiated the young girls as soon as they reached puberty.[2]

Noyes, like all too many perfectionists, simply adapted moral
standards to suit his own preferences. Rather than acknowledge
that sexual desire outside of marriage is sin and accept the corol-
lary that his own lust proved he was not yet perfect, he devised
a doctrine that permitted him and the others at Oneida to indulge
their fleshly passions and still claim they had attained sinlessness.

The Oneida Community was certainly one of the more heinous examples of how perfectionism is abused. But in all types of

perfectionism the same tendency exists. Ultimately all perfection-ists are forced to devise down-scaled definitions of sin, holiness, and perfection that can accommodate the *im*perfections of human carnality.

Most who hold this view believe "entire sanctification" is obtained all at once through a second work of grace.

The Holiness movement is a more typical variety of perfection-ism than the fanatical extremes of Oneida. So-called "Holiness doc-trine" is rooted in Wesleyan theology and may be found in traditional Methodism (but not necessarily in the liberal branch of the denomination), the Salvation Army, the Church of the Nazarene, and many charismatic denominations. Most who hold this view believe "entire sanctification" is obtained all at once through a second work of grace. The believer is thereby elevated to a position of "perfect" holiness in which he or she no longer sins— at least not consciously or intentionally. Ordinary failings are called "mistakes," or "temptations," not sins. Only deliberate, premeditated, and grotesque acts are labeled sin. Sin is thus externalized. Evils clearly named as *sin* in Scripture are reduced to misdemeanors. And conscience must be dampened in order to cope with the doctrine.

H. A. Ironside, former pastor of Moody Church, Chicago, wrote a book about his struggle with perfectionist doctrine as a young Sal-vation Army officer. Ironside ultimately left the organization and abandoned his belief in perfectionism. He described perfectionism as a conscience-shattering doctrine:

> The teaching of holiness in the flesh [perfectionism] tends to
> harden the conscience and to cause the one who professes it to
> lower the standard to his own poor experience. Any who move
> much among those in this profession will soon begin to realize
> how greatly prevalent are the conditions I have described. Holi-
> ness professors are frequently cutting, censorious, uncharitable

and harsh in their judgment of others. Exaggerations, amounting to downright dishonesty, are unconsciously encouraged by and often indulged in in their "testimony" meetings.

. . . .

Holiness advocates have all the little unpleasant ways that are so trying in many of us: they are no more free from penuriousness, tattling, evil-speaking, selfishness, and kindred weaknesses, than their neighbors.

And as to downright wickedness and uncleanness, I regret to have to record that sins of a positively immoral character are, I fear, far more frequently met with in holiness churches . . . than the outsider would think possible. I know whereof I speak; and only a desire to save others from the bitter disappointments I had to meet leads me to write as I do.[3]

All perfectionism is essentially a disastrous misunderstanding of how God works in *sanctification*. Sanctification is a process by which God—working in believers through the Holy Spirit—gradually moves them toward Christlikeness (2 Cor. 3:18). The process of sanctification hones the believer's conscience and keeps it from vanishing. That the transformation is gradual, not instantaneous—and never complete in this lifetime—is confirmed by many verses of Scripture.

As we noted at the outset of this chapter, for example, the apostle Paul wrote near the end of his ministry that he was not yet perfect (Phil. 3:12). He told the Romans, "Be [constantly being] transformed by the renewing of your mind" (Rom. 12:2). And to the Galatians he wrote that he labored with them "until Christ is formed in you" (Gal. 4:19). Sanctification will not end "until we all attain to the unity of the faith, and of the knowledge of the Son of God, to a mature man, to the measure of the stature which belongs to the fulness of Christ" (Eph. 4:13). He urged the Ephesians to stop being children, susceptible to error and trends. How were they to do that? By seeking a sudden experience? No, he wrote, "*grow up* in all aspects into Him, who is the head, even Christ" (4:14–15, emphasis added).

Likewise Peter instructed believers to "grow in the grace and knowledge of our Lord and Savior Jesus Christ" (2 Pet. 3:18). He wrote, "like newborn babes, long for the pure milk of the word, that by it you may grow in respect to salvation" (1 Pet. 2:2).

> *All perfectionism is essentially a disastrous misunderstanding of how God works in sanctification. Sanctification is a process by which God—working in believers through the Holy Spirit—gradually moves them toward Christlikeness (2 Cor. 3:18).*

The Bible clearly teaches that Christians can never attain sinless perfection in this life. "Who can say, 'I have cleansed my heart, I am pure from my sin'?" (Prov. 20:9). "For we all stumble in many ways. If anyone does not stumble in what he says, he is a perfect man, able to bridle the whole body as well" (Jas. 3:2). "For the flesh sets its desire against the Spirit, and the Spirit against the flesh; for these are in opposition to one another, so that you may not do the things that you please" (Gal. 5:17). "If we say that we have no sin, we are deceiving ourselves, and the truth is not in us" (1 Jn. 1:8).

Sanctification is therefore never complete in this lifetime. In heaven alone are the spirits of righteous people made perfect (Heb. 12:23). And at the return of Christ, "when He appears, we shall be like Him, because we shall see Him just as He is" (1 Jn. 3:2). "We ourselves groan within ourselves, waiting eagerly for our adoption as sons, the redemption of our body" (Rom. 8:23). Those verses describe *glorification*, the immediate and instantaneous completion of our sanctification.

In his masterful work against perfectionism, B. B. Warfield characterized perfectionists as "impatient souls" who "tolerate more readily the idea of an imperfect perfection than the admission of lagging perfecting. They must at all costs have all that is coming to them at once."[4] In other words, perfectionists reject the idea that sanctification is a lifelong process. They insist it is something God does all at once. And so they are forced by sheer reality to conclude that God's work in sanctifying must stop short of true conformity to the perfect likeness of Christ. They give up the pursuit of authentic biblical sanctification in exchange for a quick and dirty substitute. And in order to do so, they must inevitably tone down their consciences.

Perfectionism's Key Error

Warfield explains the common theological roots of all modern perfectionism:

> It was John Wesley who infected the modern Protestant world with this notion of "entire instantaneous sanctification." In saying this we are not bringing a railing accusation against him. There was no element of his teaching which afforded him himself greater satisfaction. There is no element of it which is more lauded by his followers, or upon their own possession of which they more felicitate themselves. . . . As wave after wave of the "holiness movement" has broken over us during the past century, each has brought, no doubt, something distinctive of itself. But a common fundamental character has informed them all, and this common fundamental character has been communicated to them by the Wesleyan doctrine. The essential elements of that doctrine repeat themselves in all these movements, and form their characteristic features. *In all of them alike justification and sanctification are divided from one another as two separate gifts of God.* In all of them alike sanctification is represented as obtained, just like justification, by an act of simple faith, but not by the same act of faith by which justification is obtained, but by a new and separate act of faith, exercised for this specific purpose. In all of them alike the sanctification which comes on this [second] act of faith, comes immediately on believing, and all at once, and in all of them alike this sanctification, thus received, is complete sanctification. In all of them alike, however, it is added, that this complete sanctification does not bring freedom from all sin; but only, say, freedom from sinning; or only freedom from conscious sinning; or from the commission of "known sins." And in all of them alike this sanctification is not a stable condition into which we enter once for all by faith, but a momentary attainment, which must be maintained moment by moment, and which may readily be lost and often is lost, but may also be repeatedly instantaneously recovered.[5]

The error Warfield describes—this tendency to make a radical separation between sanctification and justification—is the key mistake of perfectionism. Virtually all perfectionists treat sanctification as if it were a second conversion experience. Under this scheme, holiness must be obtained by a separate act of faith that occurs sometime after initial salvation—a "second blessing," as it is often called.

Biblically, as we shall see, sanctification begins immediately at justification and continues its work—despite our frequent failings—all the way to the end of life. In my book, *Faith Works*, I examined this very issue from a totally different perspective.[6] In that book I was answering the error of those who say sanctification is optional. Here, however, my purpose is to examine *how* the process of sanctification works in the lives of believers as they wage their lifelong battle against the sin in their own flesh. Interestingly, the issues are virtually identical. That is because the key to sound doctrine in the matter of sanctification is a correct understanding of the close relationship between sanctification and justification.

Contrary to the perfectionists, contrary to the so-called "deeperlife" teachers, and contrary to the prevailing notion of what it means to be Spirit-filled, sanctification is not something that begins with a crisis experience sometime after conversion. Sanctification begins at the very moment of conversion and continues throughout the Christian's earthly life. As Dr. Warfield was suggesting in the above quotation, sanctification is obtained by the very same act of faith with which we lay hold of justification. Jesus Christ becomes to all who believe, "wisdom from God, and *righteousness and sanctification*, and redemption" (1 Cor. 1:30, emphasis added). If sanctification did not occur at the moment of salvation, it could not be said of all believers, "you were washed . . . you were sanctified . . . you were justified" (1 Cor. 6:11).

---

*Biblically, as we shall see, sanctification
begins immediately
at justification and continues its work
—despite our frequent failings—
all the way to the end of life.*

This is not doctrine for advanced Christians only. Nothing in the Christian life is more practical than a right understanding of how the Holy Spirit works to conform us to Christ's image. Conversely, it is hard to imagine anything that undermines spiritually healthy Christian living more disastrously than a *mis*understanding of sanctification.

How Does Sanctification Work?

The word *sanctify* in Scripture comes from Hebrew and Greek words that mean "set apart." To be sanctified is to be set apart from sin. At conversion, all believers are disengaged from sin's bondage, released from sin's captivity—set apart unto God, or sanctified. Yet the process of separation from sin is only begun at that moment. As we grow in Christ, we become more separated from sin and more consecrated to God. Thus the sanctification that occurs at conversion only initiates a lifelong process whereby we are set apart more and more from sin and brought more and more into conformity with Christ—separated from sin, and separated unto God.

Maturing Christians never become self-justifying, smug, or satisfied with their progress. They do not pursue self-esteem; they seek instead to deal with their sin. And the more we become like Christ, the more sensitive we are to the remaining corruptions of the flesh. As we mature in godliness our sins become more painful and more obvious to ourselves. The more we put away sin, the more we notice sinful tendencies that still need to be put away. This is the paradox of sanctification: the holier we become, the more frustrated we are by the stubborn remnants of our sin. The apostle Paul vividly described his own anguish over this reality in Romans 7:21–24:

> I find then the principle that evil is present in me, the one who wishes to do good. For I joyfully concur with the law of God in the inner man, but I see a different law in the members of my body, waging war against the law of my mind, and making me a prisoner of the law of sin which is in my members. Wretched man that I am! Who will set me free from the body of this death?

Romans 7 poses a number of difficult challenges for Bible interpreters, but surely the most difficult question of all is how Paul could say those things *after* he wrote in chapter 6, "Our old self was crucified with Him, that our body of sin might be done away with, that we should no longer be slaves to sin; for he who has died is freed from sin" (Rom. 6:6–7).

These are vital truths for the Christian to understand. They hold the formula for a healthy spiritual walk, and they give much practical insight into how we should battle sin in our own lives. In order to understand them better, we must go back into Romans 6. According to Dr. Warfield, Romans 6 "was written for no other purpose than to assert and demonstrate that justification and sanctification are indissolubly bound together."[7] Or, in Paul's own imagery, dying with Christ (justification) and living with Christ (sanctification) are both necessary results of true faith. Those who think grace makes holiness optional are tragically deceived. Those who think they have experienced all the sanctification they need are equally deluded. Those who think self-esteem is more important than holiness are blind to the truth. If we would know God's principles for dealing with sin, we must understand that it is a life-and-death struggle to the end. To be content with good feelings about oneself is to be content with sin.

Shall We Continue in Sin?

God's grace does not mean holiness is optional. There have always been people who abuse God's grace by assuming it grants leeway for sin. Paraphrasing that philosophy, Paul writes, "What shall we say then? Are we to continue in sin that grace might increase?" (6:1). If grace abounds most where sin is worst (Rom. 5:20–21), then doesn't our sin only magnify the grace of God? Should we continue in sin so that God's grace can be magnified?

God's grace does not mean holiness is optional.

"May it never be!" Paul answers in a phrase so emphatic that the King James Version renders it "God forbid!" The notion that anyone would use such an argument to condone sin was clearly offensive to Paul. "How shall we who died to sin still live in it?" (Rom. 6:3).

Paul wrote elsewhere, "I have been crucified with Christ; and it is no longer I who live, but Christ lives in me" (Gal. 2:20).

But in what sense are we dead to sin? All honest Christians will testify that we are still tempted, we still fall, we are still guilty of sin all the time. What does Paul mean by saying believers have "died to sin"?

He is talking about our union with Christ. All believers are joined to Christ by faith:

> Do you not know that all of us who have been baptized into Christ Jesus have been baptized into His death? Therefore we have been buried with Him through baptism into death, in order that as Christ was raised from the dead through the glory of the Father, so we too might walk in newness of life. For if we have become united with Him in the likeness of His death, certainly we shall be also in the likeness of His resurrection (Rom. 6:3–5).

The phrase "baptized into Christ Jesus . . . baptized into His death" has nothing to do with water baptism. Paul is using the expression *baptizō* in the same way he employed it in 1 Corinthians 10:2, where he spoke of the Israelites as having been "baptized into Moses." *Baptized into* in that sense means "identified with," "linked to." In Galatians 3:27, Paul says, "All of you who were baptized into Christ have clothed yourselves with Christ" (Gal. 3:27). Again, he is speaking of *union with Christ*: "The one who joins himself to the Lord is one spirit with Him" (1 Cor. 6:17).

Our union with Christ is the premise on which justification, sanctification, and every other aspect of God's saving work hinge. If we would understand our salvation, we must first grasp what it means to be united with Christ. About this doctrine, Martyn Lloyd-Jones wrote,

> We are actually in union with Christ and to him. You cannot have read the New Testament even cursorily without noticing this constantly repeated phrase—"in Christ"—"in Christ Jesus." The apostles go on repeating it and it is one of the most significant and glorious statements in the entire realm and range of truth. It means that we are joined to the Lord Jesus Christ; we have become a part of him. We are in him. We belong to him. We are members of his body.

And the teaching is that God regards us as such; and this, of course, means that now, *in this relationship, we are sharers in, and partakers of, everything that is true of the Lord Jesus Christ himself.*[8]

"As in Adam all die, so also in Christ all shall be made alive" (1 Cor. 15:22). "In Adam" describes the state of the unregenerate person still in bondage to sin, dying, unable to please God in any way. But "in Christ" describes precisely the opposite state, the position of every true believer in Christ. We are free from sin's tyranny, able to love and obey God from the heart, partakers in all the blessedness of Christ Himself, the objects of God's loving favor, destined for a glorious eternity. "There is therefore now no condemnation for those who are in Christ Jesus" (Rom. 8:1).

Our union with Christ results in some very dramatic changes. First of all, we are justified. Justification takes place in the court of God. It is a divine "not guilty" verdict. The term *justification* does not describe the actual change in the sinner's character; it describes the change in his or her standing before God.

Our union with Christ is the premise on which justification, sanctification, and every other aspect of God's saving work hinge.

But because we are united with Christ, changes in our very nature occur as well. *Regeneration, conversion,* and *sanctification* are the words that describe that change. We are born again—*regenerated*—given a new heart, a new spirit, and a new love for God (Ezek. 36:26; 1 Jn. 4:19–20). We become partakers of the divine nature (2 Pet. 1:3–4). We are raised to walk in newness of life (Rom. 6:4). And the old sinful self is put to death: "Knowing this, that our old self was crucified with Him, that our body of sin might be done away with, that we should no longer be slaves to sin; for he who has died is freed from sin" (Rom. 6:6–7).

Freed from Sin—Or Are We?

Here is precisely where the challenge in understanding Romans 6 and 7 comes in. What is this "old self" that is said to be crucified? If the old self is done away, why do we still struggle so much with sin? And if "He who has died [in Christ] is freed from sin" (Rom. 6:7), why does Paul later write, "Wretched man that I am! Who will set me free from the body of this death?" (Rom. 7:24).

It helps to understand the terms Paul is using here. *"The old self"* refers to the unregenerate nature, who we were when we were "in Adam." It is not the dark side of a Jekyll-Hyde disposition. It is not half of a dual temperament unique to Christians. It is not an "old nature" that battles with our new nature for control of our wills. It is simply who we used to be before we were born again. The old self is no more. It has been crucified, slain, put off, laid aside. All of those expressions are used in Scripture.

For example, Paul told the Ephesians: "In reference to your former manner of life . . . lay aside the old self, which is being corrupted in accordance with the lusts of deceit, and . . . be renewed in the spirit of your mind (Eph. 4:22–23, emphasis added). The Greek verb tenses there are infinitives, not imperatives. They could be translated "you have laid aside" and "you are renewed"—not as commands, but as statements of fact. That seems to make better sense of what Paul is saying. Certainly it is the only way we can possibly read the parallel passage, Colossians 3:9–10: "Do not lie to one another, since *you laid aside the old self* with its evil practices, and *have put on the new self* who *is being renewed* to a true knowledge according to the image of the One who created him," (emphasis added). Taking all these verses together, it becomes very clear that the old self—the old unregenerate "I"—is "crucified with Christ; and it is no longer I who live, but Christ lives in me" (Gal. 2:20).

The flesh (Rom. 6:19; 7:18) is like the corpse of the old self. Though dead, it continues to influence and infect all it touches with decay, filthiness, rottenness, the stench of death, and a putrefying contamination.

When I was a small boy living in Philadelphia, a family friend died. As the custom was, his body remained in the living room of his house for several days. This was to be a tribute to him and allow the family and friends to ease the separation. I thought it was bizarre—a dead man in the living room of a small house! His presence influenced everything. He was dead, but he was still there exercising influence over all the activities.

When Paul speaks of "the flesh," he is referring to the remains of our sinfulness: our mortal weakness, our selfishness, and our tendency to sin and failure. These will not be eradicated until we are finally glorified.

But we are not entirely at sin's mercy, as was the case under our former bondage. "Walk by the Spirit, and you will not carry out the desire of the flesh. For the flesh sets its desire against the Spirit, and the Spirit against the flesh; for these are in opposition to one another, so that you may not do the things that you please" (Gal. 5:16–17).

"Flesh" in such contexts does not refer to the physical body. Nor does it describe a specific part of our being. Paul is not setting up a dualism between the material and the immaterial part of humanity, or between the body and the soul. "Spirit" in those verses refers to the Holy Spirit. "Flesh" refers to the sinfulness that remains in us while we are on this earth. It is a corruption that permeates and influences every aspect of our being—body, mind, emotions, and will. It is what makes us susceptible to sin even after we are made partakers in the divine nature (cf. 2 Pet. 1:4). Though sin does not *reign* in us, it nevertheless *remains* in us. It is *dethroned*, but not *destroyed*.

"The flesh," then, is not the body, or the soul, or any other *part* of our beings. It is a *principle* that works in us. It is the source and stimulus of our sin. Though deprived of its dominion, it has not been divested of its potency, passions, or persuasive ability. The flesh wages battle against our godly desires with the fervor of a deposed monarch seeking to regain his throne.

Unbelievers are said to be "in the flesh" (cf. Rom. 8:8–9). Christians are no longer *in* the flesh. We are in the Spirit. But we are still "of flesh" (1 Cor. 3:1)—that is, we are still fallen humans. Paul even says, "I am of flesh, sold into bondage to sin" (Rom. 7:14).

That verse underscores the dilemma between Romans 6 and 7. As we have noted, Paul has already stated explicitly that believers are "freed from sin" (6:7). Now he seems to be stating the opposite. This has made many commentators assume that Romans 7 describes Paul's life before his salvation. But as usual, the context makes very clear his meaning. Romans 7:23 shows what kind of "bondage" he has in mind in this chapter: "I see a different law in the members of my body, waging war against the law of my mind, and making me a prisoner of the law of sin which is in my members." This speaks not of the fatal soul-bondage to sin Paul referred to in 6:7. Here he is speaking of a persistent spiritual weakness in his "members"—his body, mouth, mind, emotions, imagination, and so on. This "bondage" is a persistent snare that keeps tripping him up and pulling him back into the sin he hates. This is the experience of all Christians.

In what sense, then, are believers "freed from sin" (Rom. 6:7)? What does Paul mean when he says our old self is crucified so that "our body of sin might be done away with" (v. 6)? "Done away with" almost sounds as if he were saying sin is eradicated, wiped out, "destroyed" (KJV), annihilated. But the Greek word (*katargeō*) literally means "to render inoperative," "nullify" (cf. Rom. 3:3, 31; 4:14). The word for "freed" in 6:7 is *dikaioō*, the word usually translated "justified." In other words, believers are delivered from the dreadful penalty and condemnation of sin. Because they are justified—declared not guilty and covered with the perfect righteousness of Christ—sin and death have no claim over them.

Moreover, because they have been justified from sin's penalty, they are also sanctified—liberated from sin's absolute tyranny. The old self is crucified and the body of sin nullified. That speaks of the change of character that is wrought in regeneration. Believers are emancipated from the total corruption of their natures that rendered them unable to do anything *but* sin. They are free to love and obey God.

Believers are emancipated from the total corruption of their natures that rendered them unable to do anything but sin. They are free to love and obey God.

But they are *not* yet totally free from sin's reach. They are still prone to sin's seductive power. They are unable to break free of sin's presence. They are still vulnerable to sin's enchantment. They still carry in their corrupt flesh a tendency to sin.

It Is No Longer I Who Sin

One comment of Paul's is frequently misunderstood. In Romans 7 he writes,

> For that which I am doing, I do not understand; for I am not practicing what I would like to do, but I am doing the very thing I hate. But if I do the very thing I do not wish to do, I agree with the Law, confessing that it is good. So now, *no longer am I the one doing it, but sin which indwells me.* For I know that nothing good dwells in me, that is, in my flesh; for the wishing is present in me, but the doing of the good is not. For the good that I wish, I do not do; but I practice the very evil that I do not wish. But if I am doing the very thing I do not wish, *I am no longer the one doing it, but sin which dwells in me* (vv. 15–20, emphasis added).

It is important to understand that Paul was not disclaiming responsibility for his sin. He was not using a dualistic argument—ascribing all his sin to an "old nature" or a wicked alter ego. Above all, he was not trying to evade the blame for his own sin.

He was simply saying that sin is contrary to the impulses of his new disposition as a believer. Before salvation, we are all defined by our sinfulness. We are enemies of God, in bondage to sin, in love with sin, incapable of anything *but* sin, sinful to the very core of our beings. But when we become believers that old self dies. We are born again with a new nature that loves God and desires to do righteousness. We "agree with the Law." "The wishing [to obey] is present" in us. Sin no longer defines our character; it is "the very thing [we] hate." Our new "I" (cf. Gal. 2:20) craves righteousness and abhors sin.

When we sin, therefore, it is a contradiction of everything we stand for as believers. It is no longer "I" that sins—meaning sin is no longer an expression of our true character.

Why do we sin? Because the corrupt principle of the flesh remains in us. And that is what drags us into disobedience. We are certainly responsible for our sins. But when we sin, it is no longer because of *what we are*. It is because of the stubborn flesh-principle that remains in us and exerts its continual influence until we are transformed to heavenly glory. As Paul says, "I find then the principle that evil is present in me, the one who wishes to do good" (Rom. 7:21).

Both Scripture and experience prove that all Christians struggle with sinful weaknesses and carnal tendencies as long as they live. Sin's absolute tyranny has been broken; we are loosed from its clutches. But we still succumb to sin's temptations. We carry our own flesh—the sin-principle that remains in us ("the body of this death," Rom. 7:24)—like a ball and chain. We are wholly new creations, redeemed and empowered by the Holy Spirit, filled with all the fullness of God—yet incarcerated in sinful flesh. We "groan within ourselves, waiting eagerly for our adoption as sons, the redemption of our body" (Rom. 8:23).

The sin within ourselves, therefore, although a "conquered enemy," still must be vigorously opposed throughout our lives. We are freed from sin, but we must remain on guard. Perfectionism, moreover, only undoes the process of sanctification. We are not perfect. We are human. We still groan.

While we groan and wait for that glorious day, we must continue to wage battle against the defeated enemy within. Scripture gives clear instructions about how we are to carry on our campaign against sin in the flesh. In Part III, we turn to the practical means that are available to us to gain victory over sin in our daily walk.

Part III

Handling Sin

Part III provides many practical solutions to gaining victory over sin in our daily walk.

Chapter 7, "Hacking Agag to Pieces," describes the necessity and the "how-to" of continuously mortifying the sin in our lives, lest it keep sprouting up again to wound us.

Chapter 8, "Handling Temptation," examines society's glorification of the seven deadly sins. It suggests ways of overcoming temptation by looking at its means, nature, and extent. It shows how God sends not temptation but tests, which we can learn from and which are not beyond our endurance.

Chapter 9, "Keeping a Pure Mind," examines the dangers of a sinful thought life and gives suggestions for guarding against sins of thought by watching over our hearts and knowing how the mind sins.

Chapter 10, "Holding to the Mystery of Faith with a Clear Conscience," emphasizes how modern evangelicalism has forgotten the exceeding sinfulness of sin and instead preoccupied believers with the pursuit of "feeling good." It examines the Bible's stance on the intrinsic worth of individuals and modern psychology's hostility to the doctrine of sin. It concludes with showing specific and practical principles to assist our consciences to detect and cope with the presence of sin in our lives.

7

Hacking Agag to Pieces

Mortification abates [sin's] force, but doth not change its nature. Grace changeth the nature of man, but nothing can change the nature of sin. . . . Destroyed it may be, it shall be, but cured it cannot be. . . . If it be not overcome and destroyed, it will overcome and destroy the soul.

And herein lies no small part of its power. . . . It is never quiet, [whether it is] conquering [or] conquered.

. . . .

Do you mortify; do you make it your daily work; be always at it whilst you live; cease not a day from this work; be killing sin or it will be killing you.

John Owen[1]

If sin is a defeated enemy, how can it cause us so much trouble? If sin's dominion has been broken, why does sin so often seem to dominate us? Why have the forces of secular humanism, the new hedonism, the New Age, self-esteem teaching, and bad theology all made such an impact among *believers*? Why is the conscience seemingly vanishing even in the evangelical world?

Every honest Christian will testify that the tendency to sin is not erased by becoming a believer. We still derive pleasure from sin. We still struggle with sinful habits. Some of those habits are so deeply ingrained that we still battle them after years of spiritual warfare against them. We fall into appalling, shameful sins. The truth is, we sin daily. Our thoughts are not what they ought to be. Our time is often wasted on frivolous and worldly pursuits. From time to time our hearts grow cold to the things of God. Why does all this happen if sin's dominion is broken?

We fall into appalling, shameful sins.
The truth is, we sin daily.

This section of our book examines the biblical antidote to the influence of sin in the believer's life. Here we see that Scripture urges us to avoid any lackadasical approach to dealing with our sin. We must put to death sin and its influence throughout our lifetime. It is here that our study becomes most practical.

God's Anger Against Amalek

An Old Testament illustration may help to shed light on our relationship to sin. In 1 Samuel 15, we read that Samuel anointed Saul and solemnly gave him these instructions from the Lord: "Now go and strike Amalek and utterly destroy all that he has, and do not spare him; but put to death both man and woman, child and infant, ox and sheep, camel and donkey" (v. 3).

God's command was clear. Saul was to deal ruthlessly with the Amalekites, killing even their infant children and animals. Their whole tribe was to be utterly and mercilessly leveled—no hostages taken.

What would make a God of infinite love mete out such a severe judgment? The Amalekites were an ancient nomadic race, descendants of Esau (Gen. 36:12). They inhabited the southern part of Canaan and were perennial enemies of the Israelites. They were the same tribe that viciously attacked Israel at Rephidim shortly after the Exodus, in the famous battle when Aaron and Hur had to support Moses' arms (Exod. 17:8–13). They ambushed Israel from behind, massacring the stragglers who were most weary (Deut. 25:18). It was a cowardly attack by the most powerful and savage tribe in the whole region. God supernaturally delivered Israel that day, and the Amalekites fled into hiding. At the conclusion of that skirmish, God swore to Moses, "I will utterly blot out the memory of Amalek from under heaven" (v. 14). He actually made it a point of the Mosaic law that Israel was to destroy Amalek:

> Remember what Amalek did to you along the way when you came out from Egypt, how he met you along the way and attacked among you all the stragglers at your rear when you were faint and weary; and he did not fear God. Therefore it shall come about when the Lord your God has given you rest from all your surrounding enemies, in the land which the Lord your God gives you as an inheritance to possess, you shall blot out the memory of Amalek from under heaven; *you must not forget*" (Deut. 25:17–19, emphasis added).

The Amalekites were fearful warriors. Their intimidating presence was one of the reasons the Israelites disobeyed God and balked at entering the Promised Land at Kadesh-barnea (Num. 13:29).

God's anger burned against the Amalekites for their wickedness. He constrained even the corrupt prophet Balaam to prophecy their doom: "Amalek was the first of the nations, but his end shall be destruction" (Num. 24:20). The Amalekites used to harass Israel by coming into the land after crops had been sown and moving through the farmland with their tents and livestock, razing everything in their path (Judg. 6:3–5). They hated God, detested Israel, and seemed to delight in wicked and destructive acts.

God's instructions to Saul, therefore, fulfilled the vow He swore to Moses. Saul was to wipe out the tribe forever. He and his armies were the instrument through which a righteous God would carry out His holy judgment on a sinister people.

The Folly of Partial Obedience

But Saul's obedience was only partial. He won a crushing defeat against the Amalekites, routing them "from Havilah as you go to Shur, which is east of Egypt" (1 Sam. 15:7). As commanded, he killed all the people, but "he captured Agag the king of the Amalekites alive" (v. 8). "Saul and the people spared Agag and the best of the sheep, the oxen, the fatlings, the lambs, and all that was good, and were not willing to destroy them utterly; but everything despised and worthless, that they utterly destroyed" (v. 9). In other words, motivated by covetousness, they kept all the best possessions of the Amalekites, collecting the spoils of victory, willfully disobeying the Lord's instructions.

Why did Saul spare Agag? Perhaps he wanted to use the humiliated king of the Amalekites as a trophy to display his own power. Saul seemed motivated only by pride at this point; he even set up a monument to himself at Carmel (v. 12). Whatever his reasons, he disobeyed the clear command of God and allowed Agag to live.

The sin was so serious that God immediately deposed Saul and his descendants forever from the throne of Israel. Samuel told him, "Because you have rejected the word of the Lord, He has also rejected you from being king" (v. 23).

Then Samuel said, "Bring me Agag, the king of the Amalekites" (v. 32).

Agag, evidently thinking that his life had been spared and feeling pretty confident, "came to him cheerfully." "Surely the bitterness of death is past," he said.

But Samuel was not amused. He told Agag, "As your sword has made women childless, so shall your mother be childless among women." Scripture simply says, "And Samuel hewed Agag to pieces before the Lord at Gilgal" (v. 33).

Our minds instinctively recoil from what seems a merciless act. But it was *God* who commanded that this be done. This was an act of divine judgment to show the holy wrath of an indignant God against wanton sin. Unlike his countrymen and their king, Samuel was determined to carry out the Lord's command entirely. As it was, the battle that was supposed to exterminate the Amalekites forever ended before the goal was accomplished. Scripture records that only a few years later, the reinvigorated tribe raided the southern territory and took all the women and children captive—including David's family (1 Sam. 30:1–5).

When David found the marauding Amalekites, "Behold, they were spread over all the land, eating and drinking and dancing because of all the great spoil that they had taken from the land of the Philistines and from the land of Judah" (v. 16). He slaughtered them from twilight until the next evening, killing all but four hundred who escaped on camels (v. 17).

The Amalekites make an apt illustration of the sin that remains in the believer's life. That sin—already utterly defeated—must be dealt with ruthlessly and hacked to pieces, or it will revive and continue to plunder and pillage our hearts and sap our spiritual strength. We cannot be merciful with Agag, or he will turn and try to devour us. In fact, the remaining sin in us often becomes more fiercely determined after it has been overthrown by the gospel.

That sin—already utterly defeated—must be dealt with ruthlessly and hacked to pieces, or it will revive and continue to plunder and pillage our hearts and sap our spiritual strength.

Scripture commands us to deal with our sin by putting it to death: "Mortify therefore your members which are upon the earth; fornication, uncleanness, inordinate affection, evil concupiscence, and covetousness, which is idolatry: for which things' sake the wrath of God cometh on the children of disobedience" (Col. 3:5-6, KJV). We cannot obey partially or halfheartedly as we seek to eliminate sin from our lives. We cannot stop while the task remains incomplete. Sins, like Amalekites, have a way of escaping the slaughter, breeding, reviving, regrouping, and launching new and unexpected assaults on our most vulnerable areas.

Life in the Spirit

In Romans 8:13 Paul also wrote of "putting to death the deeds of the body." After declaring victory over sin in Romans 6, then describing the ongoing struggle with sin in chapter 7, he describes the triumphant experience of life in the Spirit throughout chapter 8. In the midst of that chapter, the apostle declares that the distinctive behavior of those who are led by the Spirit is that they continually put their evil deeds to death.

It is significant that the Holy Spirit is mentioned only once in the introduction to the epistle (1:4, "the spirit of holiness"), then not mentioned again until Romans 8:1. In Romans 8 alone there are at least twenty references to the Holy Spirit.

Romans 8 portrays the Holy Spirit as the divine agent who frees us from sin and death (vv. 2–3), enables us to live righteously (4–13), assures and comforts us in our affliction (14–19), preserves and sustains us in Christ (20–28), and guarantees our final victory in eternal glory (29–39). Right in the context of this profound teaching about the Holy Spirit's role in the Christian's life, Paul has some important things to say about mortifying sin. He begins by contrasting life in the Spirit with life in the flesh and under the law. It is important to understand these truths in their proper context:

What the Law could not do, weak as it was through the flesh, God did: sending His own Son in the likeness of sinful flesh and as an offering for sin, He condemned sin in the flesh, in order that the requirement of the Law might be fulfilled in us, who do not walk according to the flesh, but according to the Spirit. Those who are according to the flesh set their minds on the things of the flesh, but those who are according to the Spirit, the things of the Spirit. For the mind set on the flesh is death, but the mind set on the Spirit is life and peace, because the mind set on the flesh is hostile toward God; for it does not subject itself to the law of God, for it is not even able to do so; and those who are in the flesh cannot please God. *However, you are not in the flesh but in the Spirit, if indeed the Spirit of God dwells in you.* But if anyone does not have the Spirit of Christ, he does not belong to Him. And if Christ is in you, though the body is dead because of sin, yet the spirit is alive because of righteousness. But if the Spirit of Him who raised Jesus from the dead dwells in you, He who raised Christ Jesus from the dead will also give life to your mortal bodies through His Spirit who indwells you (vv. 3–11, emphasis added).

In other words, life in the Spirit is markedly different from the life of the unbeliever. *All* true Christians are "in the Spirit." They "do not walk according to the flesh, but according to the Spirit." Those who walk according to the flesh are unbelievers, and Paul is quite definite in making that clear: "If anyone does not have the Spirit of Christ, he does not belong to Him" (v. 9). Later he adds, "For all who are being led by the Spirit of God, these are sons of God" (v. 14).

The Holy Spirit changes our basic disposition when we are born again. He brings us into accord with Himself.

That means there are only two kinds of people in the world—those who are in accord with the flesh, and those who are in accord with the Spirit. Of course, there are in-the-Spirit people at many different levels of spiritual maturity. In-the-flesh people also come in varying degrees of wickedness. But everyone is either "in the flesh" (v. 8) or "in the Spirit" (v. 9). There is no category called "in between."

What Paul is suggesting is that the Holy Spirit changes our basic disposition when we are born again. He brings us into accord with Himself. He actually indwells us (vv. 9, 11). We become partakers of the divine nature (2 Pet. 1:4). Our orientation to God changes. Where there was enmity, there is now love (cf. Rom. 8:28). In the flesh we could not please God (v. 8) but now the righteous requirement of the law is fulfilled in us (v. 4). Central to all of this is the reality that our whole mind-set is new. Whereas the mind set on the flesh meant death, the mind set on the things of the Spirit results in life and peace (v. 6).

If your mind-set—the fundamental orientation of your understanding, its bent, its dispositions, its thought patterns—did not change when you made a profession of faith in Christ, something is seriously wrong. That is not to suggest that Christians cannot fall into old patterns and habits. But it *does* mean that our thoughts toward God, sin, and righteousness are radically different now that we are "in the Spirit" from when we were "in the flesh." We have new holy affections and longings for godliness. We have a love for God that transcends our attachment to this world (Jas. 4:4). We can no longer blithely "indulge the flesh in its corrupt desires" (2 Pet. 2:10). We no longer have anything in common with those "who set their minds on earthly things. For our citizenship is in heaven" (Phil. 3:19–20). And it is toward heaven that our minds are now inclined. We set our minds on the things of the Spirit (Rom. 8:5). Even when we fail or fall to earthly temptations, we "joyfully concur with the law of God in the inner man" (7:22). That is our basic orientation and mind set.

In contrast, "the mind set on the flesh is death" (v. 6). Paul does not say that the mind set on the flesh *causes* death. He declares that it *is* death. The state of mind that is dominated by fleshly desires is a condition of spiritual death. In other words, those whose thoughts and desires are altogether fleshly are *already* "dead in [their] trespasses and sins" (Eph. 2:1). This cannot be a description of the true believer in Christ.

As we noted in chapter 6, Christians are no longer "in the flesh": "You are not in the flesh but in the Spirit, if indeed the Spirit of God dwells in you. But if anyone does not have the Spirit of Christ, he does not belong to Him" (Rom. 8:9). The Greek word translated "dwells" is *oikeō*, which means "to inhabit." Paul is saying that the very Spirit of God indwells every person who trusts in Jesus Christ. The Spirit is in us, and we are "in the Spirit." We are not "in the flesh."

Death in the Physical Body

But we are still "of flesh," and therefore our physical bodies deteriorate and die. The germ of death inhabits us all. Because of the curse of sin, we begin to die as soon as we are born.

For the Christian, however, there is more to this earthly life than death: "If Christ is in you, though the body is dead because of sin, yet the spirit is alive because of righteousness" (Rom. 8:10). In other words, the human body is subject to death (and is already dying) because of sin, but the believer's spirit is already alive in Christ. Eternal life is our present possession. Though the body is dying, the spirit is already endowed with incorruptibility.

For the Christian, however, there is more to this earthly life than death.

Here the word "body" clearly refers to the actual physical body (not the flesh-principle), and the expression "dead" speaks of physical death. (See the discussion in Appendix 1 of how Paul often uses "flesh" and "body" to refer to the sin-tendency in believers.) Notice that verses 10 and 11 use the word "body" (*sōma*) instead of "flesh" (*sarx*)—the word Paul used throughout the first nine verses. By contrasting "the body" and "the spirit" in this way, he makes his meaning inescapable. In verse 10, "the spirit is alive" refers to the human spirit, the immaterial part of our being. The body may be dying because of sin, but the believer's spirit is fully alive and thriving "because of righteousness"—because we are justified and therefore already have "passed out of death into life" (Jn. 5:24). Paul is simply saying here what he also told the Corinthians, "Though our outer man is decaying, yet our inner man is being renewed day by day" (2 Cor. 4:16).

In fact, the indwelling Spirit also promises "life to [our] mortal bodies" in a future resurrection with a glorified body (Rom. 8:11).

Paul's point is that the body apart from the Spirit of God has no future. It is subject to death. Therefore we have no duty to the mortal side of our beings: "So then, brethren, we are under obligation, not to the flesh, to live according to the flesh—for if you are living according to the flesh, you must die; but if by the Spirit you are putting to death the deeds of the body, you will live" (Rom. 8:12–13). Here Paul uses the word *sarx* ("flesh") in the sense of "sin principle"—and equates it with "the deeds of the body." If you live in accord with the flesh—if you live in response to sinful impulses—you "must die."

Paul is once more drawing the line of distinction as clearly as possible between Christians and non-Christians. He is by no means warning believers that they might lose their salvation if they live according to the flesh. He has already made the point that true believers do not and *cannot* live in accord with the sin principle (vv. 4–9). Besides, Paul began chapter 8 with the statement, "There is therefore now no condemnation for those who are in Christ Jesus" (8:1). He will end it with the promise that nothing can separate us from the love of God in Christ Jesus (vv. 38–39). A warning of the possibility of falling away would contradict the very purpose for which he was writing.

Paul is simply reiterating what he says again and again throughout his New Testament epistles—that those whose lives and hearts are altogether fleshly are not true Christians. They are already spiritually dead (v. 6), and unless they repent they are headed for eternal death. Meanwhile, their earthly lives are a kind of abject bondage to sin. They are enslaved to their own flesh, constrained to cater to its sensual desires.

What Is Mortification?

Christians, on the other hand, have a different obligation—not to the flesh, but to the new principle of righteousness embodied in the Holy Spirit. Therefore they labor by the power of the Spirit to mortify sin in the flesh—to "[put] to death the deeds of the body." If you are doing this, he says, "you will live" (Rom. 8:13).

Nothing is more natural than for people "led by the Spirit of God" (v. 14) to mortify their sin.

Of course, Paul is not suggesting that anyone can obtain life or merit God's favor by the process of mortification. He is saying it is characteristic of true believers that they put to death the deeds of the body. Nothing is more natural than for people "led by the Spirit of God" (v. 14) to mortify their sin. One of the proofs of our salvation is that we do this. It is expected of believers. It is the expression of the new nature.

In other words, the true believer is not like Saul, who wanted to pamper and preserve Agag, but like Samuel who hacked him to pieces without mercy and without delay. Saul may have wanted to make a lap dog of Agag, but Samuel knew that was utterly impossible. Similarly, we will never tame our flesh. We cannot mollycoddle our sin. We must deal with it quickly and severely.

It was Jesus who said,

> If your right eye makes you stumble, tear it out, and throw it from you; for it is better for you that one of the parts of your body perish, than for your whole body to be thrown into hell. And if your right hand makes you stumble, cut it off, and throw it from you; for it is better for you that one of the parts of your body perish, than for your whole body to go into hell (Matt. 5:29–30).

Jesus was not speaking in literal terms, of course, though many have misunderstood this passage. No less than the great theologian Origen had himself castrated in a misguided effort to fulfill this command literally. Jesus was *not* calling for self-mutilation, but for mortification of the deeds of the body. Mortification, in the words of Puritan John Owen, means that the flesh, "with [its] faculties, and properties, [its] wisdom, craft, subtlety, strength; this, says the apostle, must be killed, put to death, mortified,—that is, *have its power, life, vigour, and strength, to produce its effects, taken away by the Spirit.*"[2]

Romans 8:12–13, the verses where Paul introduces the idea of mortifying sin, signal a major turning point in the logical thread that runs through this chapter. Martyn Lloyd-Jones said,

> It is here for the first time, in this chapter, that we come to the realm of practical application. All we have had up to this point has been a general description of the Christian—his character, his position. But now the Apostle has really come explicitly to the doctrine of sanctification. *Here we are told exactly how, in practice, the Christian becomes sanctified.* Or, to state it differently, here we are told in detail and in practice how the Christian is to wage the battle against sin.[3]

Paul does not promise immediate freedom from sin's harassment. He does not describe a crisis-moment sanctification, where the believer is immediately made perfect. He does not tell the Romans to "let go and let God" take over while they sit idle. He does not suggest that a turning-point "decision" will solve the matter once and for all. On the contrary, he speaks of a continuous struggle with sin, where we are persistently, perpetually "putting to death the deeds of the body."

The language is often misunderstood. Paul is not calling for a life of self-flagellation. He is not saying believers should starve themselves, literally torture their bodies, or deprive themselves of life's basic needs. He is not telling them to mutilate themselves or live monastic lives or anything of the sort. The mortification Paul speaks of has nothing to do with external self-punishment. It is a spiritual process accomplished "by the Spirit."

Paul is describing a way of life where *we seek to throttle sin and crush it from our lives, sapping it of its strength, rooting it out, and depriving it of its influence.* That is what it means to mortify sin.

How Do We Mortify Sin?

Mortification involves the cultivation of new habits of godliness, combined with the elimination of old sinful habits from our behavior. It is a constant warfare that takes place within the believer. Although we should expect our triumph over sin to be ever-increasing, our mortification can never be wholly complete before we are glorified. We are to remain perpetually committed to the task. We must see sin as a sworn enemy, and commit ourselves to slaying it wherever and whenever it rears its head.

Obviously, mortification is the work of believers only. Unbelievers are called to repent and flee to Christ. Those still enslaved to sin have no means by which to put sin to death. The Holy Spirit— the agent of mortification—does not indwell them. Their only hope is the salvation that is offered to those who will trust Jesus Christ and entrust themselves to Him. No one can mortify sin who is not "in Christ" and "in the Spirit."

Scripture offers several practical means whereby believers can mortify their sin. Our growth in grace depends on our obedience to these duties. None of them are fleshly or mechanical formulas. They are not religious activities or rituals. John Owen observed that most of the Roman Catholic religious system consists of "mistaken ways and means of mortification. . . . Their vows, orders, fastings, penances, are all built on this ground; they are all for the mortifying of sin. Their preachings, sermons, and books of devotion, they look all this way."[4]

Although we should expect our triumph over sin to be ever-increasing, our mortification can never be wholly complete before we are glorified.

But sin cannot be annihilated through legalism, monasticism, pietism, asceticism, pharisaism, celibacy, self-flagellation, confessional booths, rosary beads, hail Marys, or any other external means. The instrument of mortification is the Holy Spirit, and His power is the energy that works in us to carry out the process. All the means of mortification are simple commands of Scripture that we are to obey. Some of the key commands are highlighted below:

Abstain from fleshly lusts. Peter wrote, "Beloved, I urge you as aliens and strangers to abstain from fleshly lusts, which wage war against the soul" (1 Pet. 2:11). In other words, stop lusting. Abstain from it. Stay away from it. "Flee immorality" (1 Cor. 6:18). What could be more direct?

Do you want to put to death the lusts in your heart? Then stop entertaining them. Peter does not prescribe a program of therapy. He does not suggest that such sin be treated as an addiction. He simply says abstain. Quit doing it. You have no business indulging such thoughts. Put them away at once. *You yourself* must do this; it cannot be done for you. There is no point waiting for some heavenly power to erase this sin automatically from your life. You are to stop it, and stop it immediately. Martyn Lloyd-Jones said,

> I do not know of a single scripture—and I speak advisedly—
> which tells me to take my sin, the particular thing that gets me

down, to God in prayer and ask him to deliver me from it and then trust in faith that he will.

Now that teaching is also often put like this: you must say to a man who is constantly defeated by a particular sin, "I think your only hope is to take it to Christ and Christ will take it from you." But what does Scripture say in Ephesians 4:28 to the man who finds himself constantly guilty of stealing, to a man who sees something he likes and takes it? What am I to tell such a man? Am I to say, "Take that sin to Christ and ask him to deliver you?" No, what the apostle Paul tells him is this: "Let him that stole, steal no more." Just that. Stop doing it. And if it is fornication or adultery or lustful thoughts, again: Stop doing it, says Paul. He does not say, "Go and pray to Christ to deliver you." No. You stop doing that, he says, as becomes children of God.[5]

Here is perhaps the most straightforward, obvious means of mortifying our sin: *stop doing it.* Too many people think they must wait for an extraordinary experience, a miracle from heaven, a sign from the Lord, or whatever. They think some special divine intervention is necessary to free them from a sinful practice or pattern of thinking. No, that is precisely the error Romans 6 refutes. You *are* free from sin; now stop doing it. You are dead to sin; now put to death the sin that remains. How? "Abstain." Reckon yourself dead to sin, and don't do it anymore. "Resist the devil and he will flee from you" (Jas. 4:7). It is as simple as that.

Make no provision for the flesh. In Romans 13:14 Paul writes, "Put on the Lord Jesus Christ, and make no provision for the flesh in regard to its lusts." In other words, simply refuse to accommodate fleshly lusts. If you struggle with gluttony, don't load up on junk food when you shop at the market. If you are tempted with sexual desire, don't fill your mind with images that feed your lust. If you don't want to fall, don't walk where it is slippery. Refuse to furnish your mind with the means to entertain evil thoughts. Make no preparations for the possibility of sin. Thus you can slay sin before it breeds.

Fix your heart on Christ. The apostle John wrote, "We know that, when He appears, we shall be like Him, because we shall see Him just as He is. And everyone who has this hope fixed on Him purifies himself, just as He is pure" (1 Jn. 3:2–3). It is an inexorable spiritual law that you become like the object of your worship. Psalm 135 says,

> The idols of the nations are but silver and gold, the work of man's hands. They have mouths, but they do not speak; they have eyes, but they do not see; they have ears, but they do not hear; nor is there any breath at all in their mouths. *Those who make them will be like them*, yes, everyone who trusts in them. (vv. 15–18, emphasis added).

If the heathen become like the lifeless gods they worship, how much more will we be made like Christ, who have the Holy Spirit in us working to accomplish that very goal? As we fix our hearts on Christ, we discover our worship has the effect of conforming us to His image: "But we all, with unveiled face beholding as in a mirror the glory of the Lord, are being transformed into the same image from glory to glory, just as from the Lord, the Spirit" (2 Cor. 3:18).

Meditate on God's Word. The psalmist wrote, "Thy word I have treasured in my heart, that I may not sin against Thee" (Ps. 119:11). The Lord told Joshua, "This book of the law shall not depart from your mouth, but you shall meditate on it day and night, so that you may be careful to do according to all that is written in it; for then you will make your way prosperous, and then you will have success" (Josh. 1:8). Do you want to have success in the battle against sin? Familiarize yourself with the Word of God. Meditate on it "day and night" (cf. Ps. 1:2). Let it be a lamp to your feet and a light to your path (Ps. 119:105). As the truth begins to penetrate your heart and mind, it will confront and attack sin.

Jesus prayed, "Sanctify them in the truth; thy word is truth" (Jn. 17:17). The truth of God's Word is the medium the Holy Spirit uses in our sanctification. Load your mind with it. Fill your heart with it. Ponder it carefully and let it direct your walk. "Whatever is true, whatever is honorable, whatever is right, whatever is pure, whatever is lovely, whatever is of good repute, if there is any excellence and if anything worthy of praise, let your mind dwell on these things" (Phil. 4:8). "Let the word of Christ richly dwell within you" (Col. 3:16). You will discover that "the sword of the Spirit, which is the word of God" (Eph. 6:17) is the most effective weapon for hacking the flesh to pieces.

Pray without ceasing. On the night Jesus was betrayed, He took His disciples with Him to Gethsemane and told them, "Pray that you may not enter into temptation" (Lk. 22:40). Later He found them sleeping and rebuked them for their prayerlessness. He told them, "Keep watching and praying, that you may not enter into temptation; the spirit is willing, but the flesh is weak" (Matt. 26:41).

Prayer must include confession and repentance if it is to be effective in mortifying our sin.

"Lead us not into temptation" was part of the model prayer He gave the disciples (Lk. 11:4). Prayer is an effective and necessary means for heading off sinful temptations *before* they can attack. Look at prayer as a preemptive strike against fleshliness. By drawing us near to the Lord and focusing our thoughts on Him, prayer both steels us against fleshly temptation, and weakens the temptations when they come.

Watch and pray. Identify the circumstances that lead you into sin, and pray specifically for strength to face those situations. Pray for a holy hatred of sin. Pray that God will show you the real state of your sinful heart. The psalmist prayed this prayer for sanctification:

> Who can discern his errors? Acquit me of hidden faults. Also keep back Thy servant from presumptuous sins; let them not rule over me; then I shall be blameless, and I shall be acquitted of great transgression. Let the words of my mouth and the meditation of my heart be acceptable in Thy sight, O Lord, my rock and my Redeemer (Ps. 19:12–14).

Prayer must include confession and repentance if it is to be effective in mortifying our sin. John wrote, "If we confess our sins, He is faithful and righteous to forgive us our sins and to cleanse us from all unrighteousness" (1 Jn. 1:9). And the writer of Hebrews says,

"Let us therefore draw near with confidence to the throne of grace, that we may receive mercy and may find grace to help in time of need" (Heb. 4:16).

Exercise self-control. Self-control is a fruit of the Spirit (Gal. 5:23)—and it is also one of the means through which the Spirit enables us to mortify the deeds of the body. Paul wrote,

> Everyone who competes in the games exercises self-control in all things. They then do it to receive a perishable wreath, but we an imperishable. Therefore I run in such a way, as not without aim; I box in such a way, as not beating the air; but I buffet my body and make it my slave, lest possibly, after I have preached to others, I myself should be disqualified (1 Cor. 9:25–27).

The word "buffet" in that passage is a translation of the Greek word *hupōpiazō*, meaning "to strike under the eye." Athletes discipline their bodies for mere earthly prizes. If they are willing to do that, shouldn't we also be willing to exercise a similar kind of self-control for the heavenly prize?

Paul is not speaking here of punishing the body through self-flagellation or neglect. He certainly is not advocating anything that would physically weaken or injure the body. No athlete would do such things.

I once met a man who wore a belt studded with nails that constantly tore at his flesh. He felt he was punishing his body and atoning for his own sins. Lots of misguided people over the ages have attempted similar means of dealing with the body. Martin Luther almost destroyed his body with excessive fasting as a young monk before he discovered that God's Word says, "The just shall live by faith" (Rom. 1:17, KJV). In the Philippines at Easter each year, there are men who actually have themselves crucified in a bloody ritual that they believe makes them holy.

That is not at all the spirit of what Scripture calls for. Self-control is a watchful discipline that refuses to pander to the appetites of the body at the soul's expense. Jesus said, "Be on guard, that your hearts may not be weighted down with dissipation and drunkenness and the worries of life, and [the Day of the Lord] come on you suddenly like a trap" (Lk. 21:34).

Be filled with the Holy Spirit. "Do not get drunk with wine, for that is dissipation," Paul wrote, "but be filled with the Spirit" (Eph. 5:18). To be Spirit-filled is to be controlled by the Holy Spirit, just as to be drunk is to be under the influence of alcohol. Believers are to be utterly yielded to the Spirit's control.

Now this brings us full circle to where we began in Romans 8:13. We mortify sin "by the Spirit." It is the Holy Spirit's power in us that actually does the work of mortification in those who are yielded to Him. I must emphasize again, however, that this does not mean we are passive in the process. As John Owen wrote,

> He doth not so work our mortification in us as not to keep it still an act of our *obedience*. The Holy Ghost works in us and upon us, as we are fit to be wrought in and upon; that is, so as to preserve our own liberty and free obedience. He works upon our understandings, wills, consciences, and affections, agreeably to their own natures; he works *in us* and *with us*, not *against us* or *without us*; so that his assistance is an encouragement as to the facilitating of the work, and no occasion of neglect as to the work itself.[6]

In other words, as we have noted repeatedly, we cannot abandon our own responsibility and passively wait for God to mortify sin on our behalf. The Spirit-filled life is an active, vigorous, working endeavor, where we work out our own salvation with fear and trembling (Phil. 2:12). When we obey, we then discover it is actually God who is at work in us "both to will and to work for His good pleasure" (v. 13). In other words, God both molds our wills to obey and then gives us the energy to work according to whatever pleases Him. That is the Spirit-filled life.

In other words, God both molds our wills to obey and then gives us the energy to work according to whatever pleases Him. That is the Spirit-filled life.

There are many more duties related to mortifying sin—such as clothing oneself with humility (1 Pet. 5:5); having the mind of Christ (Phil. 2:5); putting away spiteful feelings toward others (Eph. 4:31–32); putting on the armor of God (Eph. 6:11–17); laying aside sinful attitudes (Col. 3:8–9); adding the graces of spiritual growth to one's life (2 Pet. 1:5–7); following the *know, reckon, yield, obey, serve* pattern of Romans 6 (see Appendix 1)—and many similar responsibilities the New Testament assigns to believers. These may *all* be subsumed under this basic category of being filled with the Spirit.

It is really as simple as this: "Walk by the Spirit, and you will not carry out the desire of the flesh" (Gal. 5:16). The fruit of the Spirit will overgrow and choke out the works of the flesh.

"Let us [therefore] cleanse ourselves from all defilement of flesh and spirit, perfecting holiness in the fear of God" (2 Cor. 7:1).

Strike Sin at Its Head

John Owen wrote, "He that is appointed to kill an enemy, if he leave striking before the other ceases living, doth but half his work."[7] We must be always at the task of mortifying sin. We may slaughter a whole tribe of Amalekites, but if we deliberately permit one Agag to escape, God will not be pleased with our efforts.

The flesh is very subtle and deceptive, as we know. A particular sin may leave us alone for awhile to make us think we are rid of it. But it can come back with a hellish fury if we are not on our guard. Sin perpetually stalks us; we must be continually mortifying it. This is a duty we cannot rest from until we rest in glory.

Give sin an inch, it will take a mile. If it can gain a footing in our lives, it will send forth roots and grow like kudzu. It will use us and abuse us and inflict as much disaster as possible. Owen wrote,

> Every unclean thought or glance would be adultery if it could; every covetous desire would be oppression, every thought of unbelief would be atheism, might it grow to its head. . . . It proceeds toward its height by degrees, making good the ground it hath got by hardness. . . . Now nothing can prevent this but mortification; that withers the root and strikes at the head of sin every hour, so that whatever it aims at it is crossed in. *There is*

not the best saint in the world but, if he should give over this duty,
would fall into as many cursed sins as ever did any of his kind.[8]

Later, he added, "Sin sets itself against every act of holiness, and against every degree we grow to. Let not that man think he makes any progress in holiness while he walks not over the bellies of his lusts."[9]

We are not ignorant of Satan's devices, the apostle declares (2 Cor. 2:11). Neither should we be naive about the subtleties of our own flesh. When Agag comes to us cheerfully, saying, "Surely the bitterness of death is past" (1 Sam. 15:32); when he wants to make friends and declare an end to hostilities—that is when it is most imperative that we turn on him and cut him ruthlessly to pieces before the Lord. Sin is not mortified when it is merely covered up, internalized, exchanged for another sin, or repressed. It is not mortified until the conscience has been appeased.

Sin is not mortified when it is merely covered up. You can obscure your sin from others' sight, but that is not the same as mortification. If a sin has simply been papered over with hypocrisy, what good is there in that? If conscience has only been daubed, we are in a much more dangerous state than before. "He who conceals his transgressions will not prosper, but he who confesses and forsakes them will find compassion" (Prov. 28:13). You have not done your duty with regard to your sin until you have confessed and forsaken it.

Sin is not mortified when it is only internalized. If you forsake the outward practice of some evil yet continue to ruminate on the memory of that sin's pleasures, beware. You may have moved your sin into the privacy of your imagination, where it is known only to you and to God. But that sin has not been mortified. If anything it has been made more deadly by being married to pretended righteousness. Jesus rebuked the Pharisees for this very thing. They avoided murder but tolerated hate. They refrained from fornication, but indulged in lustful thoughts. Jesus declared them worthy of eternal hell (Matt. 5:21–28).

Sin is not mortified when it is exchanged for another sin. What good is it to trade the lust of the flesh for the lust of the eyes? That lust has not been mortified; it has only changed form. Puritan Thomas Fuller said, "Some think themselves improved in piety, because they have left prodigality and reel into covetousness."[10] If you succumb to this tactic, your heart is in danger of being hardened by the deceitfulness of sin (Heb. 3:13).

Sin is not mortified until the conscience has been appeased. The goal is "love from a pure heart and a good conscience and a sincere faith" (1 Tim. 1:5). As long as the conscience remains defiled, it affects our testimony. "Sanctify Christ as Lord in your hearts, always being ready to make a defense to everyone who asks you to give an account for the hope that is in you, yet with gentleness and reverence; *and keep a good conscience* so that in the thing in which you are slandered, those who revile your good behavior in Christ may be put to shame" (1 Pet. 3:15–16, emphasis added).

Part of the process of mortification is working through the issue of our guilt. Those who attempt to evade the guilt have not properly confessed their sin; therefore they cannot be cleansed and fully forgiven.

If you want to mortify sin, John Owen wrote, "*Load thy conscience with the guilt of it.*"[11] Contrary to the popular wisdom of our day, he believed the pangs of guilt were a natural and healthy consequence of wrongdoing. "Be ashamed," he wrote,[12] for he saw shame as an advantage in the mortification of sin. He correctly understood Paul's meaning in 2 Corinthians 7:10: "The sorrow that is according to the will of God produces a repentance without regret."

Those who give a nod of the head to their guilt, claim the promise of forgiveness, quickly reassure themselves, and then think no more of their wrongdoing are subjecting themselves to the heart-hardening deceit of sin—especially when the sin threatens to become a habit. Let sorrow do its full work in your heart to produce a deep, honest repentance, and those sins will be severely weakened.

Sin is not mortified when it is merely repressed. Some people use diversions to avoid dealing with their sin. They try to drown their conscience with alcohol or drown out their guilt with entertainment and other distractions. When temptation surfaces they do not give a biblical answer, as Jesus did (Matt. 4:4, 7, 10). Instead they seek a fleshly escape route. Of this tendency Martyn Lloyd-Jones said,

If you merely repress a temptation or this first motion of sin within you, it will probably come up again still more strongly. To that extent I agree with the modern psychology. Repression is always bad. "Well, what do you do?" asks someone. I answer: When you feel that first motion of sin, just pull yourself up and say, "Of course I am not having any dealings with this at all." Expose the thing and say, "This is evil, this is vileness, this is the thing that drove the first man out of Paradise." Pull it out, look at it, denounce it, hate it for what it is; then you have really dealt with it. You must not merely push it back in a spirit of fear, and in a timorous manner. Bring it out, expose it, and analyse it; and then denounce it for what it is until you hate it.[13]

That is sound advice. We should deal with our sin courageously, striking at its head. Subduing it a little bit is not enough. We need to exterminate it, hack it in pieces—seek by the means of grace and the power of the Spirit to wring the deadly life from it.

It is a lifelong task, in which our progress will always be only gradual. That may make the fight seem daunting at first. But as soon as we set ourselves to the work, we discover that sin shall *not* be master over us, for we are under grace (Rom. 6:14). That means it is God who is at work in us both to will and to work for His good pleasure (Phil. 2:13). And having begun His good work in us, He "will perfect it until the day of Christ Jesus" (1:6).

8

Handling Temptation

The Christian. . . knows that he cannot embrace that cross, or, more important, embrace the Christ who died on it and now lives for ever in the service of God, without renouncing all known sin. We cannot serve two masters—a crucified Christ who died for our sin, and sin for which he died. The more we rejoice in the way of salvation, therefore, the more we will mortify sin. That will not make us perfect, because there is no complete mortification in this life. But it will bring us joy in walking in the power of Christ and being delivered from the power of sin. This, in part, is the answer to our common perplexity: How can we keep our way pure?

Sinclair Ferguson[1]

At the beginning of this book, I noted that our culture seems to have abandoned the notion of sin. Recently, however, MTV aired a special program titled "The Seven Deadly Sins." I watched a video-tape of the program, and it more than confirmed my worst fears about the state of contemporary culture, especially how it perceives traditional sources of temptation.

The seven deadly sins are pride, covetousness, lust, anger, envy, gluttony, and sloth. That is not a biblical list, but a classifica-tion of medieval theology. Some monastic theologians probably first set forth that grouping of sins, trying to systematize and identify all the *root* sins, not necessarily the most serious ones. The seven deadly sins, along with seven cardinal virtues (faith, hope, love, jus-tice, prudence, temperance, and fortitude) receive much emphasis in Roman Catholic theology.

People love their sin. They will go to any lengths to rationalize it and defend it.

On MTV, however, the sins were portrayed as anything but deadly. Sound bites featuring celebrities, cartoon characters, ex-cerpts from well-known movies, punk rockers, rappers, and inter-views with people in the mall were all edited together to provide a running commentary on pop culture's attitude toward sin. Most of them described sin as a positive reality.

"Pride is a sin?" exclaimed rap singer Queen Latifah. "I wasn't aware of that."

Actress Kirstie Alley agreed: "I don't think pride is a sin, and I think some idiot made that up. Who made all these up?"

A rocker from the group Aerosmith stated, "Lust is what I live for. It's what I got into the band for—little girls in the front row."

Rapper Ice-T said of anger, "It's necessary. You have to release this tension because life brings tension. We release our anger when we do records. When we did 'Cop Killer,' we were angry—and the cops got angry back."

"Greed is good," says the Michael Douglas character from the movie *Wall Street*.

And of course there was the inevitable appeal to pop psychology to defend these sins as essential to one's self-esteem. Ice-T said, "Pride is mandatory. That's one of the problems of the inner city—kids don't have enough pride. I got into a gang because of pride."

A perceptive article in *U.S. News & World Report* summed up the program's flavor:

> Instead of the language of moderation and self-control, everybody seems to speak the therapized language of feelings and self-esteem. "Pride isn't a sin—you're supposed to feel good about yourself." "Envy makes you feel bad about yourself." When you have sex with a woman, one rocker says, "she makes you feel good about yourself, but I don't know if it saves you in the end." Even the repentant gay basher is totally committed to self-talk: "Forgiving myself has been the challenge of my life."

> There's a vague sense that sin, if it exists, is surely a problem of psychology. Kurt Loder, the narrator, tells us at the start of the program that we are dealing with compulsions: "The seven deadly sins are not evil acts but, rather, universal human compulsions that can be troubling and highly enjoyable." Discussion of gluttony quickly deteriorates into chatter about addictions. That's the way all habits and attachments are discussed in the pop therapies the MTV generation grew up on. "I'm addicted to my girlfriend," one male says about gluttony. Someone else says that the twelve-step self-help program is God's gift to the twenty-first century.[2]

"The repentant gay basher" referred to in the *U.S. News* article—a young man who had actually killed a homosexual—describes his feelings of remorse. He wonders if he can ever be forgiven. A chaplain has told him forgiveness is possible, but the only way the boy will know God has forgiven him is if he "feels" it someday. And so he lives each day hoping for a feeling!

Sin, it seems, is not defined as a matter of fixed morality, but instead is wholly subjective. The individual's own preferences determine the line between good and evil. The MTV program ends with an appeal for universal tolerance. The real danger of sin, according to MTV, is the damage it does to the human ego. One gets the clear idea that no sin is as evil as the killjoy attitude of those who think sin is offensive to a holy God.

The entire production reminded me that we live in a culture given over by God to its own evil lusts. People love their sin. They will go to any lengths to rationalize it and defend it.

For Christians, however, life cannot reflect our culture's values. We cannot try to excuse or tolerate sin. It was sin that put our blessed Savior on the cross to bleed and die. Sin was what set us at enmity with God. Now that that enmity has been broken, we want nothing to do with the old life. Now that we are freed from sin, we do not want to go back into bondage. And we don't have to! To choose to do so would be a denial of our Lord. As the beloved apostle wrote,

> No one who abides in Him sins; no one who sins has seen Him or knows Him. Little children, let no one deceive you; the one who practices righteousness is righteous, just as He is righteous; the one who practices sin is of the devil; for the devil has sinned from the beginning. The Son of God appeared for this purpose, that He might destroy the works of the devil. No one who is born of God practices sin, because His seed abides in him; and he cannot sin, because he is born of God. By this the children of God and the children of the devil are obvious: anyone who does not practice righteousness is not of God, nor the one who does not love his brother (1 Jn. 3:6–10).

Of course, John is speaking there about following sin as a practice. He is describing a lifestyle of unbroken, wanton sin—which no true believer is capable of.

Can We Really Overcome Temptation?

Nevertheless, even we who are Christians are besieged with constant temptation. It seems overwhelming at times. We might pose the question—is it really possible to overcome temptation in any meaningful sense? How can we be triumphant? With Satan, the world, and our own flesh against us, is there any hope for us to overcome sin's pull? Our enemies are so subtle and their strategies so sophisticated, how can we fight them? Aren't we sometimes confronted with temptations that are so effective that we frankly have no hope of defeating them? Isn't Satan so wily that we cannot possibly overcome some of his schemes? And isn't our own heart so deceitful and desperately wicked that it leaves us without a proper defense? Isn't it really folly for us to dream of victory over our sin?

Popular Christian fiction portrays the church as engaged in a fearsome satanic battle, orchestrated by a formidable conspiracy of visible and invisible evil forces that want to mow us down.

Take it a step further. With the steady stream of pastors and church leaders who have fallen into gross, disqualifying, scandalous sin, many Christians are asking if the church itself and her leaders in particular are being subjected to some level of assault for which they are no match. Indeed, several of the fallen televangelists have blamed demonic forces beyond their control for their personal moral collapse. Popular Christian fiction portrays the church as engaged in a fearsome satanic battle, orchestrated by a formidable conspiracy of visible and invisible evil forces that want to mow us down. And we know from Scripture that we *are* engaged in spiritual warfare with demons we cannot see (Eph. 6:12). If all the forces of hell are arrayed against us, are we any match for that? Or are we really just victims of overwhelming temptation that we do not have the resources to deal with?

Scripture clearly answers that question. In fact, it answers all those questions in one verse: "No temptation has overtaken you but such as is common to man; and God is faithful, who will not allow you to be tempted beyond what you are able, but with the temptation will provide the way of escape also, that you may be able to endure it" (1 Cor. 10:13).

That verse is surely one of the most welcome and comforting promises in all of Scripture. No temptation can be so overpowering that we are left helpless to resist. Satan is not so powerful; demons are not so effective; the evil conspiracy is not so cleverly devised; the flesh is not so weak; the human heart is not so deceitful—that we are left helpless to be victimized by temptation.

This verse contains principles that will help us understand how we can triumph over specific temptations through understanding more about the means by which they work, their nature, and their extent.

The Means of Temptation

First, we are told the means by which temptation works. It wants to overtake us, to ambush us when we are not prepared, and thus dominate us. It seeks control of us.

The word for "temptation" in the Greek text is *peirasmos*. It can be translated "test" or "temptation." Tests and temptations are two sides of the same thing. Life is full of trials, and each of them is a potential temptation.

An illustration might be helpful to show how this is so: A friend once told me about his new job with a very important company. After he had been on the job only a little while, one night after everyone else had left the office, he noticed that someone had left a large sum of money on his desk. He immediately took the money, put it in his briefcase and thought, *I'm going to have to return this.* He wrapped it up and the next morning walked into the boss's office, put the money on the boss's desk, and said, "Someone left this money on my desk and I don't know who it was or who will be missing it, but I wanted to turn it in as soon as I could so that no one would be distressed by its absence."

His boss looked him in the face and said, "I put the money there. It was a test. You passed."

Life offers us similar tests. Depending on how we respond, they can become temptations.

If my friend had taken the money home and counted it, and desired it, and thought through his options, he might have said to himself, *Hmm, nobody will know,* and begun to battle in his heart whether to turn it in or keep it for himself. Then the test would have become a temptation. When the heart is solicited to do evil, that is a temptation.

Life is full of tests that have the potential of becoming tempta-tions. For example, when you are in the midst of a financial setback and you say, "I'm going to trust God to meet my needs. I will cut back, live frugally, budget carefully, and be faithful to my obligations. I will live on less and trust the Lord to provide my needs"—you pass the test. But if you say, "I can take money from the till and no one will know. I can save money by cheating on my income tax. And I can cut expenses by not paying what I owe"—you have moved from a test into a temptation because your heart is being solicited to evil.

Or the test might be some personal disappointment. Perhaps you had expectations of someone who did not fulfill your hopes. You can either accept your circumstances with a trusting heart, and love that person in spite of your disappointment—or you can begin to feel animosity and bitterness in your heart. The moment those evil thoughts petition your heart, your test becomes a temp-tation.

Or you might face the test of illness, injury, or unexpected di-saster. Perhaps someone you love dies. Or your plans are thwarted. Or you fail to accomplish something you had dreamed for a long time. Maybe you will face a problem with no obvious solution. Or perhaps a friend will urge you to do something you know is wrong. These are the kind of tests that make up life. And when they begin to entreat us to respond with evil they become temptations. Job had to face *all* those tests at the same time.

James gives a very lucid explanation of how trials turn into temptations. He writes, "Consider it all joy, my brethren, when you encounter various trials, knowing that the testing of your faith pro-duces endurance. And let endurance have its perfect result, that you may be perfect and complete, lacking in nothing" (Jas. 1:2–4). Later, he adds, "Blessed is a man who perseveres under trial; for once he has been approved, he will receive the crown of life, which the Lord has promised to those who love Him" (v. 12).

In other words, God has a beneficent purpose in allowing us to go through trials. The trials perfect us, mold us to Christ's image, give us endurance, and bring us to the point of spiritual complete-ness. Peter said something similar: "After you have suffered for a little while, the God of all grace, who called you to His eternal glory in Christ, will Himself perfect, confirm, strengthen and establish you" (1 Pet. 5:10).

God sends us tests but not temptations. James also said, "Let no one say when he is tempted, "I am being tempted by God"; for God cannot be tempted by evil, and He Himself does not tempt anyone" (Jas. 1:13). God himself is never responsible for the solicitation to do evil.

God sends us tests but not temptations.

Then how does it happen? James 1 tells us: "Each one is tempted when he is carried away and enticed by his own lust. Then when lust has conceived, it gives birth to sin; and when sin is accomplished, it brings forth death" (vv. 14–15). It is *our own lust* that produces the solicitation to do evil. God only gives good gifts: "Do not be deceived, my beloved brethren. Every good thing bestowed and every perfect gift is from above, coming down from the Father of lights, with whom there is no variation, or shifting shadow" (vv. 16–17). God is perfect, unchanging, invariable. He is not responsible for our temptations, though He sends trials to test us.

Victory then begins with an understanding of how temptation comes. It comes when we respond wrongly to tests. It comes when we are drawn away by our own lusts. That plants the seeds for sin, and when sin bears fruit, that fruit is death. So we need to learn to respond correctly to tests.

The Nature of Temptation

We return to that wonderful promise in 1 Corinthians 10:13 to see the true nature of temptation: "No temptation has overtaken you but such as is common to man." In a word, temptation is *human*. It is not supernatural. It is not a force so powerful, so extraordinary that we are at a loss regarding how to deal with it. Temptation is common to humanity. The temptations you face are the very same ones everyone else faces. It is the same for all of us. The temptations that come to you are the same temptations that come to me. We may each have our peculiar besetting sins—areas where our habits or weaknesses frequently draw us into the same sins over and over. We may be particularly vulnerable or susceptible to different temptations. But we all get hit with the same basic temptations.

More encouraging yet, these are the very same temptations Jesus experienced. Hebrews 4:15 says Christ "has been tempted in all things as we are." Hebrews 2:17 says He was "made like His brethren in all things." He suffered all the very same temptations that are common to us. That is why He is such a faithful and merciful high priest. That is why He is touched with the feeling of our infirmities.

The Extent of Temptation

Moreover, there are limits to the amount or extent of temptation that God will allow us to face: "God is faithful who will not allow you to be tempted beyond what you are able." God knows your individual limitations. If you are a Christian, He has planned your life to guarantee your security in Christ eternally. He will never allow you to face any test that is more than you at any given point in your spiritual life can handle.

He will never allow you to face any test that is more than you at any given point in your spiritual life can handle.

We see an illustration of this principle in Jesus' dealings with the eleven disciples. On the night of His betrayal, Jesus told Peter, "Simon, Simon, behold, Satan has demanded permission to sift you like wheat; but I have prayed for you, that your faith may not fail" (Lk. 22:31–32). When Peter assured the Lord that he was ready to follow Him even to death, Jesus replied, "I say to you, Peter, the cock will not crow today until you have denied three times that you know Me" (v. 34). It happened just as Jesus prophesied. But did Peter's faith fail? No, Jesus' prayer for him was answered, and Peter was ultimately restored to full fellowship and even leadership in the early church.

On that same evening of Jesus' betrayal, while our Lord was praying in the garden, He prayed for His disciples: "While I was with them, I was keeping them in Thy name which Thou hast given Me; and I guarded them, and not one of them perished but the son of perdition, that the Scripture might be fulfilled" (Jn. 17:12). In other words, the eleven had been perpetually guarded and upheld by Jesus' sovereign, gracious keeping power. Only Judas, who never was a true believer, was left to carry out his own evil purposes.

While Jesus was praying, the disciples fell asleep (Mk. 13:37–43). When soldiers arrived with Judas, "Jesus therefore, knowing all the things that were coming upon Him, went forth, and said to them, 'Whom do you seek?' They answered Him, 'Jesus the Nazarene.' He said to them, 'I am He'" (Jn. 18:4–5). His words had a profound effect on the soldiers: "They drew back, and fell to the ground"(v. 6).

He asked them again, "Whom do you seek?" And they said, "Jesus the Nazarene" (v. 7).

Scripture says, "Jesus answered, 'I told you that I am He; if therefore you seek Me, let these go their way'" (v. 8). He was protecting the disciples. Twice He made the soldiers state whom they had come for. Then He volunteered the information that He was the one they were seeking, and He urged the soldiers to let the others go. He wanted to insure that none of the eleven were arrested, so "that the word might be fulfilled which He spoke, 'Of those whom Thou hast given Me I lost not one'" (v. 9).

This implies that if any of the disciples had been taken captive, they would have been spiritually too weak to survive such a test and would have defaulted from the faith. Therefore Jesus made sure they never had to face such a test. Peter almost messed everything up, because he took out a weapon and sliced off the ear of the high priest's servant (vv. 10–11). But Jesus miraculously healed the ear and rebuked Peter, and the disciples were able to flee (Mk. 14:50).

Through it all, Jesus Himself orchestrated all the events to make sure the disciples were not tested beyond their ability to withstand. Peter, especially, was confronted with a severe test that night. And although he sinned greatly by denying the Lord three times and even sealing his denial with a curse, Peter's faith did not fail. He was forced to look into his own soul, and he learned some valuable lessons that night. But through it all the Lord sustained him and made sure he did not fall away.

Whatever level of spiritual growth we are at, our Lord never allows us to go through any temptation beyond our ability to handle. If we are true Christians we cannot fall away. Our Lord Himself sees to that.

Furthermore, Christ prays for all true believers just as He prayed for the eleven in the garden. Hebrews 7:25 says, "He is able to save forever those who draw near to God through Him, since *He always lives to make intercession for them*" (emphasis added). He also puts limits on the extent of temptation we can undergo. He is faithful. He will not allow you to be tempted beyond your ability.

The Escape from Temptation

Best of all, when God allows us to be tested, He always provides a way out. There is always a path to victory. There is always an escape hatch. *Ekbasis* is the Greek word for "escape" in 1 Corinthians 10:13. It literally means "an exit."

Best of all, when God allows us to be tested, He always provides a way out. There is always a path to victory.

Here is a truth you may never have noticed in this verse— Paul tells us exactly what the way of escape is: God "with the temptation will provide the way of escape also, that you may be able to endure it." *The way out is through.* The way out of the temptation is to endure it as a trial and never let it become a solicitation to evil. You have been wronged. You have been falsely accused. You have been maligned or treated unkindly or dealt with unjustly. So what? Accept it. Endure it with joy (Jas. 1:2); that is the way of escape. Usually we look for a quick and easy escape route. God's plan for us is different. He wants us to count it all joy, "and let endurance have its perfect result, that [we] may be perfect and complete, lacking in nothing" (v. 4). God is using our trials to bring us to maturity.

How can we endure? There are several practical answers. I will mention only a few.

First, *meditate on the Word*: "Thy word I have treasured in my heart, that I may not sin against Thee" (Ps. 119:11). Second, *pray*: "Do not lead us into temptation, but deliver us from evil" (Matt. 6:13). In other words, ask God to keep the test from becoming a temptation. Third, *resist Satan and yield to God*: "Submit therefore to God. Resist the devil and he will flee from you" (Jas. 4:7).

There are many more I could mention, but do these begin to look familiar? They are precisely the same means of mortifying the deeds of the flesh we listed in chapter 8. The way to endure temptation *is* to be mortifying the deeds of the flesh.

There is one more key to endurance that I want to focus on, and that is faith. Hebrews 11 talks about the great heroes of faith, and their common characteristic is that they endured faithfully to the end. Of Moses, the writer of Hebrews says, "By faith he left Egypt, not fearing the wrath of the king; for he *endured*, as seeing Him who is unseen" (11:27, emphasis added). Abel, Enoch, Noah, Abraham, Sarah, Isaac, Jacob, Joseph, and Rahab all ran the race that was set before them *with endurance* (12:1). The writer of Hebrews summarizes:

> What more shall I say? For time will fail me if I tell of Gideon, Barak, Samson, Jephthah, of David and Samuel and the prophets, who by faith conquered kingdoms, performed acts of righteousness, obtained promises, shut the mouths of lions, quenched the power of fire, escaped the edge of the sword, from weakness were made strong, became mighty in war, put foreign armies to flight. Women received back their dead by resurrection; and others were tortured, not accepting their release, in order that they might obtain a better resurrection; and *others experienced mockings and scourgings, yes, also chains and imprisonment. They were stoned, they were sawn in two, they were tempted, they were put to death with the sword; they went about in sheepskins, in goatskins, being destitute, afflicted, ill-treated (men of whom the world was not worthy), wandering in deserts and mountains and caves and holes in the ground* (11:32–39, emphasis added).

Most of the heroes of faith endured incredible trials. If *our* faith is genuine, it will enable us to withstand whatever trials the Lord permits *us* to encounter. If you think your own trials are particularly severe, the writer of Hebrews reminds us, "You have not yet resisted to the point of shedding [your own] blood in your striving against sin" (Heb. 12:4).

By now we know these truths. When testing comes we must apply them. What an encouragement to our faith it is to know that no test can come to us that is more than we can bear!

Meanwhile, we must continually, faithfully mortify our sin. We must pray and ask God to deliver us from evil temptations. We must refuse to heed the lustful hankerings of our own flesh. And we must pursue God's whole purpose in allowing us to be tested—the perfecting of our faith unto endurance and spiritual maturity.

Through it all, we must look to Christ and lean on Him, our merciful and faithful High Priest, who is touched by the feeling of our infirmities, who can sympathize with our weaknesses because He was tempted in all points like we are—yet without sin (Heb. 4:15).

How can we "run with endurance the race that is set before us"? (Heb. 12:1). By "fixing our eyes on Jesus, the author and perfecter of faith, who for the joy set before Him endured the cross, despising the shame, and has sat down at the right hand of the throne of God. For consider Him who has endured such hostility by sinners against Himself, so that you may not grow weary and lose heart" (Heb. 12:2–3).

We live in a culture that is filled with temptation. Our society glorifies sin and despises God. It is certainly not an easy age in which to live. But neither was the first century. Remember, we have not yet resisted to the point of shedding blood.

Someday He may test us in a way that requires us to endure physical harm or death in our striving against sin. If that day comes, we are assured that He will sustain us through it. In the meantime, our trials are strengthening us, drawing us closer to Him, building our endurance, and conforming us to His image. What an encouragement to know that He personally insures that our temptations will not be too great for us! He sustains us so that we will not fall away. And "He Himself has said, 'I will never desert you, nor will I ever forsake you,' so that we confidently say, 'The Lord is my helper, I will not be afraid. What shall man do to me?'" (Heb. 13:5–6).

9

Keeping a Pure Mind

Seeing that sin is so sinful, it is evil even to be a thinking sinner, or a sinner though only in thought. It is too commonly said that thoughts are free. They are indeed free in respect of men, who cannot judge us for them, but God can and will. Many people who seem to be modest and sparing as to evil words and deeds will still make bold with thoughts and, as the saying is, pay it with thinking. Such are speculative, contemplative sinners.

Ralph Venning[1]

No sin is more destructive to the conscience than the sin that takes place in the arena of the mind. Sins of the mind assault the conscience like no other sins, because the conscience is their only deterrent. After all, who but God and the sinner ever knows about them? "Who among men knows the thoughts of a man except the spirit of the man, which is in him?" (1 Cor. 2:11). Many people who will not do evil deeds are nevertheless boldly evil in their thoughts. A man who abstains from fornication for fear of getting caught might convince himself it is all right to indulge in salacious fantasies because he thinks no one else will ever discover such a private sin. The sins he deliberately entertains in his mind may be a thousand times more evil than anything he would ever think of doing before others. Scripture says his guilt is the same as if he acted out his fantasies.

> *No sin is more destructive to the conscience than the sin that takes place in the arena of the mind.*

To indulge in sins of thought, therefore, is to molest the conscience directly. Those whose thoughts are impure *cannot* have pure consciences; the guilt is inherent in the evil thought. When the thoughts are defiled, the conscience immediately is, too. That is why nothing is more characteristic of unbelief than an impure mind combined with a defiled conscience: "To the pure, all things are pure; but to those who are defiled and unbelieving, nothing is pure, but *both their mind and their conscience are defiled*" (Tit. 1:15, emphasis added). In fact, nothing damages the conscience more than the habit of indulging in evil thoughts. Unfortunately, once begun, the practice becomes all too easy. This is a sin that does not have to wait for an opportunity; the mind can sin anytime, anywhere, under any circumstances. So the habit is quickly and easily established.

The Danger of a Sinful Thought Life

By engaging the inner faculties—mind, emotions, desire, memory, and imagination—thought-sins work directly on the soul to bias it toward evil. Sow a thought, reap an act. Sow an act, reap a habit. Sow a habit, reap a character. Sow a character, reap a destiny. Evil thoughts thus underlie and lay the groundwork for all other sins.

By engaging the inner faculties— mind, emotions, desire, memory, and imagination—thought-sins work directly on the soul to bias it toward evil.

No one ever "falls" into adultery. The adulterer's heart is always shaped and prepared by lustful thoughts before the actual deed occurs. Likewise, the heart of the thief is bent by covetousness. And murder is the product of anger and hatred. All sin is first incubated in the mind.

Jesus taught this truth to His disciples: "The things that proceed out of the mouth *come from the heart*, and those defile the man. For *out of the heart* come evil thoughts, murders, adulteries, fornications, thefts, false witness, slanders. *These are the things which defile the man*; but to eat with unwashed hands does not defile the man" (Matt. 15:18–19, emphasis added).

Jesus was teaching that the real point of the Mosaic Law was the moral truth embodied in the external ceremonial requirements. He downplayed the symbolic aspects of washing and abstaining from what is legally declared unclean. Instead He emphasized the moral requirement of the law. Defilement, He suggested, is not primarily a ceremonial or external problem; what is truly defiling in the spiritual sense is the wickedness that emanates from the heart. In the New Testament, "the heart" is the seat of the whole person— mind, imagination, affections, conscience, and will. "Heart" is often used as a synonym for "mind." In these verses, therefore, our Lord was condemning the wickedness of an impure thought life.

Again and again Christ rebuked the Pharisees for their fastidious observance of the external, ceremonial law and their wanton neglect of the law's moral requirements. They were utterly preoccupied with appearing to be righteous. Yet they were willing to tolerate the grossest sins of the heart. They thought no one else could ever discover what was really inside them. But our Lord knew what was in their hearts (Matt. 9:4; 12:25). He compared them to elegant crypts, beautiful on the outside but full of defilement and death on the inside:

> Woe to you, scribes and Pharisees, hypocrites! For you clean the outside of the cup and of the dish, but inside they are full of robbery and self-indulgence. You blind Pharisee, first clean the inside of the cup and of the dish, so that the outside of it may become clean also. Woe to you, scribes and Pharisees, hypocrites! For you are like whitewashed tombs which on the outside appear beautiful, but inside they are full of dead men's bones and all uncleanness. Even so you too outwardly appear righteous to men, but inwardly you are full of hypocrisy and lawlessness (Matt. 23:25–28).

The Pharisees' teaching had so inculcated this notion into people that it was commonly believed evil thoughts were not really sinful, as long as they did not become acts. That is precisely why our Lord targeted sins of the heart in His Sermon on the Mount:

> You have heard that the ancients were told, "You shall not commit murder" and "Whoever commits murder shall be liable to the court." But I say to you that everyone who is angry with his brother shall be guilty before the court. . . . You have heard that it was said, "You shall not commit adultery"; but I say to you, that everyone who looks on a woman to lust for her has committed adultery with her already in his heart (Matt. 5:21–22, 27–28).

What *should* take place in our minds and hearts? What *should* be the deepest secret of our souls? Worship to God:

> When you give alms, do not let your left hand know what your right hand is doing that your alms may be in secret; and your Father who sees in secret will repay you. And when you pray, you are not to be as the hypocrites; for they love to

stand and pray in the synagogues and on the street corners, in order to be seen by men. Truly I say to you, they have their reward in full. But you, when you pray, go into your inner room, and when you have shut your door, pray to your Father who is in secret, and your Father who sees in secret will repay you (Matt. 6:3-6).

To sin in the mind, therefore, is to desecrate the very sanctuary where our highest and best worship should be taking place.

Watch over Your Heart

It is relatively easy to confess and forsake deeds of sin, sins of omission, and unintentional sin. But the sins of our thought life are soul-coloring sins, character-damaging sins. Because they work so directly against the conscience and will, dealing with them honestly and thoroughly is one of the most difficult aspects of mortifying our sin. If we ever want to see real progress in sanctification, however, this is an area where we must attack and destroy our sinful habits with a vengeance. If we allow our thoughts to be influenced by the values of the world, our conscience will surely be dulled. Listening to and entertaining the claims of bad theologies or the self-esteem credo of modern psychology will surely deaden the conscience. Not only thoughts about lust, envy, and the other traditional sins, but also thoughts about the myriad false values and idols of an unbelieving world can be devastating obstacles to a pure mind.

The Old Testament sage wrote, "Watch over your heart with all diligence, for from it flow the springs of life" (Prov. 4:23).

God knows our hearts (Acts 15:8). "God is greater than our heart, and knows all things" (1 Jn. 3:20). David wrote, "Thou dost understand my thought from afar. . . . and art intimately acquainted with all my ways. Even before there is a word on my tongue, behold, O Lord, Thou dost know it all" (Ps. 139:2-4). Why, then, would we ever feel free to indulge in gross sins in our imagination—sins we would never act out before others—when we know that God is the audience to our thoughts? "Would not God find this out? For He knows the secrets of the heart" (Ps. 44:21).

Because they work so directly against the conscience and will, dealing with them honestly and thoroughly is one of the most difficult aspects of mortifying our sin.

Jesus told the Pharisees, "You are those who justify yourselves in the sight of men, but God knows your hearts; for that which is highly esteemed among men is detestable in the sight of God" (Lk. 16:15). Is not what we do in the sight of God infinitely more important than what we do in the sight of others?

Moreover, the thoughts of our heart are the real litmus test of our character: "As he thinks within himself, so he is" (Prov. 23:7). "A worthless person, a wicked man, is the one . . . who with perversity in his heart devises evil continually" (Prov. 6:12–14). Do you want to know who you really are? Take a hard look at your thought life. For "as in water face reflects face, so the heart of man reflects man" (27:19). External behavior is not an accurate mirror of your character; the thoughts of your heart reveal the truth. Only your conscience and God can assess the real truth about you.

Job's "comforters" falsely accused him of an impure thought life. Zophar was sure he understood Job's real problem: "Evil is sweet in his mouth, and he hides it under his tongue, though he desires it and will not let it go, but holds it in his mouth" (Job 20:12–13). The picture he painted of the evil thinker is vividly true-to-life. Evil thoughts are like candy to them. They derive great satisfaction from their imaginary sins. They savor their evil fantasies. They relish them like a choice morsel of sweetness under the tongue. They roll them around in their imagination. They return to the same wicked musings from which they can glean illicit pleasure over and over again. They mull them over like an animal chewing the cud, bringing up their favorite evil thoughts time and time again to re-enact them anew in the mind.

But Zophar misjudged Job. Job had carefully guarded himself against wicked and lustful thoughts: "I have made a covenant with my eyes; how then could I gaze at a virgin?" (Job 31:1). He knew God was audience to his thoughts: "Does He not see my ways, and number all my steps? If I have walked with falsehood, and my foot has hastened after deceit, let Him weigh me with accurate scales, and let God know my integrity" (vv. 4–6). Job denied that his heart had followed his eyes (v. 7). He denied that his heart had been enticed by another woman (v. 9). "That would be a lustful crime . . . an iniquity punishable by judges," he acknowledged (v. 11). To hide iniquity in the bosom, he said, would be to cover one's transgression like Adam (v. 33). The very thought appalled his righteous mind.

Moreover, the thoughts of our heart are the real litmus test of our character.

Clearly, Job was well aware of the danger of sinful thoughts. He had consciously, deliberately set a guard in his heart to avoid any such sin. He even offered special sacrifices to God just in case his children sinned in *their* hearts: "When the days of feasting had completed their cycle, that Job would send and consecrate them, rising up early in the morning and offering burnt offerings according to the number of them all; for Job said, 'Perhaps my sons have sinned and cursed God in their hearts.' *Thus Job did continually*" (1:5, emphasis added). Job's careful safeguarding of his thought life seems to have been the very reason God singled him out for unique blessing. "There is no one like him on the earth," the Lord told Satan. "[He is] a blameless and upright man, fearing God and turning away from evil" (1:8).

How the Mind Sins

Job understood what the Pharisees stubbornly refused to see: that just because you don't act out an evil deed, that doesn't excuse the secret desire. Lust itself is sinful. Greed alone is wicked. Covetousness, anger, pride, concupiscence, envy, discontent, hatred, and all evil thoughts are just as bad as the behavior they produce. To treasure such thoughts in the heart and relish the thought of them is an especially grievous sin against God, because it adds hypocrisy to the original evil thought. There are at least three ways the mind engages in this sin: remembering, scheming, and imagining.

Sins of remembering. One way is to cherish the memories of sins past. To bring back a lurid memory of a bygone sin is to repeat the sin all over again. Can someone who is truly repentant about a sin still harvest pleasure from the memory of that deed? The answer is yes, because of the deceitfulness of our own hearts and the sinful tendencies of our flesh.

Not long ago I baptized a man who was a former homosexual transformed by Christ. His life was changed. His circle of friends was different. And he had removed himself as much as possible from a lifestyle that would hold any temptation to return to his former sins. But he admitted to me that the most difficult problem he faced was that his own mind was filled with memories that became temptations to him every time he thought of them. He had entertained himself with many vile kinds of sexual relationships and activities, and those memories were so embedded in his brain that he would never forget them. Even though he was transformed as a Christian, Satan would bring back the memory of his former life. If he allowed himself to dwell on such thoughts, he would discover that his flesh was trying to draw him back into the sin. All his senses were stirred up easily by the memories, and the memories could be recalled unexpectedly by his senses. Some sound or smell or sight would provoke a memory in his mind, and he would find himself battling temptation.

The truth is, we all know what that is like. Sin has a way of impressing itself on our memories with vivid sensations we cannot shake off. As adults we can still remember the sins of our youth as if they occurred only yesterday. Perhaps it was just such thoughts that prompted David to pray, "Do not remember the sins of my youth or my transgressions" (Ps. 25:7). David himself remembered them all too graphically.

Don't think this problem is unique to sexual sins. Some people like to rehearse memories of the time they got angry and poured out vengeance on someone. Some enjoy thoughts of the time they lied and got away with it. All kinds of tempting memories lodge themselves in us and become new sins every time we remember them with pleasure.

Satan will take all the garbage out of your past and try to drag it back through your mind so that you relive it.

Savoring memories of one's past sin is a particularly heinous form of sin. In Ezekiel 23, the Lord condemned Israel by comparing the nation to a harlot named Oholibah. This was His charge against her: "She multiplied her harlotries, remembering the days of her youth, when she played the harlot in the land of Egypt" (v. 19).

And the spiritual devastation this practice leaves in its wake is tremendous. It hardens the conscience. It corrupts the character. It can even destroy relationships. I have talked to young couples who lived a life of fornication before they came to Christ. They become Christians and get married. Then they find it very difficult to be singly devoted to each other because they struggle with constant thoughts about all the fornication and sinful relationships they indulged in before they knew the Lord.

Satan will take all the garbage out of your past and try to drag it back through your mind so that you relive it. That is precisely why pornography is so spiritually destructive. Once you implant a lurid image in your thoughts, you cannot take it away. But it isn't only hard-core pornography that has this effect. Many of the films and television programs produced for the mass market routinely include images, themes, and story lines that tempt people to sinful thought patterns. Once the suggestive pictures and thoughts are planted in the mind, they reside there as potential temptations anytime we think of them. We would all do well to emulate Job's example, and refuse to expose our eyes to anything that might provoke such thoughts.

Sins of scheming. A second way the mind can sin is by plotting sins of the future. Scripture is full of strong condemnations of those whose minds are engaged in this kind of activity:

- "Transgression speaks to the ungodly within his heart; there is no fear of God before his eyes. For it flatters him in his own eyes, concerning the discovery of his iniquity and the hatred of it. The words of his mouth are wickedness and deceit; he has ceased to be wise and to do good. He plans wickedness upon his bed; He sets himself on a path that is not good; He does not despise evil" (Ps. 36:1–4).

- "Hide me from the secret counsel of evildoers, from the tumult of those who do iniquity, who have sharpened their tongue like a sword. They aimed bitter speech as their arrow, to shoot from concealment at the blameless; suddenly they shoot at him, and do not fear. They hold fast to themselves an evil purpose; they talk of laying snares secretly; they say, 'Who can see them?' They devise injustices, saying, 'We are ready with a well-conceived plot'; for the inward thought and the heart of a man are deep. But God will shoot at them with an arrow; suddenly they will be wounded" (Ps. 64:2–7).
- "A good man will obtain favor from the Lord, But He will condemn a man who devises evil" (Prov. 12:2).
- "Deceit is in the heart of those who devise evil" (Prov. 12:20).
- "Will they not go astray who devise evil? But kindness and truth will be to those who devise good" (Prov. 14:22).
- "Evil plans are an abomination to the Lord, But pleasant words are pure" (Prov. 15:26).
- "The Lord hates . . . a heart that devises wicked plans (Prov. 6:16–18).
- Do not be envious of evil men, nor desire to be with them; for their minds devise violence, and their lips talk of trouble" (Prov. 24:1–2).
- "He who plans to do evil, men will call him a schemer. The devising of folly is sin, and the scoffer is an abomination to men" (Prov. 24:8–9).
- For a fool speaks nonsense, and his heart inclines toward wickedness, to practice ungodliness and to speak error against the Lord, to keep the hungry person unsatisfied and to withhold drink from the thirsty. As for a rogue, his weapons are evil; he devises wicked schemes to destroy the afflicted with slander, even though the needy one speaks what is right. But the noble man devises noble plans; and by noble plans he stands (Isa. 32:6–8).

Some people love to dream of sins they will commit, evil they long to do, and sinister plots they want to hatch. Their thoughts vent their anger, hatred, lust, greed, envy, pride, and every evil desire. Their minds and hearts are full of wickedness, and God condemns them for it.

But even Christians can fall into this habit if they are not careful. This is what Paul was warning against when he wrote, "Put on the Lord Jesus Christ, and make no provision for the flesh in regard to its lusts" (Rom. 13:14). We are not to make plans that will cater to our fleshly desires. We are not to devise evil plans in our minds.

Sins of imagining. A third kind of sin that takes place in the mind is the purely imaginary sin. This is what Jesus referred to when he said, "Everyone who looks on a woman to lust for her has committed adultery with her already in his heart" (Matt. 5:28). You may have no intention of ever performing the deed, but Jesus says if you even imagine it, you are guilty.

That sets the standard extremely high—but this is the level of purity we must maintain if we are to have a clear conscience. Every imagined sin offends the healthy conscience. Those who tolerate this kind of sin in their hearts as a habit give irrefutable evidence of a defiled and hardened conscience. It is here that our self-examination becomes most convicting. But it is here that we must train our consciences to be most sensitive.

People fantasize about sins they long to commit. They imagine what it would be like to indulge their favorite lusts, or wreak revenge on a despised enemy, or hurt someone they loathe. They act out a robbery in their minds, or fantasize about an illicit relationship, or visualize killing someone.

But many imaginary sins are not so heinous. People dream covetous thoughts about winning the lottery. They imagine themselves with great power, wealth, or prestige. They daydream about what it would be like to be married to someone else, or muse about a luxury vacation, or indulge their gluttony in an imaginary binge. Modern society is filled with temptations to those kinds of sins. The entire advertizing industry thrives on appealing to such lusts. And most of the entertainment industry is focused on creating those kinds of images. The result is that literally millions of people live in a fantasy world of sin.

Are such sins really that disastrous? Yes, they defile us (Matt. 15:18–20). They are an abomination to God: "The thought of foolishness is sin" (Prov. 24:9, KJV). Any thought that is not God-honoring, Christ-exalting, and representative of full obedience to the Word of God is sin. Covetousness, the basis of most of our evil fantasies, is expressly forbidden by the Tenth Commandment.

We dare not think of these thought-sins as mere peccadillos. They open the door to actual deeds of sin. James 1:15 says, "When lust [evil desire] has conceived, it gives birth to sin." Puritan Ralph Venning wrote in 1669:

> Evil deeds are the offspring and children of evil thoughts, the branches and fruit which grow out of this root. Thoughts are the first-born of the soul; words and actions are only younger brothers. They are the oil that feeds and maintains the wick, which would otherwise go out; life-sins receive their juice and nourishment from thought-sins. St. James speaks as if our thoughts were the belly and womb where sin is conceived (Jas. 1:15). . . . As Job [cursed] the day and place of [his] birth, the womb that bore [him]; so should you curse sin even in the very womb that bore it, laying the axe to the root of this tree.
>
> The wickedness of men's lives is charged upon their thoughts, that it has its root and rise there: murders, adulteries, etc., all come out of the heart, as out of the belly of a Trojan horse (Gen. 6:5; Mat. 12:35; 15:19). One would wonder (as we do at some birds, where they nest all winter) to see so many flocks and herds of wickedness. One would wonder from what corner of the world they come. Why, they all come out of the heart, the rendezvous of wickedness, the inn where lodge all the thieves and travelling lusts that are in the world and that do so much mischief in it. All the unclean streams flow from this unclean fountain, this ocean and sea of sin.[2]

That is why David cried out for God to help him at the very front line of defense: "Create in me a clean heart, O God" (Ps. 51:10). It was an appeal for a sound conscience arising from a pure mind.

Discerning the Thoughts and Intents of the Heart

Do you realize that the difference between a sincere, Spirit-controlled, devoted, godly, obedient Christian and a defeated, weak, struggling Christian is what takes place in the mind? They may be attending the same church, active in the same ministries, and externally doing the same things, but one is defeated and the other lives a spiritually fruitful life. The difference is the thought life.

Do you realize that the difference between a sincere, Spirit-controlled, devoted, godly, obedient Christian and a defeated, weak, struggling Christian is what takes place in the mind?

One day the difference will be made manifest. Paul told the Corinthians that when the Lord comes, He "will both bring to light the things hidden in the darkness and disclose the motives of men's hearts" (1 Cor. 4:5). Jesus said something similar: "Nothing is hidden that shall not become evident, nor anything secret that shall not be known and come to light" (Lk. 8:17). And, "Beware of the leaven of the Pharisees, which is hypocrisy. But there is nothing covered up that will not be revealed, and hidden that will not be known" (Lk. 12:1–2).

I urge you to look deeply into the mirror of God's Word (Jas. 1:23–24), which is a powerful "discerner of the thoughts and intents of the heart" (Heb. 4:12, KJV). As Jeremiah counseled Israel, "Wash your heart from evil, O Jerusalem, that you may be saved. How long will your wicked thoughts lodge within you?" (Jer. 4:14). And "let us cleanse ourselves from all defilement of flesh and spirit, perfecting holiness in the fear of God" (2 Cor. 7:1).

Taking Every Thought Captive to Obedience

How *can* we deal with the problem of evil thoughts? The process is like mortifying any other sin; it involves taking the following steps:

First confess and forsake the sin. "Let the wicked forsake his way, *and the unrighteous man his thoughts*; and let him return to the Lord, and He will have compassion on him; and to our God, for He will abundantly pardon" (Isa. 55:7, emphasis added). If your thought life harbors sins of immorality, sins of anger toward someone, sins of vengeance, sins of bitterness, sins of covetousness, or whatever— confess them to God. Repent and ask forgiveness. If we confess, He is faithful and just to forgive and keep on cleansing (1 Jn. 1:9).

Refuse to entertain those thoughts. Purpose to abandon your wrong thought patterns immediately and begin to build new, righteous habits. If you find yourself slipping into old ways of thinking, confess your sin and refuse once again to give place to evil thoughts. Consciously direct your mind to fix itself on pure things: "Whatever is true, whatever is honorable, whatever is right, whatever is pure, whatever is lovely, whatever is of good repute, if there is any excellence and if anything worthy of praise, let your mind dwell on these things" (Phil. 4:8). In other words, reprogram your mind with truth and righteousness.

Feed on the Word of God. "Thy word I have treasured in my heart, that I may not sin against Thee" (Ps. 119:11). The Word insulates the mind. It strengthens the heart. It occupies the soul and fortifies it against evil thoughts. Only as we use the sword of the Spirit skillfully can we mortify our fleshly imaginations (Eph. 6:17).

Avoid evil attractions. Don't expose yourself to activities, images, or conversation that provoke evil thoughts. Like Job, make a covenant with your eyes (Job 31:1)—or with your ears, or with whatever sensations lead you into evil thoughts. Refuse to feed any tendencies that draw your imagination into wickedness. This is what Jesus meant figuratively when He said, "If your right eye makes you stumble, tear it out, and throw it from you; for it is better for you that one of the parts of your body perish, than for your whole body to be thrown into hell. And if your right hand makes you stumble, cut it off, and throw it from you; for it is better for you that one of the parts of your body perish, than for your whole body to go into hell" (Matt. 5:29–30).

Cultivate the love of God. David said in Psalm 119:97, "O how I love Thy law! It is my meditation all the day." And then four verses later he said, "I have restrained my feet from every evil way." If we set our minds on things above, things on the earth will cease to hold the same fascination for us (Col. 3:2). "Where your treasure is, there will your heart be also" (Matt. 6:21)—and where your affections are set, your thoughts will be there as well.

David ended Psalm 19, his great paean to the sufficiency of Scripture, with these words:

> Who can discern his errors? Acquit me of hidden faults. Also keep back Thy servant from presumptuous sins; let them not rule over me; then I shall be blameless, and I shall be acquitted of great transgression. Let the words of my mouth and the meditation of my heart be acceptable in Thy sight, O Lord, my rock and my Redeemer (vv. 12–14).

That is the state of mind of every truly godly person. It is also the goal of biblical instruction: "love from a pure heart and a good conscience and a sincere faith" (1 Tim. 1:5).

How's *your* thought life?

10

Holding to the Mystery of Faith with a Clear Conscience

It is a very evil choice for any soul under heaven to choose the least sin rather than the greatest affliction. Better be under the greatest affliction than be under the guilt or power of any sin. . . . There is more evil in sin than in outward trouble in the world; more evil in sin than in all the miseries and torments of hell itself.

Jeremiah Burroughs[1]

One of the great tragedies of contemporary culture is that we have lost any concept of the exceeding sinfulness of sin. Puritan Jeremiah Burroughs wrote an entire book on the subject, titled, *The Evil of Evils*. Burroughs's thesis was that it is better to choose the sufferings of affliction than sin. The smallest sin, he pointed out, is more evil than the greatest affliction. Describing the horrors of hell, he suggested that one act of sin contains more evil than all the sufferings of eternal doom:

> Suppose that God should bring any of you to the brink of that bottomless gulf and open it to you, and there you should see those damned creatures sweltering under the wrath of the infinite God, and there you should hear the dreadful and hideous cries and shrieks of those who are under such soul-amazing and soul-sinking torments through the wrath of the Almighty. Yet, I say, there is more evil in one sinful thought than there is in all these everlasting burnings. . . . The truth is, that if it should come into competition whether we would endure all the torments that there are in hell to all eternity rather than to commit one sin, I say, if our spirits were as they should be, we would rather be willing to endure all these torments than commit the least sin.[2]

Sin, Burroughs pointed out, is contrary to the very character of God. Sin is the evil of all evils—the source from which emanates every affliction, pain, suffering, disease, and human misery. Unlike suffering, sin brings a curse from God. No one is condemned for affliction, but all are condemned for sin. Sin makes the sinner evil; affliction cannot—and so on. Burroughs argues eloquently and convincingly through sixty-seven chapters, examining the vileness of sin and showing it for what it is. His book is a masterpiece of Puritan literature, showing the depth and richness of the English Reformers' biblical mastery.

In stark contrast, today's church seems utterly to lack any notion of the profound evil of sin. We grieve over calamities. We are troubled by our miseries. The trials of life distress us. But are we equally disturbed by our sin? Do *we* believe that the least sin contains more evil than the least affliction? Few contemporary Christians, it seems, have ever entertained the thought that sin is *that* evil.

Sin and Shame

In fact, modern evangelicalism seems often to teach precisely the opposite. Today we are more concerned that people *feel* good than that they *do* good. Affliction, we believe, is to be avoided at all costs. Sin, on the other hand, is thought to be easily forgivable. Therefore to offend God is viewed as the lesser of evils when the other choice is to endure some kind of personal pain or affliction. We see *shame* as a worse evil than the *sin* that causes it. This is precisely the mentality behind the massive self-esteem movement.

Today's church seems utterly to lack any notion of the profound evil of sin.

At the opposite end of the spectrum from Burroughs's work is another book I recently read. This one was written by a modern seminary professor who is very well known for his popular books on human relationships, psychology, religion, and related topics. His latest book deals with the subject of human shame. He begins by recounting his saintly mother's death. As she lay dying she told him, "I'm so glad that the Lord forgives me all of my sins; I've been a great sinner, you know."

"Great sinner?" he writes incredulously. "As far back as I can remember, she was on her knees scrubbing people's kitchen floors most days, up to her neck in the frets of five fussing children every evening, and, when late night fell, there she was on her knees again . . . asking the Lord for strength to do it again for one more day."[3]

His assessment was that his mother was inflicted with "a classic case of unhealthy shame." He writes, "It saddens me still that such a triumph of a woman should have to die feeling like a wretch. Her shame was totally out of touch with her reality. She did not deserve to be stuck with so much shame."[4]

Yet the professor acknowledges that in both her living and her dying, his mother was "wondrously serene. She was given a grace to turn her shame into peace with a life tougher than she deserved."[5]

Evidently her statements about being a "great sinner" reflected nothing but the godly response of a chastened and transformed heart. Her lament was only an echo of what we all should feel when we realize the nature and the profound depth of our sinfulness (Rom. 7:24). Why this man concluded his mother's shame was "unhealthy" and undeserved is not entirely clear.

After all, didn't even the apostle Paul describe himself as foremost of all sinners (1 Tim. 1:15)? Peter fell on his face before Christ and said, "Depart from me, for I am a sinful man, O Lord" (Lk. 5:8). Isaiah, the most godly man in all Israel, said, "Woe is me, for I am ruined! Because I am a man of unclean lips, and I live among a people of unclean lips" (Isa. 6:5). The greatest saints of history have all felt the same deep sense of shame.

But this professor suggests that we really are not so vile after all. In fact, he believes we are *worthy* of divine grace: "If grace heals all our shame, it must be a grace that tells us we are worthy to have it. We need, I believe, to recognize that we are accepted not only in spite of our undeserving but because of our worth."[6] He distinguishes between "deserving" and "worthy" like this: "If I deserve some good that comes my way, it is because I *did* something to earn it. If I am worthy, it is because I *am* somebody of enormous value."[7]

But does Scripture portray sinful humanity as inherently "worthy" of God's favor? Not at all. Nowhere in Scripture are we told we are "accepted . . . because of our worth." Grace is *grace* precisely because it comes to people who are utterly ineligible for any favor from God: "While we were still *helpless* . . . Christ died for the ungodly. . . . While we were yet *sinners*, Christ died for us. . . . While we were *enemies*, we were reconciled to God through the death of His Son" (Rom. 5:6, 8, 10, emphasis added). Paul's very point in those verses is to suggest the supreme marvel of God's grace—that it should be extended to helpless, sinful, undeserving, even loathsome, adversaries.

Look, for example, at Daniel's prayer of repentance: "Righteousness belongs to Thee, O Lord, but to us *open shame*, as it is this day—to the men of Judah, the inhabitants of Jerusalem, and all Israel, those who are nearby and those who are far away in all the countries to which Thou hast driven them, because of their unfaithful deeds which they have committed against Thee. *Open shame belongs to us, O Lord, to our kings, our princes, and our fathers, because we have sinned against Thee"* (Dan. 9:7–8, emphasis added). Daniel would hardly have been an advocate of self-esteem theology!

The reasons for God's grace to sinners are a mystery. We certainly are never told that God loves us because we are worthy.

The Bible simply does not speak of sinners as intrinsically worthy of God's grace. The Prodigal Son, Jesus' illustration of a repentant sinner, admitted his unworthiness (Lk. 15:21). Even John the Baptist—who by Jesus' own testimony was the greatest prophet who ever lived (Matt. 11:11)—said he was *unworthy* to carry the shoes of the Savior (3:11). "What is man, that Thou dost take thought of him? And the son of man, that Thou dost care for him?" (Ps. 8:4). The reasons for God's grace to sinners are a mystery. We certainly are never told that God loves us because we are worthy. That notion is simply an echo of worldly self-esteem doctrine.

The focus of Scripture is entirely on *God's* worth, *His* majesty, *His* glory, *His* holiness, and *His* grace and mercy. Our worth as Christians is a *product* of God's grace, certainly not the *reason* for it. If people were inherently worthy of salvation, God would be unrighteous not to save everyone.

As we noted in chapter 4, Adam's sin plunged the whole human race into sin, so we are born guilty. Shame is not an undeserved emotion, but an honest reflection of who we are. Human beings have felt shame ever since that first sin (cf. Gen. 2:25; 3:10). Sometimes our shame may be misplaced, irrational, or even emotionally unbalanced—but shame itself is certainly not undeserved. No one is "too good" to feel he or she is a miserable sinner. That is, after all, precisely what we are.

This doctrine is in serious decline these days, to the detriment of the church. We change the words of great hymns so that they don't refer to us as "wretches" or "worms." We buy into the self-esteem lie. We want to minimize our sin, eliminate our sense of shame, boost our ego, and feel good about ourselves. We want, in other words, all those things which deaden the conscience. We abhor shame, however justified. We abhor repentance because it is too hard. We avoid guilt. We want the easy street.

Sin and Psychology

The rush to embrace psychology has done much to contribute to these trends. Psychology itself is hostile to the biblical doctrine of sin, and the move to marry Scripture with psychotherapy has certainly not changed this. One well-known and widely used handbook of psychology for pastoral counselors included the following under the heading "original sin." Though it is rather lengthy I include the entire section entitled "Original Sin," because it shows how psychology can corrupt the biblical doctrine of sin:

> No reputable psychologist would hold the ancient theological and anthropological theory that sin is passed on from generation to generation. The term "sin" is now reserved for conscious and deliberate acts of a person against accepted norms or mores of his society and the ideals associated with a moral God. Sin is thus a *responsible* misdemeanor. Original sin has, however, an element of psychological validity, viz., the fact that weaknesses of personality ingredients have a history beyond the pale of conscious responsibility.
>
> Our inherited drives, for example, are our equipment. As such they are amoral. They function for biological purposes. When in conflict with standards of conduct they make for trouble and become easy predispositions to (deliberate) sin. Add to this the disorders provoked by early environment—beyond the will of the individual—and there is the picture of a handicap on the kind of social adjustment called "moral."
>
> If it is true that all of us have genetically come out of the forest primeval with a long standing equipment to employ in the hard struggle for survival in a world not too easy (temperature changes, wild animals, floods, disease germs, etc.) and in the course of social development have attained a kind of set of interpersonal social relationships which call for softer dealings with others, then it is easy to see how difficult it is to adjust elemental

drives useful for one kind of hardfisted world to another which demands their curbing. Biologically, elemental drives have a way of persisting in spite of an environment calling for their softening. "Original sin" is an unhappy term for the elemental failings of man to live as he ought to live in a social order where virtues of altruism are supposed to eliminate selfishness. But there is this truth in "original sin," viz., that man's long history has not been erased in spite of ideals emphasized in developing society. So long as there is this disparity (for which the individual person is not responsible) there is more than a myth in the doctrine that we are not easily made into saints.[8]

Notice how this passage absolves people from responsibility for all inherited drives, all evil desires, all sinful tendencies, all the "elemental failings of man"—and it even excuses us from original sin itself! The only things deemed sin are "conscious and deliberate acts of a person against accepted norms or mores of his society and the ideals associated with a moral God." How far that is from the biblical definition! But does anyone notice? Does anyone still know?

Sin and the Church

Martyn Lloyd-Jones suggested years ago that the doctrine of sin was fast disappearing from evangelical teaching and preaching. He said,

When we are dealing with the unconverted, we tend to say: "Ah, you need not worry about sin now, that will come later. All you need to do is to come to Christ, to give yourself to Christ. Do not worry your head about sin—of course you cannot understand that now. Do not worry either whether or not you have got a sense of sin or deep conviction, or whether you know these things. All you need to do is to come to Christ, to give yourself to Christ, and then you will be happy."

Then when we are dealing with those who have so come, our tendency, again, is to say to them, "Of course, you must not look at yourself, you must look to Christ. You must not be for ever analysing yourself. That is wrong, that is what you did before you were converted. You were thinking in terms of yourself and of what you had got to do. The only thing you must do is to keep looking to Christ and away from yourself." We imagine, therefore, that all that is needed by Christians is a certain amount of comfort and encouragement, of preaching about the love of God and about his general providence and perhaps a certain amount of moral and ethical exhortation. And so, you see, the doctrine of sin is, as it were, crowded out. We fail to emphasise it both before and after conversion, and the result is that we hear very little about it.[9]

Martyn Lloyd-Jones suggested years ago that the doctrine of sin was fast disappearing from evangelical teaching and preaching.

An entire generation of believers is now virtually ignorant about sin. When they hear *any* mention of sin, they think it is harsh, unloving, ungracious. The trends toward user-friendly churches and seeker-sensitive ministry have only heightened this problem.[10]

Sin and the Christian

We desperately need to recover a holy hatred of sin. We need to do this corporately as a church, but we also need to do it individually as believers. Sin is surely not a pleasant subject to study or preach on, but it is necessary. Here in the midst of an increasingly worldly church it is *critical*. We must see our sin for what it is. An inadequate view of one's own sinfulness is spiritually debilitating. Those who don't see themselves as despicably sinful will never take the necessary steps to lay sin aside.

We desperately need to recover a holy hatred of sin.

God has clearly indicted us for our own sin and assigned full responsibility to each individual sinner. The proof of that is the biblical doctrine of hell—the awful reality that each damned and unforgiven sinner will pay forever in hell the terrible price for his or her own sins. In no way can this guilt be escaped by blaming others. Clearly, God does not see us as a race of victims! If He saw us as victims, He would punish someone else. But every condemned sinner will pay the full price in eternal torment for his or her own deeds—because each one is fully responsible.

No one's conscience will be silent then. It will turn on the sinner with a fury, reminding him that he alone is responsible for the agonies he will suffer eternally. John Blanchard writes,

> Things will be very different in hell [for those who have numbed their consciences here on earth] . . . Their consciences will be their worst tormentors. Nor will there be any way in which they can be stifled or silenced. As John Flavel wrote in the seventeenth century, "Conscience, which should have been the sinner's curb here on earth, becomes the whip that must lash his soul in hell. Neither is there any faculty or power belonging to the soul of man so fit and able to do it as his own conscience. That which was the seat and centre of all guilt, now becomes the seat and centre of all torments."
>
> Conscience will make the sinner acutely aware that he deliberately, freely and gladly chose the lifestyle that led him to hell, that he is there because of his willfulness and obstinacy. In addition, it will force him to admit the truth of every charge it brings, and the justice of every pain he suffers, so that, in Flavel's words, "In all this misery, there is not one drop of injury or wrong." As if this were not horrifying enough, the castigation will be uninterrupted; the sinner will have "No rest day or night" (Rev. 14:11). As never before, he will discover the truth of God's words that "There is no peace . . . for the wicked" (Isa. 48:22).[11]

If you find your conscience vanishing, you must realize the seriousness of your condition and repent, beseech God for a clear, functioning conscience, and set yourself to the task of laying aside sin in your own life.

I want to leave you with a very practical list of principles that will assist you in that task. Many of these simply review and restate issues that we have seen throughout this book, but they are essential nevertheless. And perhaps this final checklist will give you a place to start as you seek to recover a healthy conscience:

Don't underestimate the seriousness of your sin. Surely this is the primary reason most people tolerate sin in their lives. If they saw their sin as God sees it, they could not continue indifferently in ways of known sin. Sin violates God's holiness, it brings His discipline, it destroys our joy, and it causes death. If we really understood, as Jeremiah Burroughs said, that the smallest sin contains more evil than all the torments of hell, we could not remain unconcerned about mortifying our sins. God gave the law precisely so that the exceeding sinfulness of sin would be evident (Rom. 7:13).

Purpose in your heart not to sin. Make a solemn vow to oppose all sin in your life. The psalmist did that: "I have sworn, and I will confirm it, that I will keep Thy righteous ordinances" (Ps. 119:106). Unless you have that kind of determination in your life, you will find you are easily entangled by sin. In fact, it is that kind of bold affirmation and earnest heart that is at the root of all holy living. Until you make that kind of conscious commitment to the Lord, you're going to battle the same things over and over—and be defeated.

That same psalm contains this wonderful verse: "I shall run the way of Thy commandments, for Thou wilt enlarge my heart" (v. 32). Distance runners' hearts are usually larger than average. The many miles running in training actually conditions the heart to enable it to pump blood more efficiently during long periods of exercise. David was saying that God would equip him spiritually with a heart that fit him to run the race he had committed himself to. In other words, God will honor your commitment to lay aside sin.

Be suspicious of your own spirituality. Paul said, "Let him who thinks he stands take heed lest he fall" (1 Cor. 10:12). "The heart is more deceitful than all else and is desperately sick; who can understand it?" (Jer. 17:9). The seducing subtlety of our own heart will sometimes ensnare us at the very moments of our greatest spiritual victories. We can all be deceived quite easily; except for the grace of God, we would fall into any and every sin. Learn to seek that grace and never become confident in your own flesh (Phil. 3:3).

---

*We can all be deceived quite easily;
except for the grace of God,
we would fall into any and every sin.*

Resist the first hint of evil desire. "When lust has conceived, it gives birth to sin; and when sin is accomplished, it brings forth death" (Jas. 1:15). The time to stop sin is at conception, not after it has been born and gets a life of its own. At the first suggestion of lust, exterminate the thought before it hatches and begins to bring forth its own diabolical offspring.

Meditate on the Word. "The mouth of the righteous utters wisdom, and his tongue speaks justice. *The law of his God is in his heart; his steps do not slip*" (Ps. 37:30, emphasis added). When the heart is controlled by the Word, the steps are sure and steady. The Word of God fills the mind and controls the thinking, and that strengthens the soul against temptation. Scripture acts as a powerful restraint in the heart given over to its truth.

Be instantly repentant over your lapses. When Peter sinned his great sin, denying Christ three times, Scripture says, "He went out and wept bitterly" (Matt. 26:75). We shudder at his sin, but we must admire him for the immediacy of his remorse. Unconfessed sin contaminates and hardens the conscience. "If we confess our sins, He is faithful and righteous to forgive us our sins and to cleanse us from all unrighteousness" (1 Jn. 1:9). And when you confess your sin, name it. Let your ear hear the specific sin you are repenting for. That's one way to develop a high degree of accountability to God and keep from falling into the same sins over and over again. If you hold back from naming your sin, it may be that you secretly want to do that same sin again.

Continually watch and pray. After all the armor of Ephesians 6 is itemized, Paul writes, "With all prayer and petition pray at all times in the Spirit, and with this in view, be on the alert" (Eph. 6:18). He told the Colossian believers, "Devote yourselves to prayer, keeping alert in it" (Col. 4:2). Jesus Himself said, "Keep watching and praying, that you may not enter into temptation; the spirit is willing, but the flesh is weak" (Matt. 26:41).

Be part of a church with other believers who hold you accountable. We all struggle with the same temptations (1 Cor. 10:13). That is why Paul told the Galatians, "Bear one another's burdens, and thus fulfill the law of Christ" (Gal. 6:2). We need each other. Can we keep each other from sinning? Not always. But we can encourage one another (Heb. 3:13; 1 Thess. 5:11). We can stimulate one another to love and good works (Heb. 10:24–25). And "even if a man is caught in any trespass, you who are spiritual, restore such a one in a spirit of gentleness; each one looking to yourself, lest you too be tempted" (Gal. 6:1).

This is a very important reason the church was instituted. We are to hold one another accountable, lovingly pursue those who sin (Matt. 18:15–17), love one another, and serve one another. All of this works corporately to help us as individuals mortify our sin.

Sin and God

Remember that God hates sin. Remember that it was sin that put His beloved Son on the cross. Remember that His eyes are too pure to approve evil (Hab. 1:13). And remember that His own perfect holiness is the standard He calls us to.

Will we reach that goal? Not in this lifetime, but He guarantees that we *will* reach it. "For whom He foreknew, He also predestined to become conformed to the image of His Son" (Rom. 8:29). We already "are being transformed into the same image from glory to glory, just as from the Lord, the Spirit" (2 Cor. 3:18). And "we know that, when He appears, we shall be like Him, because we shall see Him just as He is" (1 Jn. 3:2). "Whom He predestined, these He also called; and whom He called, these He also justified; and whom He justified, these He also glorified" (Rom. 8:30).

Meanwhile, we dare not become discouraged and give up the fight. We dare not yield an inch to sin and temptation. And above all, we must keep our conscience pure and undefiled.

"And the work of righteousness will be peace, and the service of righteousness, quietness and confidence forever" (Isa. 32:17).

Appendix 1

Gaining Victory over Sin—A Closer Look at Romans 6

We must never think that grace, wonderful as it is, either permits or encourages us to go on sinning. . . . "Shall we go on sinning so that grace may increase?" asked Paul. He answered, "By no means! We died to sin; how can we live in it any longer?" (Rom. 6:1–2).

This is why the ending of the story of Jesus and the woman trapped in adultery is so important, though it is often overlooked. [Having forgiven her, Jesus] added, "Go now and leave your life of sin." This always follows upon forgiveness. . . . If we are saved, we must stop sinning.

At the same time, we can be grateful that Jesus spoke as he did. For we notice that he did not say, "Leave your life of sin, and I will not condemn you." If he had said that, what hope for us could there be? Our problem is precisely that we do sin. There could be no forgiveness if forgiveness was based upon our ceasing to sin. Instead of that, Jesus actually spoke in the reverse order. First, he granted forgiveness freely, without any conceivable link to our performance. Forgiveness is granted only on the merit of his atoning death. But then, having forgiven us freely, Jesus tells us with equal force to stop sinning.

James M. Boice[1]

Lazarus had been dead four days when the Lord arrived at his grave. Although Jesus loved Lazarus and his family intensely, He had purposely delayed coming so that He might exhibit God's glory through an unprecedented miracle that would demonstrate His power over death. Mary and Martha, sisters of Lazarus, knew that if Jesus had come in time He could have healed Lazarus and kept him from dying (Jn. 11:21, 32). Jesus waited, however, because He wanted them to understand and believe the full scope of His power.

He went to Lazarus' tomb, a cave with a rock over the opening, and instructed the mourners to remove the stone. Martha, assuming the worst, warned Him, "Lord, by this time he stinketh: for he hath been dead four days" (Jn. 11:39, KJV).

Jesus nevertheless cried out with a loud voice, "Lazarus, come forth" (v. 43).

The sight that greeted the bewildered mourners might have been humorous if it were not so poignant. Lazarus, "bound hand and foot with wrappings; and his face . . . wrapped around with a cloth," waddled to the cave opening. There he stood, wrapped like a mummy, but alive!

"Unbind him, and let him go," Jesus commanded them (v. 44). As long as the grave clothes enshrouded Lazarus, the aura of death clung to him and hindered him from the full expression of his new life.

The story of Lazarus offers a particularly graphic illustration of our predicament as believers. We have been raised to walk in newness of life (Rom. 6:4). We "joyfully concur with the law of God in the inner man" (Rom. 7:22). Yet we cannot do what we desire (Gal. 5:17). "The wishing is present in [us], but the doing of the good is not" (Rom. 7:18). We are held prisoner by the remnants of the very fallenness from which we have been redeemed (7:22). It is as if we were still bound in our grave clothes. This appendix compares our situation and that of Lazarus in casting off the binding remnants of sin. It offers the apostle Paul's instructions (in Romans 6) for liberation, which involve knowing, reckoning, yielding, obeying, and serving.

We Being Raised Yet Stink

There is, however, an important difference between our situation and the raising of Lazarus. His mummy suit came off immediately. It was merely a linen shroud. Fortunately, the corruption of death—such as the awful stench Martha feared—did not follow Lazarus forth from the grave.

Our predicament, however, cannot be resolved so quickly. It is not just a linen shroud that fastens itself to us, but a full-fledged carcass—Paul calls it "the body of this death" (Rom. 7:24). It is the fleshly sin-principle that casts its pall over our glorious new lives throughout our earthly pilgrimage. It befouls our spiritual atmosphere, surrounding us with the fetid stink of sin. It no longer can dominate us like a ruthless tyrant, but it will plague us with temptation, torment, and grief until we are finally glorified.

That is precisely why we "groan within ourselves, waiting eagerly for our adoption as sons, the redemption of our body" (Rom. 8:23).

While we wait for that final glorious deliverance from sin's presence, we must not live as we did when sin was lord over us. Sin's mastery is broken. Our old self is crucified, so that "we should no longer be slaves to sin" (Rom. 6:6).

While we wait for that final glorious deliverance from sin's presence, we must not live as we did when sin was lord over us.

Don't be confused by the language of that verse. "Should" there does not indicate that emancipation from sin's absolute control is a yet-future *possibility*. Paul is declaring that because our old self is dead, freedom from sin is already an accomplished *reality*. A few verses later, he makes it very clear that this is the present state of every true believer: "Thanks be to God that though you were slaves of sin, you became obedient from the heart to that form of teaching to which you were committed, *having been freed from sin, you became slaves of righteousness*" (Rom. 6:17–18; emphasis added). He reiterates the point once more in verse 22: "Now *having been freed from sin* and enslaved to God, you derive your benefit, resulting in sanctification, and the outcome, eternal life" (emphasis added). "He who has died"—that is, he who is joined with Christ in His death—"is freed from sin" (v. 7). The liberation he is describing is a *fait accompli.*

But as we have seen repeatedly, he is not suggesting that Christians are sinless—or even that they can be. Nor is he suggesting that sin is no longer the problem in Christians' lives. Paul is simply teaching that all believers are released from sin's absolute domination.

We can experience that liberation practically. We can live lives that reflect our new natures. We can shed ourselves of fleshly tendencies by mortifying the deeds of the flesh. Let's look a little more closely at Romans 6 as a way of summarizing and reviewing the practical means by which we can attack and mortify the remnants of sin in our lives.

Know

Fundamental to everything is sound knowledge. "Do you not *know* . . . ?" Paul asks at the outset of the whole discussion. Growth in righteousness and godly living are based on spiritual principles that must be *known* before they can do us any good.

Notice how many times in these verses Paul uses the word *know* and its cognates: "Do you not *know* that all of us who have been baptized into Christ Jesus have been baptized into His death?" (v. 3). "*Knowing* this, that our old self was crucified with Him, that our body of sin might be done away with, that we should no longer be slaves to sin" (v. 6). "*Knowing* that Christ, having been raised from the dead, is never to die again; death no longer is master over Him" (v. 9). "Do you not *know* that when you present yourselves to someone as slaves for obedience, you are slaves of the one whom you obey . . . ?" (v. 16). "Do you not *know*, brethren . . . that the law has jurisdiction over a person as long as he lives?" (7:1; cf. also vv. 7, 14, 18).

It is popular in some circles to denigrate knowledge and elevate passion, mysticism, brotherly love, blind faith, or whatever. Christian doctrine is often set against practical Christianity, as if the two were antithetical. Truth is ignored and harmony exalted. Knowledge is scorned while feeling is elevated. Reason is rejected and sentiment put in its place. Understanding is disdained and gullibility encouraged. That eats away at genuine spiritual maturity, which is always grounded in sound doctrine (cf. Tit. 1:6–9).

Knowledge alone is no virtue, of course. If someone "knows the right thing to do, and does not do it, to him it is sin" (Jas. 4:17). Knowledge without love corrupts the character: "Knowledge makes arrogant, but love edifies" (1 Cor. 8:1). Knowledge not mixed with obedience hardens the heart: "If we go on sinning willfully after receiving the knowledge of the truth, there no longer remains a sacrifice for sins" (Heb. 10:26). Knowledge can be destructive when not tempered with other virtues: "If someone sees you, who have knowledge, dining in an idol's temple, will not his conscience, if he is weak, be strengthened to eat things sacrificed to idols? For through your knowledge he who is weak is ruined, the brother for whose sake Christ died" (1 Cor. 8:10–11).

But *lack* of knowledge is even more deadly. Israel rejected Christ because they had zeal without knowledge (Rom. 10:2). Hosea recorded the Lord's complaint against Israel's spiritual leaders: "My people are destroyed for lack of knowledge. Because you have rejected knowledge, I also will reject you from being My priest. Since you have forgotten the law of your God, I also will forget your children" (Hos. 4:6). Isaiah recorded a similar indictment: "Israel does not know, My people do not understand" (Isa. 1:3).

All spiritual growth is based on *knowledge of truth*. Sound doctrine is crucial to a successful spiritual walk (Tit. 2:1, ff.). Paul told the Colossians that the new self is renewed to true knowledge (Col. 3:10). Knowledge is foundational to our new position in Christ. The entire Christian life is established on knowledge of divine principles, sound doctrine, and biblical truth. Those who repudiate knowledge in effect jettison the most basic means of spiritual growth and health, while leaving themselves vulnerable to a host of spiritual enemies.

And as Paul suggests in Romans 6, if we are to experience victory over sin, it must begin with knowledge. What, specifically, are we to know? Our position in Christ: "Knowing this, that our old self was crucified with Him, that our body of sin might be done away with, that we should no longer be slaves to sin; for he who has died is freed from sin" (Rom. 6:6–7). We must understand the very truths we have focused on throughout this book: that we are united with Christ in His death and resurrection and therefore free from our former enslavement to sin.

Reckon

Fine, you may be thinking to yourself. *Now I know those truths. But like Paul himself I still find myself unable to shake free of sin's influence. What do I do now?* Paul tells us, "Reckon . . . yourselves to be dead indeed unto sin, but alive unto God through Jesus Christ our Lord" (Rom. 6:11, KJV). The word translated "reckon" ("consider" in the NASB) is *logizomai,* which literally means "to calculate or number something." It is the same word Jesus used when He quoted Isaiah 53:12: "He was numbered with transgressors" (Lk. 22:37).

Reckoning in this sense goes beyond knowledge. It moves our faith out of the realm of the purely intellectual and makes it supremely practical. Paul is suggesting that our union with Christ ought to be something more than a theoretical truth. We are to count on it, deem it a reality, consider it done—and act accordingly. "Consider yourselves to be dead to sin, but alive to God in Christ Jesus [and] do not let sin reign in your mortal body that you should obey its lusts" (Rom. 6:11–12).

Reckoning our old self dead is certainly not an easy thing. So much in our experience seems to argue against the truth we know in our hearts. We may be free from sin's dominion, but our daily battle with sin often seems very much like the old slavery. Nevertheless, we must reckon ourselves dead to sin but alive to God. We cannot live as if the old self were still in control.

Nevertheless, we must reckon ourselves dead to sin but alive to God. We cannot live as if the old self were still in control.

It may seem at this point that Paul's advice has something in common with the ideology of the modern "positive thinking" and self-esteem cults. But Paul was not proposing that we play a mere mind game. He was not saying we should seek to convince ourselves of something that is not true. He was not suggesting that we should elevate ourselves in our own minds to a spiritual level we have not actually attained. He was not advising us to shut down our rational minds and dream of something that hasn't really occurred.

On the contrary, he was affirming the absolute truth of the believer's union with Christ, and assuring us that we can live our lives in light of that truth. Our old self *is* dead. God's Word declares it. We must regard it as true.

Too many Christians fail at this point. They think of themselves as hopelessly enslaved to sin. They have been taught that the old nature is still alive in all its fury. They do not understand that Christ has broken the power of sin. And therefore they cannot live victoriously. They do not consider themselves genuinely dead to sin.

That is precisely why I oppose the two-nature dualism that was popularized by *The Scofield Reference Bible*. Since this is probably the predominant view in American evangelicalism today, it is helpful to examine what is being taught.

Scofield believed all Christians have two active natures—"the old or Adamic nature, and the divine nature received through the new birth."[2] These, he taught, are equal but opposing realities that operate in every believer. The old Adamic nature—with its love for sin, its thoroughgoing depravity, all its evil propensities, and its inability to love God or do good—is still alive and powerful. The new divine nature is given only to believers, but once implanted within, it competes with the old nature for control of the will. Therefore, according to this view, every Christian still has the old sinful nature to contend with—but now has a new, godly nature as well. It is a kind of spiritual schizophrenia. It views conversion as not so much a *transformation* of the person but rather the *addition* of a new nature.

One writer who shared Scofield's views on the two natures wrote,

> When the "New Man" is born in the heart of the Believer the "Old Man" does not die. He is still there and very much alive. There are now two natures, diametrically opposed, fighting for the possession of the same body, like two tenants fighting for the possession of the same dwelling house. . . . We must remember that we cannot get rid of the "Old Nature" until the death of our body of "Flesh."[3]

The dualism of that view inevitably frustrates Christian growth. After all, if our old nature is just as alive and powerful as ever, how can we truly consider ourselves dead to sin but alive to God? In fact, it would seem rather dangerous to deem the old self dead if it is actually still "very much alive."

Some people even use the two-nature view as an excuse for their sin. "It is only the old nature that sins," they claim—as if they personally were not responsible.

Indeed, those who hold to the two-nature view have a very hard time with Paul's instructions in Romans 6:11. Because they believe the old sinful self still lives on, by definition they *cannot* reckon themselves dead to sin. They *cannot* regard the old nature as crucified with Christ or believe that the body of sin has been nullified. This is obvious in their writings. The same author I quoted above wrote, "We must remember that while we may starve the Old Man, and he may become very feeble and cause little trouble, and we may reckon him dead, he is *not dead*, and if we begin to feed him again he will revive and recover his strength and give us trouble."[4] That quotation illustrates perfectly why those who hold the two-nature view of the Christian dare not reckon the old self dead. Their system tells them the old man is *not really* dead, and therefore those who *consider* him to be dead feel they may be actually placing themselves in a dangerous position of presumption.

Some people even use the two-nature view as an excuse for their sin. "It is only the old nature that sins," they claim—as if they personally were not responsible. Such a notion wreaks havoc on the conscience and seriously stunts spiritual growth. It disallows personal responsibility and thus dulls the conscience.

R. L. Dabney argued against an early form of the two-nature view more than a century ago. He noted the doctrine's "antinomian tendencies":

If one believes that he has two "real men," or "two natures" in him, he will be tempted to argue that the new man is in no way responsible for the perversity of the old. Here is a perilous deduction. . . . [And if] the old nature never loses any of its strength until death; then the presence, and even the flagrancy of indwelling sin need suggest to the believer no doubts whatever, whether his faith is spurious. How can it be denied that there is here terrible danger of carnal security in sin? How different this from the Bible which says Jas. ii:18, "Show me thy faith without thy works; and I will show thee my faith by my works." If then any professed believer finds the "old man" in undiminished strength, this is proof that he has never "put on the new man."[5]

Scripture does not support the dualistic view. Romans 6:6 clearly says that our old self was crucified with Christ. The person we were before we trusted Christ is no more. The tyranny of sin is nullified. Our nature is *changed*, transformed. We are new creations, not merely the same old creatures with a new side to our personalities. We have a new heart—not an added one, but a whole different one. This, after all, is the promise of the New Covenant: "I will give you a new heart and put a new spirit within you; and *I will remove the heart of stone* from your flesh and give you a heart of flesh" (Ezek. 36:26, emphasis added). This new heart has a *conscience*. It can take charge.

You can count on it. Reckon it to be so. Consider it accomplished.

Yield

"Yield" is the next key word in our quest for freedom from sin: "Let not sin therefore reign in your mortal body, that ye should obey it in the lusts thereof. Neither yield ye your members as instruments of unrighteousness unto sin: but *yield yourselves unto God*, as those that are alive from the dead, and your members as instruments of righteousness unto God" (Rom. 6:12–13, KJV, emphasis added).

As we have noted repeatedly, Christians are no longer dominated and controlled by sin. We are finally able to say no to sin's edicts. We are free from its absolute control. Before we were born again, we did not have that capability. But now sin has no authority to command us.

It can, however, beguile, tantalize, threaten, intimidate, and use every ploy it knows to tempt us. Although overthrown and defeated, it has not been eliminated. It still poses dangers. It does not give up easily. It taunts and torments us. It rages and storms. *But it no longer reigns over us.* And we do not have to yield to it.

Rather we must yield ourselves to a new Lord. "Present yourselves to God as those alive from the dead, and your members as instruments of righteousness to God" (v. 13). The surrender this calls for is a conscious, active submission of all our members to God as instruments of righteousness. In other words, we can use for God's glory the very faculties that sin once dominated.

Notice that Paul speaks of "your mortal body" (v. 12) and "the members of your body" (v. 13). But he has in mind not merely the corporeal body and its physical members. He is actually speaking more particularly of the soul's faculties, such as the mind, emotions, imagination, appetites, and will. Colossians 3:5 spells out precisely what he means: "Mortify therefore your members which are upon the earth; fornication, uncleanness, inordinate affection, evil concupiscence, and covetousness, which is idolatry" (Col. 3:5, KJV). "Members" in that verse clearly does not refer primarily to the physical extremities. It speaks instead of the faculties and activities of "the hidden person of the heart" (cf. 1 Pet. 3:4).

In our thinking, terms like *flesh*, *members*, and *body* tend to represent only the physical components of our beings. We contrast those terms with *heart*, *soul*, and *mind*, which we associate with the immaterial, or spiritual, part of our beings. But Scripture often refers to "the body" when it means the whole person—both the material and immaterial parts included—making no distinction between body and soul. James wrote, "The tongue . . . defiles the entire body" (Jas. 3:6)—that is, it debases the whole person. Jesus said, "The lamp of the body is the eye; if therefore your eye is clear, your whole body will be full of light. But if your eye is bad, your whole body will be full of darkness. If therefore the light that is in you is darkness, how great is the darkness!" (Matt. 6:22–23). "If therefore your whole body is full of light, with no dark part in it, it shall be wholly illumined, as when the lamp illumines you with its rays" (Lk. 11:36). In those verses, the expression "your whole body" refers to the entire mortal soul—the *complete person*—not the literal, tangible flesh and blood.

Likewise throughout Romans 6 and 7 Paul uses the terms *body* and *members* to describe the entire person who is yet unglorified—body, mind, emotions, and will—not just the physical side.

In places the wording can be hard to understand. Paul writes, for example, "I joyfully concur with the law of God in the inner man, but I see a different law in the members of my body, waging war against the law of my mind, and making me a prisoner of the law of sin which is in my members" (Rom. 7:22–23). There he seems to be contrasting the "inner man" with the physical body, as if he were suggesting that his flesh and blood wage war against his mind. Some readers wrongly assume this means the mind is good but the physical body is evil. That is the very kind of dualism the gnostic heretics preached. But that is not at all the point Paul was making. He was simply saying that his mortal members—including his body, his passions, his appetites, his emotions, and surely in some sense even his mind—were in conflict with his "inner man"—the new, immortal, vibrant, Spirit-wrought principle of righteousness that made him love and affirm the law of God. He was using the expressions "members of my body" and "inner man" as a convenient shorthand to contrast the flesh principle with the new person.

Our mortality—"the mortal body," as Paul uses the term—is the only ground on which sin can attack us. Sin cannot claim our eternal souls. One day our mortal selves—body and mind—will be "swallowed up by life" (2 Cor. 5:4). The perishable will put on imperishability (1 Cor. 15:53–54). That is what we wait eagerly for: "the redemption of our body" (Rom. 8:23). "The Lord Jesus Christ . . . will transform the body of our humble state into conformity with the body of His glory" (Phil. 3:20–21). Then, and only then, we will be forever out of sin's reach. But while we are still mortal, we are subject to corruption.

This "body of our humble state" and all its faculties are still susceptible to the lure of sin. We wage a continual warfare against sin in our mortal minds and bodies. We must not "go on presenting [our members] to sin as instruments of unrighteousness" (Rom. 6:13). Instead, we must "present [our] bodies a living and holy sacrifice, acceptable to God, which is [our] spiritual service of worship" (Rom. 12:1). We must "present [ourselves] to God as those alive from the dead, and [our] members as instruments of righteousness to God" (6:13).

"Sin shall not be master over you, for you are not under law, but under grace" (Rom. 6:14).

Paul inserts a glorious promise at this point: "Sin shall not be master over you, for you are not under law, but under grace" (v. 14). We are free from sin's condemnation because of our justification. But grace also frees us from sin's day-to-day domination, so that we can become "slaves of righteousness" (v. 18)—so that we can obey a new Lord.

Obey

The very purpose of grace is to free us from sin—"so we too might walk in newness of life" (v. 4). Grace is much more than mere forgiveness for our sins, or a free ride to heaven. Grace certainly does not leave us under sin's dominion. Saved by grace, "we are [God's own] workmanship, created in Christ Jesus for good works, which God prepared beforehand, that we should walk in them" (Eph. 2:10). Grace "[instructs] us to deny ungodliness and worldly desires and to live sensibly, righteously and godly in the present age" (Tit. 2:12). This is the very reason Christ gave Himself for us: "That He might redeem us from every lawless deed and purify for Himself a people for His own possession, zealous for good deeds" (v. 14).

Yet it seems there have always been those who have corrupted the grace of God by turning it into lasciviousness (cf. Jude 4). They characterize grace as total freedom, but they themselves are enslaved to corruption (2 Pet. 2:19). Thus they nullify the grace of God (cf. Gal. 2:21).

"The true grace of God" (cf. 1 Pet. 5:12) does not offer freedom from moral restraint. Grace is no sanction for sin. On the contrary, it grants the believer freedom *from* sin. It frees us from the law and from sin's penalty, but it also liberates us from sin's absolute control. It frees us to obey God.

Anticipating the thoughts of those who misunderstand God's grace, Paul echoes his query from Romans 6:1: "What then? Shall we sin because we are not under law but under grace?" (v. 15). And he answers once again emphatically, "May it never be!"

His argument against the objection is an appeal to common sense: "Do you not know that when you present yourselves to someone as slaves for obedience, you are slaves of the one whom you obey, either of sin resulting in death, or of obedience resulting in righteousness?" (v. 16). In other words, if you present yourself as a slave to do sin's bidding, you only demonstrate that you are still under sin's dominion. The clear implication is that those truly saved by grace would not willingly choose to return to the old slavery.

In fact, the phrase "present yourselves" suggests a conscious, active, willing *choice* of obedience. It pictures a soldier who presents himself with all his weapons to his commander, prepared to do the master's bidding. It is a voluntary, deliberate surrender of oneself and one's members to a life of service—either to "sin resulting in death, or [to] obedience resulting in righteousness." Here Paul is calling for a deliberate, willful, conscious choice of obedience. For unbelievers, there is no choice. They are enslaved to sin and cannot choose otherwise. Here Paul is suggesting that genuine Christians also have only one choice.

In other words, those who choose to serve sin as its slaves are in fact still enslaved to sin—they have never experienced God's grace. "When you present yourselves to someone as slaves for obedience, you are slaves of the one whom you obey." That at first may sound like a tautology, but a paraphrase may help explain the apostle's meaning: "When you voluntarily relinquish yourself to sin and its service, you give evidence that you were never freed from sin's dominion to begin with. Your pattern of life proves who your true master is—whether sin unto death, or obedience that results in righteousness." Or, as Peter wrote, "By what a man is overcome, by this he is enslaved" (2 Pet. 2:18–19).

In Romans 5 Paul made precisely the same point, only arguing in reverse. There he suggested that sin and death reign over all those in Adam (5:12); but grace, righteousness, and eternal life reign over the one who is in Christ (vv. 17–20).

In Romans 6, Paul suggests that everyone is a slave who has a master. Fallen man likes to declare that he is the master of his fate and the captain of his soul. But no one really is. All people are either under Satan's lordship and in bondage to sin, or they are under

Christ's lordship and servants of righteousness. There is no neutral ground, and no one can serve two masters (Matt. 6:24). "If we would know to which of these two families we belong, we must inquire to which of these two masters we yield our obedience."[6]

His point is that true Christians cannot be anything but slaves of righteousness.

Again, Paul is not telling the Romans that Christians *ought to be* slaves of righteousness. His point is that true Christians *cannot be anything but* slaves of righteousness. They were taken out of sin's servitude for precisely that purpose: "Thanks be to God that though you were slaves of sin, you became obedient from the heart to that form of teaching to which you were committed, and having been freed from sin, you became slaves of righteousness" (Rom. 6:17–18). That corresponds exactly to what the apostle John wrote: "No one who is born of God practices sin, because His seed abides in him; and he cannot sin, because he is born of God. By this the children of God and the children of the devil are obvious: anyone who does not practice righteousness is not of God" (1 Jn. 3:9–10).

For the Christian, the life of slavery to sin is *past*. Sin cannot continue to be the chief characteristic of our lives. Fleshly disobedience interrupts the new life frequently and we do sin. At times sin may *appear* to dominate a Christian's life completely (as was the case when David sinned). But all true believers still have a new and holy nature. They hate their sin and love righteousness. They cannot live in unbroken sin or hardened rebellion against God and enjoy it. That would be a contradiction of who they are (cf. 1 Jn. 3:9).

Serve

Paul makes very clear that the obedience he is calling for is a lifelong servitude to God:

> Just as you presented your members as slaves to impurity and to lawlessness, resulting in further lawlessness, so now present

your members as slaves to righteousness, resulting in sanctification. For when you were slaves of sin, you were free in regard to
righteousness. Therefore what benefit were you then deriving
from the things of which you are now ashamed? For the outcome of those things is death. But now having been freed from
sin and enslaved to God, you derive your benefit, resulting in
sanctification, and the outcome, eternal life (Rom. 6:19–22).

In other words, Christians should serve righteousness exactly like
we once served sin—as slaves.

Paul has moved from the issue of our position ("consider yourselves to be dead to sin," v. 11) to the matter of our practice ("now
present your members as slaves to righteousness," v. 19). Obviously,
our position ought to determine our practice.

> ## *In other words, Christians should serve righteousness exactly like we once served sin—as slaves.*

Just as sin once led us into impurity and lawlessness, "resulting in further lawlessness" (v. 19), now righteousness results in
our ever-increasing progress in sanctification. Martyn Lloyd-Jones
wrote,

> As you go on living this righteous life, and practising it with all
> your might and energy, and all your time . . . you will find that
> the process that went on before, in which you went on from bad
> to worse and became viler and viler, is entirely reversed. You
> will become cleaner and cleaner, and purer and purer, and ho-
> lier and holier, and more and more conformed unto the image of
> the Son of God.[7]

It is impossible to stand still spiritually and morally. Everyone is
moving one way or the other—either sinking deeper into sin and
degradation, or gloriously progressing toward Christlikeness.

After all, life in Christ *should* be dramatically different from our lives before conversion: "When you were slaves of sin, you were free in regard to righteousness." If what you really desire now is freedom from moral restraint, you are no Christian. You are still a servant of sin.

True righteousness can neither command nor instruct those who are still captive to sin. They serve a different master. Though many of them put on a show of *self*-righteousness—as was true of Paul himself before his conversion—the works of the flesh have absolutely nothing to do with real righteousness. Scripture uses some of its strongest language to condemn such fleshly efforts. Isaiah wrote, "All our righteous deeds are like a filthy garment"—literally, "like a menstrual cloth" (Isa. 64:6). Paul called his pre-Christian self-righteousness "dung" (Phil. 3:8, KJV).

The real fruit of sin's mastery includes "immorality, impurity, sensuality, idolatry, sorcery, enmities, strife, jealousy, outbursts of anger, disputes, dissentions, factions, envying, drunkenness, carousing, and things like these." And the ultimate result is eternal condemnation: " . . . of which I forewarn you just as I have forewarned you that those who practice such things shall not inherit the kingdom of God" (Gal. 5:19–21). "Therefore what benefit were you then deriving from the things of which you are now ashamed? For the outcome of those things is death" (Rom. 6:21).

True faith bears exactly the opposite fruit. "Now having been freed from sin and enslaved to God, you derive your benefit, resulting in sanctification, and the outcome, eternal life" (v. 22).

"Freed from sin and enslaved to God" is as good a description of the Christian life as any I know. Of course it does not mean believers are incapable of sinning. But it *does* mean they are no longer enslaved to sin, no longer helpless to answer its attacks, no longer loving darkness rather than light.

What Paul has given us in this brief chapter is a courageous call to stand firm in the face of sin's onslaughts. Believers need to *know* that they are united with Christ in His death and resurrection, and therefore freed from sin's dominion. They need to *reckon* that their union with Christ means the old self is dead, nullified, no longer able to demand obedience to its sinful lusts. They need to *yield* themselves to God and surrender all their members—body, mind, emotions, and the whole person—to God as instruments of righteousness. They need to *obey* Him as their new Lord. And they need to *serve* Him with the same unquestioning obedience they once gave to sin.

Though sin is a defeated enemy, though we wage our battle against it from a position of victory, it is still a life-and-death struggle.

That is Paul's formula for victory. It calls for boldness, determination, and an intelligent, informed faith. It assumes that we love God and desire to see His righteousness working in our lives. It offers freedom from sin's absolute authority and the means to defeat sin in our daily walk.

But it does not assume that the process is easy or that glorious victory will always be our daily experience. Paul certainly was not suggesting that the Christian walk is never marked by defeat or failure. As we have noted throughout, all we need to do is read on to Romans 7, and it becomes evident that Paul's experience with his own sin was often deeply frustrating to him: "I am not practicing what I would like to do, but I am doing the very thing I hate" (v. 15). "That which I am doing, I do not understand . . . for I know that nothing good dwells in me, that is, in my flesh; for the wishing is present in me, but the doing of the good is not" (vv. 15, 18). "The good that I wish, I do not do; but I practice the very evil that I do not wish" (v. 19). "Evil is present in me, the one who wishes to do good" (v. 21). "Wretched man that I am! Who will set me free from the body of this death?" (v. 24).

The truth is, when we look into our own hearts, every one of us must echo those words of frustration. Though sin is a defeated enemy, though we wage our battle against it from a position of victory, it is still a life-and-death struggle. And it is a battle we must continue to take to the enemy as we mortify sin and attack its remaining influence in our lives.

Appendix 2

An Appeal for a Good Conscience

by Richard Sibbes[1]

And corresponding to that, baptism now saves you—not the removal of dirt from the flesh, but an appeal to God for a good conscience—through the resurrection of Jesus Christ (1 Pet. 3:21).

The context of these words from 1st Peter is this: the blessed apostle had just spoken of those who perished in the flood, and of Noah's salvation in the ark ("few, that is, eight persons, were brought safely through the water"). Then he mentions baptism ("corresponding to that, baptism now saves you").

Christ is the same yesterday, today, and forever (Heb. 13:8). He has always taken care to save His Noahs in the midst of destruction. Salvation is a work that He has carried since the beginning of the world. There were two cities prefigured in Cain and Abel. And God has always communicated Himself differently to the citizens of the two cities. "The Lord knows how to rescue the godly" (2 Pet. 2:9). All who were ever saved were saved by Christ, and all had different sacrifices that foreshadowed Christ.

For those who are not His, those of Cain's posterity, God communicates Himself in a contrary way to them: He destroys them.

But to come to the words "and corresponding to that, baptism now saves you. . . . " The saving of Noah in the ark was an illustration of baptism; for as baptism pictures Christ, so did the saving of Noah in the ark. They correspond to one another in many things.

First, as everyone who was not in the ark perished, so shall everyone perish who is not in Christ (those not engrafted into Him by faith). Baptism is an emblem of that engrafting.

Second, as the same water in the flood *preserved* Noah in the ark and *destroyed* all the old world, so the same blood and death of Christ kills all our spiritual enemies. They are all drowned in the Red Sea of Christ's blood, but it preserves His children. There were three main deluges in the Old Testament, which all prefigure Christ: the flood that drowned the old world; the passing through the Red Sea; and the waters of Jordan. In all these God's people were saved and the enemies of God's people destroyed. That is what Micah the prophet alludes when he says, "Thou wilt cast all their sins into the depths of the sea" (7:19). He alludes to Pharaoh and his host drowned in the bottom of the sea. They sunk as lead; so all our sins, which are our enemies if we be in Christ, they sink as lead.

Third, as Noah was mocked by the wretched world while he was making the ark, so all are derided who flee to Christ for salvation.

Yet Noah was thought a wise man when the flood came. Likewise when destruction comes, they are wise who have secured their standing in Christ before. There are many such resemblances between the ark and baptism. I name but a few, and move on.

Outward Ritual Is Not Enough

"Corresponding to that, baptism now saves you." Here, first of all, in a word, is a description of the means of salvation, how we are saved: "baptism now saves you."

Then he anticipates an objection: "—not the removal of dirt from the flesh," the outward part of baptism.

Then he sets down *how* baptism saves us: "but an appeal to God for a good conscience."

And then the ground of it: "through the resurrection of Jesus Christ."

All that I pass over, so that I may come to that which I specially intend. I come, therefore, to the anticipated objection, which I will not speak much of. But I will say something, because it is a useful point.

The ritual of baptism does not save. When he said that baptism saves us, he said it is *not* that baptism which is a removal of dirt from the flesh—insinuating that baptism has two parts. There is a double baptism: the outward, which is the washing of the body; the inward, which is the washing of the soul. The outward does not save without the inward. Therefore he deflects the notion, lest they should think that all who are baptized outwardly with water are saved by Christ.

The danger of looking too much to externals. The apostle knew that people are naturally prone to give too much to outward things. The devil is an extremist. He labors to bring people to extremes, to make the outward rituals idols, or to make them idle rituals. That is, he wants us to focus so intently on the external aspects of our faith (such as baptism and the Lord's Supper) that we make the ceremonies themselves objects of idolatry—or else get us to care so little for them that they mean nothing at all. The devil gets what he wants either way.

The apostle knew the disease of the times, especially in his time. People attributed too much to outward things. The apostle Paul, writing to the Galatians, twice repeats it: "Neither is circumcision anything, nor uncircumcision, but a new creation" (Gal. 6:15; cf. 5:6). You stand too much on outward things, he was saying. What counts with God is the "new creation."

Likewise in the Old Testament, when God prescribed both outward and inward worship, they attributed too much to the outward, and let the inward alone. As in Psalm 50:16–17, God complains how they served Him: "What right have you to tell of My statutes, and to take My covenant in your mouth? For you hate discipline, and you cast My words behind you." Also in Isaiah 1:13–14 and 66:3, we see God's decisive dealing with them: "Bring your worthless offerings no longer, incense is an abomination to Me. . . . I hate your new moon festivals and your appointed feasts." And, "He who kills an ox is like one who slays a man; he who sacrifices a lamb is like the one who breaks a dog's neck; he who offers a grain offering is like one who offers swine's blood; he who burns incense is like the one who blesses an idol"— yet these were sacrifices anointed by God Himself. What was the reason for this? They played the hypocrites with God, and gave Him only the shell. They brought Him outward performances. They attributed too much to that, and left the spiritual part that God most esteems.

Notice also how our Savior Christ rebukes the Pharisees: "Do not suppose that you can say to yourselves, 'We have Abraham for our father'" (Matt. 3:9). They boasted too much of their outward privileges. You see throughout the Scriptures that people who don't belong to God are especially apt to attribute too much to outward things. They ought to combine that with the inward, which they neglect.

Why people overemphasize external religion. There are always two parts of God's service, outward and inward. The inward aspect is hard for flesh and blood to lay hold of. As in baptism there are two parts, outward and inward washing; and hearing the Word involves both the outward man and the inward soul, bowing to hear what God says; so in the Lord's Supper, there is outward receiving of bread and wine, and inward making of a covenant with God. Now people give too much to the outward, and think that God owes them something for it. But they neglect the inward because they are protecting their own lust.

But more particularly, the reason is in corrupt nature.

First, because the outward part is easy and glorious to the eye of the world. Everyone can see the sacrament administered, everyone can see when one comes and hears the Word of God.

Second, people rest in the outward ritual because it does something to mollify the conscience, which would clamor if they did nothing religious, or if they were direct atheists. Therefore they say, *We will hear the Word, and perform the outward things.* But being loath to search into the bottom of their conscience, they stop with the outward things, and satisfy conscience by that. Those and similar reasons explain why so many people attend to external religion only.

Application. Let us take notice of this tendency to focus on externals; let us know that God does not regard the outward without the inward. More than that, He abhors it. If God can despise the worship that He Himself appointed, how much more must He loathe the empty devices and ceremonies of men's own devising? The liturgy of papal religion, for example, is but a barren external. They labor to *put off* God with the work done. Their doctrine is tailor-made for corrupt human nature. They teach that the sacrament administered confers grace regardless of the person's state of heart. In their system the elements themselves confer grace, as if grace could be transmitted through a lifeless substance. The whole process makes people dote too much on outward things. But our text shows that the outward part of baptism without the inward is nothing: "not the removal of dirt from the flesh, but an appeal to God for a good conscience," says Peter.

Let us labor, therefore, in all our services to God, to rivet our hearts especially on the spiritual part. As Samuel told Saul, "Behold, to obey is better than sacrifice, and to hearken than the fat of rams" (1 Sam. 15:22). And God said through the prophet Hosea, "I delight in loyalty rather than sacrifice, and in the knowledge of God rather than burnt offerings" (Hos. 6:6). Too many Christians are content to do the externals, which is the easy part of religion.

But what is not done in the heart is not truly done. "God is spirit, and those who worship Him must worship in spirit and truth" (Jn. 4:24). There is a kind of divine power necessary in all true worship that goes beyond anything the outward person can bring. In *hearing* divine truth a divine power is required to make a person hear as he or she should (1 Cor. 2:9–15). Similarly in *worship*, more is required than the outward man is able to supply. There is both form and power in all the parts of religion. Let us not rest in the form, but labor for the power.

We see what kind of persons those were in 2 Timothy 3:5: "Holding to a form of godliness, although they have denied its power." Paul names a catalogue of sins there: they were "lovers of pleasure rather than lovers of God." Nevertheless, these people wanted a form of religion, although they denied the power of it. But I hasten to the issue I want to dwell on.

Appealing to God for a Good Conscience

After removing people's false confidence in external religion, Peter positively sets down what it is that *does* save: It is "an appeal to God for a good conscience." The holy apostle might have said, "Not water baptism, but the baptism by the Spirit into Christ's Body" (1 Cor. 12:13). He might have said, "Not putting off the filth of the body, but putting off the filth of the soul." Instead he names the act of the soul that lays hold of God's gracious salvation—"an appeal to God for a good conscience." Of course he is speaking of *faith*.

God must be satisfied before conscience can be satisfied. God is satisfied with the death of the mediator; so when we are sprinkled with the blood of Christ—when the death of Christ is applied to us— our conscience is satisfied too. That is how "the blood of Christ, who through the eternal Spirit offered Himself without blemish to God, cleanse[s our] conscience from dead works to serve the living God" (Heb. 9:14).

The "appeal to God for a good conscience," then, is the same thing as faith. Peter is describing the attitude of those who engage themselves to believe and to live as Christians.

When we believe, our conscience is made good. If Satan lays anything to our charge, we can answer with a good conscience. "Who will bring a charge against God's elect? God is the one who justifies; who is the one who condemns? Christ Jesus is He who died, yes, rather who was raised, who is at the right hand of God, who also intercedes for us" (Rom. 8:33–34). We may, with a heart sprinkled with the blood of Christ, answer all objections, and triumph against all enemies. We may "draw near with confidence to the throne of grace, that we may receive mercy and may find grace to help in time of need" (Heb. 4:16).

"A good conscience" in the sense Peter employs the term, then, is a conscience cleansed from the defilement of sin, set free to serve God. Only true Christians have such a conscience. It is a conscience that looks to God and will ultimately answer to Him. How can we know if we are "in Christ," recipients of God's saving grace and favor? Conscience is set in us for this very purpose, to tell us what we are doing, and with what motives we are doing it, and what our standing is before God. If you want to test your spiritual health, ask simply whether your conscience is set toward God.

If you are righteous, honorable, and good because your conscience responds to God's commands, it is a good conscience. But if you are doing good works or religious ritual just so that others will see, those are not from a good conscience (Matt. 6:5–6, 16–18). A good conscience holds us accountable simply because God commands it. The conscience is God's deputy in the heart of a believer.

Therefore what we do from a good conscience we do from the heart. When we do something grudgingly, not out of love, and not from the heart, that is not from a good conscience. A healthy conscience looks not merely to *what* we do, but it examines *why* we do it as well—whether it is out of love for God and a desire to obey, or from a sense of resentful obligation.

A good conscience renounces and denies *all* sin. Those, therefore, who labor to feed their corruptions while thinking they are Christians contradict their profession of faith. Those who feed their eyes with vanity and their ears with filthy discourse; those who allow their feet to carry them to places where they infect their souls; those who, instead of renouncing their sins, maintain them—what shall we think of them? Can they think to be saved by Christ when they live with a defiled conscience?

David prayed, "Restore to me the joy of Thy salvation, and sustain me with a willing spirit" (Ps. 51:12). He lost that joy and willingness by sin. For when we deliberately sin against conscience, we stop the mouth of our prayers, so that we cannot go to God. We stop the mouth of conscience, so that we cannot go *boldly* to God. Let us labor to be pliable to the Spirit. Let us submit to God in all that we are exhorted to do. And let us yield the obedience of faith to all His promises. That is what it means to have a good conscience. Therefore let us resolve to take this course if we would attain a good conscience.

Let us examine ourselves carefully so that our consciences may be convinced of the sin that is in us. Let us put questions to ourselves: *Do I believe? Or have I merely placated my own heart without satisfying God? Do I obey? Do I willingly cast myself into the mold of God's Word and willingly obey all that I hear? Or am I deceiving myself?* Put those questions to your own heart. "For God is greater than our heart, and knows all things" (1 Jn. 3:20). If we answer God with reservations (*I will obey God in this, but not in that; I will go along with Christ as long as I don't have to give up a favorite sin*) that is not the answer of a good conscience. What is done for God must be done wholeheartedly and without reservation. If our hearts balk, we do not have a good conscience. Partial obedience is no obedience at all. To single out easy things that do not oppose our lusts or threaten our pride is not the obedience God calls for. Our obedience must be universal to all His commands. Therefore let us search ourselves, and propound searching questions to ourselves, whether we believe and obey or not, and what are our motives in doing so.

The life of many is nothing but a breach of their profession of faith. What will they have to look for at the hour of death, and in the day of judgment? Can they possibly hope that God should keep His promise with them to give them life everlasting, when they never had grace to keep any commitment to Him? How can they look for God's grace then, when they have spurned His grace here, and their whole life has been a satisfying of their base lusts? If your profession of faith is meaningless now, it will be meaningless at the judgment. Fetch that argument against sin when you are tempted.

On the other hand, when you fail, do not let Satan tempt you to discouragement, but come and cast yourself on Christ. Faith and repentance are not one-time acts; you must live your life believing and repenting.

The Advantage of a Pure Conscience

What a comfort to have a good conscience! It will uphold us in sickness, in death, and at the day of judgment. Let the devil object what he can; let our own unbelieving thoughts object what they can—if we have a renewed, sanctified conscience, it can answer all.

Appendix 2: An Appeal for a Good Conscience

Though we be ever so vexed in this world, we are never truly over-come until our conscience is cracked. If our conscience stands up-right, we conquer, and are more than conquerors.

Conscience is either the greatest friend or the greatest enemy in the world. When it knows we have obeyed God in all things, con-science is a friend that speaks to God on our behalf. Then again at the hour of death, what a comfort a good conscience will be! And especially at the day of judgment—a sincere heart, a conscience that has labored to obey the gospel—it can look God in the face.

A Christian that has the answer of a good conscience, has Christ to be his ark in all deluges. Christ saves us not only from hell and damnation, but in all the miseries of this life.

But for those who live in rebellion and thus defile their con-science, alas! What comfort can such as these have? Their con-science tells them that their lives do not witness for God, but they rebel against Him. Their hearts tell them they cannot look to heaven for comfort. They carry a hell in their bosom, a guilty con-science. Those that have their conscience thus stained, especially those who deliberately live in sin—they can look for nothing but vengeance from God.

In times of trouble, and at the hour of death it is shown that they are the wisest people who kept their conscience pure and kept their covenant with God. Their faith is not external ceremony only—it emanates from a pure heart and a clear conscience. Let us bind our consciences to closer obedience.

Appendix 3

Searching Your Conscience

by Jonathan Edwards[1]

Search me, O God, and know my heart: try me, and know my thoughts: and see if there be any wicked way in me, and lead me in the way everlasting (Ps. 139:23–24, KJV).

Psalm 139 is a meditation on the omniscience of God. God views and perfectly knows *everything*. The psalmist represents that perfect knowledge by affirming that God knows all our *actions* ("Thou dost know when I sit down and when I rise up," v. 2); all our *thoughts* ("Thou dost understand my thought from afar," v. 2); all our *words* ("Even before there is a word on my tongue, Behold, O Lord, Thou dost know it all," v. 4).

Then he illustrates the impossibility of fleeing from the divine presence:

> Where can I go from Thy Spirit? Or where can I flee from Thy presence? If I ascend to heaven, Thou art there; if I make my bed in Sheol, behold, Thou art there. If I take the wings of the dawn, if I dwell in the remotest part of the sea, even there Thy hand will lead me, and Thy right hand will lay hold of me. If I say, "Surely the darkness will overwhelm me, and the light around me will be night," even the darkness is not dark to Thee, and the night is as bright as the day. Darkness and light are alike to Thee (vv. 7–12).

Then he speaks of the knowledge God had of him before he was even born:

> Thou didst form my inward parts; thou didst weave me in my mother's womb. . . . My frame was not hidden from Thee, when I was made in secret, and skillfully wrought in the depths of the earth. Thine eyes have seen my unformed substance; and in Thy book they were all written, the days that were ordained for me, when as yet there was not one of them (vv. 13, 15–16).

After this the psalmist observes what must be inferred as a necessary consequence of God's omniscience: He will slay the wicked (v. 19).

Finally, the psalmist makes a practical application of his meditation on God's omniscience: he begs God to search and test him, and see if there is any wicked way in him, and lead him in the everlasting way.

Obviously, the psalmist was not imploring God to search him so that *God* could gain any information. The whole point of the psalm is to declare that God already knows everything. Therefore, the psalmist must be praying for God to search him so that *the psalmist himself* might see and be informed of the sin in his own heart.

David obviously had examined his own heart and ways, but he did not trust that. He was still fearful that there might be some unknown sin in him that had escaped his own searching, so he cried to God to examine him.

Elsewhere, David wrote, "Who can discern his errors? Acquit me of hidden faults" (Ps. 19:12). By "hidden faults" he meant sins that were secret to himself—those sins that were in him that he was not aware of.

All of us ought to be concerned to know whether we live in ways of sin without even knowing it. Whether we entertain some secret lust or neglect some spiritual duty, our hidden sins are just as offensive to God and just as dishonoring to Him as the open, flagrant, known sins. Since we are prone to sin anyway and our natural hearts are full of sin, we must take special care to avoid those sins that are presumptuous, unintentional, and done in ignorance.

Why People Live in Sin Without Knowing It

Our trouble in seeing whether there be any wicked way in us is not because we lack external light. God has certainly not failed to tell us plainly and abundantly what wicked ways are. He has given us ample commandments to show us what we ought to do or not do, and these are clearly set before us in His Word. So our difficulty in knowing our own hearts is *not* because we lack the proper guidelines.

How *can* people live in ways that displease God—yet seem completely insensitive and go on utterly oblivious to their own sin? Several factors contribute to this evil tendency of humanity:

The blinding, deceitful nature of sin. The human heart is full of sin and corruption, and corruption has a spiritually blinding effect. Sin always carries a degree of darkness with it. The more it prevails, the more it darkens and deludes the mind. It blinds us to the reality of what is in our own hearts. Again, the problem is not at all that we lack the light of God's truth. The light shines clearly enough around us, but the fault is in our own eyes; they are darkened and blinded by a deadly disability that results from sin.

Sin easily deceives because it controls the human will, and that colors the judgment. Where lust prevails, it disposes the mind to approve. Where sin influences our preferences, that sin seems pleasing and good. The mind is naturally prejudiced to think whatever is pleasing is right. Therefore when a sinful desire gains the will, it also prejudices the understanding. And the more a person walks in sin, the more that person's mind will probably be darkened and blinded. That is how sin gains its mastery of people.

Therefore when people are unaware of their own sin, it can be extremely difficult to make them see the wrongness of it. After all, the same evil desires that lead them into sin blind them in it. The more an angry person gives in to malice or envy, the more those sins blind the understanding to approve of them. The more a man hates his neighbor, the more he will be disposed to think that he has good cause to hate, and that the neighbor is hateful, and that he deserves to be hated, and that it is not his duty to love him. The more a man's impure lust prevails, the more sweet and pleasant the sin will appear, and the more he will be inclined to think there is no evil in it.

Likewise, the more a person covets material things, the more likely he is to think himself excusable in doing so. He will tell himself that he *needs* certain things and cannot do without them. If they are necessary, he reasons, it is no sin to desire them. All the lusts of the human heart can be justified in such a way. And the more they prevail, the more they blind the mind and influence the judgment to approve of them. That is why Scripture calls worldly appetites "lusts of deceit" (Eph. 4:22). Even godly people may for a time be blinded and deluded by lust, so that they live in a way which is displeasing to God.

Lusts also stir up the carnal mind to invent excuses for sinful practices. Human nature is very subtle when it comes to rationalizing sin. Some people are so strongly devoted to their wickedness that when conscience troubles them about it, they will rack their brains to find arguments to stop the mouth of conscience and make themselves believe they may proceed lawfully in a sinful practice.

Self-love also prejudices people to condone their own sin. People do not like to condemn themselves. They are naturally prejudiced in their own favor. So they will look for good names by which to call their sinful dispositions and practices. They will make them virtuous—or at least they will make them innocent. They label covetousness "prudence" or call greed "business savvy." If they rejoice at another's calamity, they pretend it is because they hope it will do the person good. If they drink too much, it is because their constitutions require it. If they backbite or talk against their neighbor, they claim it is only zeal against sin. If they get into a dispute, they call their stubbornness conscience, and categorize their petty disagreements as matters of principle. Thus they find good names for all their evil ways.

People tend to shape their principles according to their practices rather than vice versa. Rather than allowing their behavior to conform to their consciences, they will expend tremendous energy trying to get their consciences to conform to their behavior.

Because sin is so deceitful, and because we have so much sin dwelling in our hearts, it is difficult for us to judge our own ways and practices righteously. On this account we should make diligent self-examination and be much concerned to know whether there is any wicked way in us. "Take care, brethren, lest there should be in any one of you an evil, unbelieving heart, in falling away from the living God. But encourage one another day after day, as long as it is still called 'Today,' lest any one of you be hardened by the deceitfulness of sin" (Heb. 3:12–13).

People more easily see faults in others than in themselves. When they see others do wrong, they immediately condemn them—even while excusing themselves for the very same sin! (cf. Rom. 2:1). We all see the specks in others' eyes better than the beams in our own. "Every man's way is right in his own eyes" (Prov. 21:2). "The heart is more deceitful than all else and is desperately sick; who can understand it?" (Jer. 17:9). We cannot trust our own hearts in this matter. Instead, we must keep a protective eye on ourselves, interrogate our own hearts carefully, and cry to God that he will search us thoroughly. "He who trusts in his own heart is a fool" (Prov. 28:26).

The subtlety of Satan. The devil works hand in hand with our own deceitful lusts. He labors to blind us to our own faults. He continually endeavors to lead us into sin, then works with our carnal minds to flatter us with the idea we are better than we are. He thus blinds the conscience. He is the prince of darkness. Blinding and deceiving have been his work ever since he began it with our first parents.

The power of habit. Some people are oblivious to the sins they practice out of habit. Habitual sins often stupefy the mind, so that sins that once pricked the conscience begin to seem harmless.

The example of others. Some people become desensitized to their own sin because they let popular opinion dictate their standards. They look to the behavior of others to discern what is right and wrong. But society is so tolerant of sin that many sins have become destigmatized. Things that displease God and are abominations in His sight appear innocent when viewed through the eyes of popular opinion. Perhaps we see them practiced by those whom we esteem highly, by our superiors, and by those who are accounted wise. That greatly slants the mind in favor of them and diminishes the sense of their evil. It is especially dangerous when godly men, respected Christian leaders, are seen engaging in sinful practices. That especially tends to harden the observer's heart and blind the mind with respect to any evil habit.

Incomplete obedience. Those who obey God halfheartedly or incompletely are in great danger of living in undetected sin. Some professing Christians neglect half of their spiritual duties while concentrating on the other half. Perhaps their thoughts will be wholly taken up with secret prayer, Bible reading, public worship, meditation, and other religious duties—while ignoring moral duties, such as their responsibilities to their spouse, their children, or their neighbors.

They know they must not defraud their neighbor, lie, or fornicate. But they seem not to consider what an evil it is to talk against others lightly, to take up a reproach against a neighbor, to contend and quarrel with people, to live hypocritically before their families, or to neglect their children's spiritual instruction.

Such people may seem very conscientious in some things—those branches of their duty on which they keep their eye—but they may entirely neglect other important branches.

How to Discover the Unknown Sin Within

As we have observed, it is naturally very difficult to assess our own sin honestly. But if we are sufficiently concerned about it, and if we are strict and thorough in searching our own hearts, we can, for the most part, discover the sin within. Persons who want to please and obey God, with all the light we enjoy, certainly do not need to go on in the ways of sin through ignorance.

It is true that our hearts are exceedingly deceitful. But God, in His holy Word, has given sufficient light for the state of darkness we are in. By thorough care and inquiry, we may know our spiritual responsibilities, and we can know whether we are living in any sinful way. Everyone with any true love for God will be glad for biblical assistance in this inquiry. Such persons are deeply concerned to walk in all things as God would have them walk, so as to please and honor Him. If their lives are in any way offensive to God, they will be glad to know it and would by no means choose to have their own sin concealed from them.

Also, those who sincerely inquire, *What shall I do to be saved?* will want to identify the sin in their lives. For their sin is what keeps them from Christ.

There are two means by which we come to the knowledge of our own sin:

Knowledge of God's law. If you desire to know whether you live in some unknown sin, you must become thoroughly acquainted with what God requires of you. In Scripture God has given us a true and perfect guide by which we ought to walk. He has expressed His precepts clearly and abundantly, so that we might be able to know—despite our own spiritual darkness and disadvantages—precisely what He requires of us. What a full and abundant revelation of God's mind we have in the Scriptures! How plain it is in instructing us how to behave! How often the precepts are repeated! And how explicitly they are revealed in so many various forms so that we might fully understand them!

But what good is all that if we neglect God's revelation and make no effort to become acquainted with it? What good is it to have godly principles yet not know them? Why should God reveal His mind to us if we don't care enough to know what it is?

Yet the only way we can know whether we are sinning is by knowing His moral law: "By the law is the knowledge of sin" (Rom. 3:20). Therefore if we don't want to go on displeasing God, we ought to study diligently the principles of right and wrong He has revealed.

We ought to read and search the Holy Scriptures much. And we ought to do it with the intention of knowing our *whole* duty, so that the Word of God may be "a lamp unto our feet, and a light unto our paths" (Ps. 119:105).

That being so, it is clear that most people are very much guilty simply because of their negligence of spiritual duties. They are blameworthy first of all because they disregard God's Word and other resources that might inform them. They act as if such study were the work of ministers only. Such ignorance is often willful, deliberate carelessness. If they are unaware of what God demands of them, it is their own fault. They have enough opportunities to know, and they *could* know if they wanted to. Furthermore, they take pains to acquire other kinds of knowledge. They are well trained in whatever worldly interests strike their fancy. They learn whatever is necessary to earn a living in this world. But they will not expend any energy in spiritual pursuits that count for eternity.

Knowledge of ourselves. Second, if you desire to know whether you are harboring secret sin, you must examine *yourself*. Compare your life with God's law to see if you conform to the divine standard. That is the primary way we must discover our own character. This is an important difference between human beings and brute creatures: a human is capable of self-reflection, contemplating his own actions, and evaluating the nature and quality of them. Doubtless it was partly for this very reason that God gave us this power—so that we might know ourselves, and consider our own ways.

We must examine ourselves until we satisfactorily discover either agreement or disagreement with the principles of Scripture. This requires the utmost diligence, lest we overlook our own irregularities, or lest some evil way in us should lie hidden under disguise.

How to Examine Yourself

You might think we would already be better acquainted with ourselves than with anything else. After all, we are always present with ourselves. We are immediately conscious of our own actions. We instantly know about everything that happens within us and everything that we do.

But in some respects the true knowledge of ourselves is harder to obtain than almost anything else. We therefore must pry diligently into the secrets of our own hearts and examine carefully all our ways and practices. Here are some guidelines to help in this process:

Always join self-reflection with your reading and hearing of God's Word. When you read the Bible or hear sermons, reflect on yourself, comparing your own ways with what you read or hear. Ponder what agreement or disagreement there is between the Word and your ways. The Scriptures testify against all kinds of sin, and contain directions for every spiritual responsibility, as Paul wrote: "All Scripture is inspired by God and profitable for teaching, for reproof, for correction, for training in righteousness; that the man of God may be adequate, equipped for *every good work*" (2 Tim. 3:16–17, emphasis added). Therefore when you read the commandments given by Christ and His apostles, ask yourself, *Do I live according to this rule? Or do I live in any way contrary to it?*

When you read in the historical parts of Scripture about the sins others have been guilty of, reflect on yourself as you go along. Ask yourself whether you are guilty of similar sins. When you read how God reproved the sins of others and executed judgments on them for their sins, ask whether you deserve similar chastisement. When you read the examples of Christ and the saints, ask yourself whether you live in ways contrary to their example. When you read how God commended and rewarded His people for their virtues and good deeds, ask whether you deserve the same blessing. Make use of the Word as a mirror in which you carefully inspect yourself—and be a doer of the Word (Jas. 1:23–25).

How few are there who do this as they should! While the minister is testifying against sin, most are busy thinking how others fail to measure up. They may hear hundreds of things in sermons that properly apply to them; yet it never so much as comes into their minds that what the preacher is saying in any way concerns them. Their minds readily fix on other people whom the message seems to fit, but they never think whether they themselves need the message.

If you do things that are generally avoided by people who are discerning and mature, be especially careful to ask yourself if

such activities might actually be sinful. Perhaps you have argued with yourself that such and such a practice is lawful; you don't see any evil in it. But if the thing is generally condemned by godly people, it certainly looks suspicious. You may be wise to consider conscientiously whether it is actually displeasing to God. If a practice is generally disapproved of by those who in such cases are most likely to be right, you ought to consider all the more carefully whether the thing in question is lawful or unlawful.

Ask yourself whether on your deathbed you will have pleasant memories of the way you have lived. Healthy people often indulge in activities they would not dare do if they thought they would soon stand before the Lord. They think of death as something in the distance, so they find it much easier to still their consciences about what they are doing today. Yet if they thought they might soon die, they would not find it so comfortable to contemplate such activities. Conscience is not so easily blinded and muffled when the end of life appears imminent.

Ask yourself solemnly, therefore, whether you are doing anything now that might trouble you on your deathbed. Think over your ways and test yourself with the sobering expectation of soon going out of the world into eternity. Earnestly endeavor to judge impartially what things you will be glad for on a deathbed—as well as what you will disapprove of, and wish you had left alone.

Consider what others may say of you. Although people are blind to their own faults, they easily discover the faults of others—and are apt enough to speak of them. Sometimes people live in ways that are not at all appropriate, yet they are blind to it themselves. They do not see their own shortcomings, though the faults are perfectly plain and evident to others. They themselves cannot see their failings, yet others cannot shut their eyes or avoid seeing where they fall short.

Some people, for instance, are very proud without knowing it. But the problem appears notorious to others. Some are very worldly; yet they seem not to be aware of it themselves. Some are malicious and envious. Others see it, and to them it appears truly hateful. Yet the very ones with the problem do not reflect on it. There is no trusting our own hearts or our own eyes in such cases. So we must hear what others say of us, observe what they charge us with, heed what fault they find with us, and strictly examine whether there is some foundation for it.

If others charge us with being proud, worldly, or spiteful and malicious—or accuse us of any other ill temper or practice—we should ask ourselves honestly whether it is so. The accusation may seem to us to be altogether groundless, and we may think that the accuser's motives or spirit are wrong. But the discerning person will see it as an occasion for self-examination.

We should especially listen to what our *friends* say to us and about us. It is foolhardy, as well as unchristian, to take offense, and resent it, when we are thus told of our faults. "Faithful are the wounds of a friend, but deceitful are the kisses of an enemy" (Prov. 27:6). We should rejoice that we are shown our spots.

But also we should heed what our *enemies* accuse us of. If they reproach and revile us to our faces—even out of a wrong attitude— we should ponder it enough to reflect inwardly, and ask ourselves whether there is any truth in it. Even if what is said comes across in a reproachful, reviling manner, there may still be much truth in it. When people criticize others, even when their motives for criticizing are wrong, they are nevertheless likely to target real faults. In fact, our enemies are likely to attack us where we are weakest and most defective, and where we have given them most grounds to criticize. They are most prone to attack us where we can least defend ourselves. Those who revile us—though they do it from an unchristian spirit and in an unchristian manner—will usually identify the very areas where we are the most blameworthy.

So when we hear of others talking against us behind our backs, no matter what the spirit of the criticism, the right response is to reflect upon ourselves, and consider whether we indeed are guilty of the faults they lay to our charge. That is certainly a more godly response than to be in a rage, to revile in return, or to despise them for their evil-speaking. Thus we may get good out of evil, and it is the surest way to defeat the designs of our enemies who revile and backbite against us. They do it from wrong motives, wanting to injure us. But in this way we may turn it to our own good.

When you see others' faults, examine whether you have the same deficiencies in yourself. Too many people are ready to speak of others' faults when they have the very same shortcomings. Nothing is more common than for proud men to accuse others of pride. Likewise it is common for dishonest men to complain of being wronged by others. Evil traits and practices in others appear much more odious in others than they do in ourselves. We can easily see how contemptible this or that sin is in someone else. We see so readily in others what a hateful thing pride is, or how evil malice can be, or how pernicious other faults can be. But though we can easily see such imperfections in others, when we look at ourselves, those things are obscured by a mirror of deceit.

Therefore when you see others' faults, when you notice how someone else acts amiss, what an unkind attitude he shows, or how unsuitable her behavior is, when you hear others speak of it, or when you find fault with others in their dealings with you—reflect. Consider whether there is any similar shortcoming in your own conduct or attitude. Realize that these things are just as unbecoming and offensive in you as they are in others. Pride, or a haughty spirit and mannerisms, are as odious in you as they are in your neighbor. Your own malicious and revengeful spirit toward your neighbor is just as despicable as his malicious and revengeful spirit toward you. It is just as sinful for you to wrong or deceive your neighbor as it is for him to wrong or deceive you. It is just as destructive and unkind for you to talk against others behind their backs as it is for them to do the same to you.

Consider how others are blind to their own sins, and ask yourself if you suffer from the same kind of blindness. You know that others are blinded by their lusts. Could it be that some carnal appetite or lust of the mind has blinded you? You see how others are blinded by their worldliness. Ask whether your own attachment to this world might be blinding you in a way that causes you to justify things in your life that are not right. You are as prone to be blinded by sinful desires as others. You have the same deceitful and desperately wicked heart. "As in water face reflects face, so the heart of man reflects man" (Prov. 27:19).

Search Your Conscience for Secret Sins

Examine the secrets of your own heart. Do you live with some hidden sin? Do you neglect some duty only you and God know about? Do you indulge in some secret practice that is offensive to the all-seeing eye of God? Examine yourself concerning all your private responsibilities: Bible reading, meditation, secret prayer. Do you fulfill those duties at all? And if so, do you fulfill them in an unsteady and careless manner? What is your behavior like when you are hid from the eye of the world—when you have no restraints other than conscience? What does your own conscience tell you?

I will mention two matters in particular:

Ask yourself whether you neglect the reading of God's Word. The Bible was surely written to be read—not only by ministers, but by the people, too. It is not enough to have read the Bible once, or to read it once in a great while. The Scriptures were given to be with us continually, to act as our rule of life. Just as the craftsman must have his yardstick and the blind man his guide, just as he who walks in darkness carries a light, so the Bible was meant to be a lamp to our feet and a light to our path (Ps. 119:105).

Joshua 1:8 says, "This book of the law shall not depart from your mouth, but you shall meditate on it day and night, so that you may be careful to do according to all that is written in it; for then you will make your way prosperous, and then you will have success." Deuteronomy 6:6–9 commanded the Israelites,

> These words, which I am commanding you today, shall be on your heart; and you shall teach them diligently to your sons and shall talk of them when you sit in your house and when you walk by the way and when you lie down and when you rise up. And you shall bind them as a sign on your hand and they shall be as frontals on your forehead. And you shall write them on the doorposts of your house and on your gates.

In the same way Christ commands us to search the Scriptures (Jn. 5:39). These are mines in which we are to dig for hidden treasures. Do you neglect this duty?

Ask yourself whether you are secretly gratifying some sensual lust. There are many ways and degrees of gratifying our carnal lusts, but every one of them is provoking to a holy God. Even if you refrain from gross indulgences, do you in some way secretly from time to time gratify your lusts and allow yourself to taste the sweets of unlawful delight?

Do you realize that it is offensive to God even when we gratify a lust only in our thoughts and imagination? Are you guilty of this sin?

The Danger of Unforsaken Sin

You have had directions laid before you on how to examine yourself for sin you may be unaware of. How are things in your own life? Do you find that you are living in some sinful way? I'm not asking whether you find yourself clear from sin. That is not expected of you, for there is no one who does not sin (1 Ki. 8:46). But is there some way of sin in which you *live*, which is your *lifestyle* or *practice*? There are doubtless some who are clear in this matter, some "whose way is blameless, who walk in the law of the Lord. . . . who observe His testimonies, who seek Him with all their heart. They also do no unrighteousness; they walk in His ways" (Ps. 119:1–3).

Let your own conscience answer how you find your own life. Are you guilty? Do you practice some sin as a matter of habit? Have you *allowed* yourself to do so? If that is the case, consider the following things:

If you have been seeking salvation and not yet found it, some way of sin in your life may be the reason. You may have wondered what is the matter when you have long been concerned about your salvation—when you have sought it diligently—yet to no avail. You have many times cried to God, yet He does not regard you. Others obtain comfort, yet you remain in darkness. But is it any wonder at all, if you have held on to your sin for so long? Isn't this a sufficient reason why all your prayers and all your pleas have been blasted?

If you are trying to retain your sin while seeking the Savior, you are not seeking salvation the right way. The right way is to turn from your ungodliness. If there is one member that is corrupt and you don't cut it off, there is danger that it will carry you to hell (Matt. 5:29–30).

If grace seems to be languishing rather than flourishing in your soul, perhaps some way of sin is the cause. The way to grow in grace is to walk in obedience, and to be very thorough in doing so. Grace will flourish in the hearts of all who live in this manner. If you live in some way of sin, however, it will be like some secret disease eating at your vitals. Sin will thus keep you poor, weak, and languishing.

Just one sin practiced habitually will suppress your spiritual prosperity and will diminish the growth and strength of grace in your heart. It will grieve the Holy Spirit (Eph. 4:30). It will prevent the good influence of God's Word. As long as it remains it will be like an ulcer, keeping you weak and lean, though you be fed the most wholesome spiritual food.

If you have fallen into great sin, perhaps some way of sin in your life was the underlying root of your greater failure. A person who does not avoid every sin and is not meticulously obedient cannot be guarded against great sins. The sin in which he lives will always be an inlet, an open door, by which Satan will find entrance. It is like a breach in your fortress through which the enemy may get in and find his way to hurt you greatly. If you have fallen into some horrible sin, perhaps this is the reason.

Or if you allow some way of sin as an outlet for your own corruption, it will be like a breach in a dam, which if left alone will grow bigger and bigger until it cannot be stopped.

If you live very much in spiritual darkness, without sensing God's presence, it may be that some way of sin is the reason. If you complain that you have little sweet communion with God; if you feel God has deserted you; if God seems to hide His face from you and seldom shows you evidences of His glory and grace; or if you seem left to grope in darkness and wander in the wilderness—this may be the reason. Perhaps you have cried to God often. Perhaps you experience sleepless nights and sorrowful days. If you are living in some way of sin, it is very probable *that* is the cause, the root of your mischief, the Achan, the troubler that offends God and brings so many clouds of darkness over your soul. You are grieving the Holy Spirit, and that is why you have no comfort from Him.

Christ promised He would disclose Himself to His disciples. But it is on the condition that they keep His commands: "He who has My commandments and keeps them, he it is who loves Me; and he who loves Me shall be loved by My Father, and I will love him, and will disclose Myself to him" (Jn. 14:21). But if you habitually live in disobedience to any of His commandments, then it is no wonder He does not give you reassuring manifestations of Himself. The way to receive God's favor is to walk closely with Him.

If you have been doubting your salvation, perhaps some way of sin in your life has stoked those doubts. The best way to gain clear evidence of your salvation is by a close walk with God. This, as we have already observed, is also the way to have grace flourishing in the soul. And the more lively God's grace is in us, the more likely it is to be seen. When Christ is disclosing Himself to us, we have the reassurance of His love and favor.

But if you live in some way of sin, it is no wonder if that greatly diminishes your assurance. After all, it subdues the exercise of grace and hides the light of God's countenance. It may be that you will never know whether you are a true Christian or not until you have wholly forsaken the way of sin in which you live.

If you have met with the frowns of Providence, perhaps some way of sin in your life explains why. When you have received sore rebukes and chastisements, it is very probable that your practicing a sinful habit or tolerating an evil act is what has caused you the trouble. Sometimes God is exceedingly severe in His dealings with His own people for their sins in this world. Moses and Aaron were not permitted to enter Canaan because they disobeyed God and sinned with their lips at the waters of Meribah. And how terrible was God in His dealings with David! What affliction did He send upon him through his family! One of his sons raped his sister; another murdered his brother; and having expelled his father out of his own kingdom in the sight of all Israel, he defiled his father's concubines on the housetop in full view of everyone. In the end he met with a terrible demise that utterly broke his father's heart (2 Sam. 18:33). Immediately after that followed the rebellion of Sheba (2 Sam. 20). Then at the end of his life, David saw another of his sons usurping the crown.

How harshly did God deal with Eli for living in the sin of not restraining his children from wickedness! Both sons were killed in one day, and Eli himself died a violent death. The ark was taken into captivity (1 Sam. 4). Eli's house was cursed forever; God Himself swore that the iniquity of Eli's house would never be purged by sacrifice and offerings (1 Sam 3:13–14). The priesthood was taken from Eli and given to another line. And there never again was an old man in Eli's family (1 Sam. 12:31).

Is the way of sin in which you live the reason for the rebukes of Providence you have met with? True, it is not the proper business of your neighbors to judge you with respect to events of Providence, but you certainly ought to inquire yourself whether God is contending with you (Job 10:2).

If death is a fearful thought for you, perhaps it is because you are living in some way of sin. When you think of dying, do you find yourself shrinking back at the thought? When you have an illness, or when something threatens your life, are you frightened? Are thoughts of dying and going into eternity alarming to you, even though you profess to be a Christian?

If you are living in some sinful way, that is probably the foundation of your fears. Sin keeps your mind sensual and worldly and hinders a lively sense of heaven and heavenly enjoyments. Sin keeps grace low and prevents the anticipation of heavenly comforts you would otherwise have. Sin prevents your having the comforting sense of the divine favor and presence. Without that, no wonder you cannot look death in the face without terror.

Don't continue in any way of sin. If you have found in reading this that you *have* lived in a way of sin, consider that from this point on if you live in the same way, you will be living in *known* sin. Whether it was known sin in the past or not, you may have inadvertently been living in it. But now that you are aware of it, if you continue in it, your sin will not be a sin of *ignorance*, but you will show yourself to be one of those who willfully live in ways of known sin.

Notes

Chapter 1 — "Whatever Happened to Sin?"

1. Karl Menninger, *Whatever Became of Sin?* (New York: Hawthorn, 1973), 13.
2. Charles Krauthammer, "From People Power to Polenta," *Time* (4 October 1993), 94.
3. Wayne W. Dyer, *Your Erroneous Zones* (New York: Funk & Wagnalls, 1976), 90–91.
4. Ibid., 105–106.
5. *The Ann Landers Encyclopedia* (New York: Doubleday, 1978), 514–17.
6. Steve Lopez, "Thief Becomes a Millionaire over a Beating," *LA Daily News* (2 December 1993), 25.
7. Barbara Sommer, "PMS in the Courts: Are All Women on Trial?," *Psychology Today* (August 1984), 36.
8. "Bitter Legacy," *Time* (26 September 1983), 19.
9. J. Rangel, "Defendant in the Killing of 10 Is Guilty of Reduced Charge," *New York Times* (27 July 1985), 1, 27.
10. Amy Wilentz, "Pondering a High-Proof Defense," *Time* (2 November 1987), 60.
11. P. Shenon, "Deaver Is Sentenced to Suspended Term and $10,000 Fine," *New York Times* (24 September 1988), 1.
12. Andrew Ferguson, "Take Off the Kid Gloves," *National Review* (1 November 1993), 80.
13. "Compulsive Gambling May Be a Handicap, and a Shield from Firing," *Wall Street Journal* (21 June 1988), 1.
14. Stanton Peele, *Diseasing of America* (Lexington, Mass.: Lexington, 1989), 2–4 (emphasis in original).
15. Bernie Zilbergeld, *The Shrinking of America* (Boston: Little, Brown, 1983), 89.
16. Ibid., 167.

17. Charles J. Sykes, *A Nation of Victims: The Decay of the American Character* (New York: St. Martin's, 1992), 13.
18. Ibid., 16.
19. Ibid., 15.
20. Wendy Kaminer, *I'm Dysfunctional, You're Dysfunctional* (Reading, MA.: Addison-Wesley, 1992), 121.
21. Ibid., 124.
22. Ibid., 124–125.
23. Ibid., 20.
24. Ibid., 18.
25. Garth Wood, *The Myth of Neurosis* (New York: Harper & Row, 1986), 9.
26. Karl Menninger, *Whatever Became of Sin?* (New York: Hawthorn, 1973).

Chapter 2—"The Soul's Automatic Warning System"

1. J. I. Packer, *Rediscovering Holiness* (Ann Arbor: Servant, 1992), 151.
2. Richard Sibbes, *Commentary on 2 Corinthians Chapter 1*, in Alexander B. Grosart, ed., *Works of Richard Sibbes*, 7 vols. (Edinburgh: Banner of Truth, 1981 reprint), 3:208.
3. Ibid., 210–211.
4. Ibid., 212 (emphasis added).

Chapter 3—"How Sin Silences the Conscience"

1. Charles W. Colson, "The Enduring Revolution: 1993 Templeton Address," (pamphlet) "Sources, No. 4" (Washington: Wilberforce Forum, 1993), 4–5.
2. Robert L. Vernon, *L. A. Justice* (Colorado Springs: Focus on the Family, 1993), 209–212.
3. Ibid., 213.
4. D. Martyn Lloyd-Jones, *The Plight of Man and the Power of God* (Grand Rapids: Eerdmans, 1945), 14.
5. Herodotus, *The Histories*, 1:31.
6. Augustine, *The City of God*, 4:31.

7. Lucian, *The Syrian Goddess*, 34.
8. Dennis A. Williams and Susan Agrest, "A School for Homosexuals," *Newsweek* (17 June 1985), 93.
9. "Quotable," *Daily News* (3 November 1993), 6.
10. Benjamin DeMott, "The Pro-Incest Lobby," *Psychology Today* (March 1980), 11.
11. Maurice Roberts, "God Gave Them Up," *The Banner of Truth* (October 1993), 3–4.

Chapter 4—"What Do You Mean, 'Totally Depraved'?"

1. J. C. Ryle, *Holiness* (Durham, England: Evangelical Press, 1979 reprint), 6. (First published in 1879.)
2. Jerry Adler, Pat Wingert, Lynda Wright, Patrick Houston, Howard Manley, and Alden Cohen, "Hey, I'm Terrific," *Newsweek* (17 February 1992), 50.
3. Charles Krauthammer, "Education: Doing Bad and Feeling Good," *Time* (5 February 1990), 70.
4. Cheryl Russell, "Predictions for the Baby Boom," *The Boomer Report* (15 September 1993), 4.
5. Adler, 50.
6. Ibid.
7. Norman Vincent Peale, *The Power of Positive Thinking* (Englewood Cliffs, NJ: Prentice Hall, 1952).
8. Ibid., viii.
9. Ibid., ix.
10. Adler, 50.
11. Ryle, 16.
12. Robert Schuller, *Self-Esteem: The New Reformation* (Waco: Word, 1982), 33.
13. Ibid., 57.
14. Ibid., 75 (emphasis in original).
15. Robert Schuller, "The Phil Donahue Show," 12 August 1980.
16. Schuller, *Self-Esteem*, 99.
17. Ibid., 14.
18. Ibid., 15.
19. Ibid., 98.

20. Ibid., 104.
21. "A Special Interview with Dr. Robert Schuller," "The White Horse Inn" radio broadcast with Michael Horton, host (1 November 1992).
22. Schuller, *Self-Esteem*, 45.
23. Ibid., 39.
24. "A Special Interview."
25. Schuller, *Self-Esteem*, 127.
26. Ibid., 31.
27. Ibid.
28. Ibid., 26–27.
29. Ibid., 64.
30. Ibid., 36.
31. Ibid., 98.
32. Ibid., 37.
33. Ibid., 39.
34. Ibid., 58.
35. Ibid., 67.
36. Ibid., 65.
37. Ibid.
38. D. Martyn Lloyd-Jones, *The Plight of Man and the Power of God* (Grand Rapids: Eerdmans, 1945), 87.
39. George F. Will, "A Trickle-Down Culture," *Newsweek* (13 December 1993), 84.
40. Dennis Prager, "The Belief That People Are Basically Good," *Ultimate Issues* (January-March 1990), 15.
41. Ibid.
42. Ryle, 9–10.

Chapter 5 — "Sin and Its Cure"

1. D. Martyn Lloyd-Jones, *The Plight of Man and the Power of God* (Grand Rapids: Eerdmans, 1945), 147
2. Tom Wolfe, *The Bonfire of the Vanities* (New York: Farrar, Straus, Giroux, 1987).
3. Jay Adams, *The Grand Demonstration* (Santa Barbara: EastGate, 1991), 16.
4. Harold S. Kushner, *When Bad Things Happen to Good People* (New York: Schocken, 1981).

5. R. L. Dabney, *Systematic Theology* (Edinburgh: Banner of Truth, 1985 reprint of 1871 original), 537–38.
6. Lloyd-Jones, 89.

Chapter 6 — *"The Conquered Enemy Within"*

1. D. Martyn Lloyd-Jones, *Sanctified Through the Truth: The Assurance of Our Salvation* (Wheaton: Crossway, 1989), 120.
2. Spencer Klaw, *Without Sin: The Life and Death of the Oneida Community* (New York: Allen Lane, 1993), 3.
3. H. A. Ironside, *Holiness: The False and the True* (Neptune, NJ: Loizeaux, 1912), 36–37.
4. B. B. Warfield, *Perfectionism*, vol. 2 (Grand Rapids: Baker, 1981 reprint of 1932 original), 561.
5. Ibid., 562 (emphasis added).
6. John MacArthur, *Faith Works: The Gospel According to the Apostles* (Dallas: Word, 1993), 105–121.
7. Warfield, 568.
8. Lloyd-Jones, 116–17 (emphasis added).

Chapter 7 — *"Hacking Agag to Pieces"*

1. John Owen, *The Works of John Owen*, 16 vols. (Edinburgh: Banner of Truth, 1967 reprint of 1853 edition), 6:177, 6:9.
2. Ibid., 6: 8 (emphasis added).
3. D. Martyn Lloyd-Jones, *Romans: An Exposition of Chapter 8:5–17: The Sons of God* (Grand Rapids: Zondervan, 1974), 92 (emphasis added).
4. Owen, 6:16–17.
5. D. Martyn Lloyd-Jones, *Sanctified Through the Truth: The Assurance of Our Salvation* (Wheaton: Crossway, 1989), 54.
6. Owen, 6:20.
7. Ibid., 6:11.
8. Ibid., 6:12 (emphasis added).
9. Ibid., 6:14.
10. Cited in I.D.E. Thomas, *A Puritan Golden Treasury* (Edinburgh: Banner of Truth, 1977), 264.
11. Ibid., 6:56.
12. Ibid., 55.
13. Lloyd-Jones, *Romans 8:5–17*, 143.

Chapter 8—"Handling Temptation"

1. Sinclair Ferguson, *Taking the Christian Life Seriously: A Study on Christian Maturity* (Grand Rapids: Zondervan, 1981), 84–85.
2. John Leo, "The Seven Video Sins," *U.S. News & World Report* (23 August 1993), 19.

Chapter 9—"Keeping a Pure Mind"

1. Ralph Venning, *The Sinfulness of Sin* (Edinburgh: Banner of Truth, 1965 reprint of 1669 original), 224.
2. Ibid., 227.

Chapter 10—"Holding to the Mystery of Faith with a Clear Conscience"

1. Jeremiah Burroughs, *The Evil of Evils* (Ligonier, PA: Soli Deo Gloria, 1992 reprint of 1654 original), 2–3.
2. Ibid., 3.
3. Lewis B. Smedes, *Shame and Grace: Healing the Shame We Don't Deserve* (San Francisco: HarperCollins, 1993), 3–4.
4. Ibid., 4.
5. Ibid.
6. Ibid., 119.
7. Ibid., 120.
8. Vergilius Ferm, *A Dictionary of Pastoral Psychology* (New York: Philosophical Library, 1955), 173–74.
9. D. Martyn Lloyd-Jones, *Sanctified Through the Truth: The Assurance of Our Salvation* (Wheaton: Crossway, 1989), 96–97.
10. My analysis of this movement is in John MacArthur, *Ashamed of the Gospel: When the Church Becomes Like the World* (Wheaton: Crossway, 1993).
11. John Blanchard, *Whatever Happened to Hell?* (Durham, England: Evangelical Press, 1993), 145.

Notes

Appendix 1 — "Gaining Victory Over Sin — A Closer Look at Romans 6"

1. James M. Boice, *Amazing Grace* (Wheaton: Tyndale, 1993), 41–42.
2. C. I. Scofield, *The Scofield Reference Bible* (New York: Oxford, 1917), 1200.
3. Clarence Larkin, *Rightly Dividing the Truth* (Philadelphia: Larkin Estate, n.d.), 210–211.
4. Ibid. (emphasis in original).
5. R. L. Dabney, *Systematic Theology* (Edinburgh: Banner of Truth, 1985 reprint of 1878 edition), 677.
6. Matthew Henry, *Commentary on the Whole Bible*, 6 vols. (Old Tappan, NJ: Revell, n.d.], 6:405.
7. D. Martyn Lloyd-Jones, *Romans: An Exposition of Chapter Six: The New Man* (Grand Rapids: Zondervan, 1972), 268–69.

Appendix 2 — "An Appeal for a Good Conscience"

1. Adapted into modern English and abridged from a sermon originally titled, "The Demand of a Good Conscience" first published in Sibbes's *Evangelical Sacrifices*, published in London in 1640.

Appendix 3 — "Searching Your Conscience"

1. Adapted and paraphrased into modern English from Edwards' tract "Christian Cautions: The Necessity of Self-Examination" (first printed 1788).

Scripture Index

Index

Subject Index

Index